Eco Instigator has in the past ten years blazed a trail in serious environmental journalism in Nigeria. It is widely quoted and referenced and it has occupied a hallowed place in the canon in Nigeria.

> – **Ike Okonta**, a Leverhulme Early Career Fellow in the
> Department of Politics, University of Oxford.

A decade of powerful contributions. Always engaging readings. Multiple approaches. Inspiring proposals. Consistent positions. Emancipatory horizons. What more can you ask for as a starting point for a fight for life worthy of humans and non-humans, which is always beginning and is permanently renewing.

Thank you Health of Mother Earth Foundation (HOMEF).

> – **Alberto Acosta**, Ecuador's former Minister of Energy and
> Mining, chairman of the constituent assembly which enshrined
> the rights of Mother Nature in its constitution

In *The Politics of Turbulent Waters*, Nnimmo Bassey, HOMEF, and many brilliant contributors chart a path through the turbulence and cross currents, beyond the rapids of the climate crisis and neoliberal corporate rule. To read this collection is to be reassured that downstream, the waters are backing up and spilling over the old dams of environmental destruction, inequity and racism, and that change will not be negotiated, rather it will burst through the widening cracks in those dams.

> – **Stephen Kretzmann**, Founder, Oil Change International

The global climate emergency confronts us all with existential and social questions, but we do not all face this crisis on equal terms. As *The Politics of Turbulent Waters* so powerfully argues, the destructive forces of climate change wreaking havoc on the African continent's peoples and environment are not so much "natural". They are profit-driven, far disproportionately impacting ordinary people in the Global South. With sharp insights and compelling conclusions, these essays not only identify the battle lines of struggle – against neoliberal "green" solutions for food sovereignty and extractivism – but give voice to the strategic visions of a people-driven solution. As the contributors make clear, a truly just transition must embrace the politics of solidarity and the urgency of system change.

> – **Lee Wengraf**, author, *Extracting Profit: Imperialism,*
> *Neoliberalism and the New Scramble for Africa*

The Politics of Turbulent Waters is a must read on how we resist tyranny.

> – **Jay Naidoo**, Founding General Secretary of the Congress
> of South African Trade Unions, Minister in the Cabinet of
> President Nelson Mandela, An Elder and Humanist

Health of Mother Earth Foundation

Politics of Turbulent Waters

Reflections on Ecological, Environmental and Climate Crises in Africa

Edited by Nnimmo Bassey

Daraja Press

Published by
Daraja Press
https://darajapress.com
Wakefield, Quebec, Canada

ISBN 9781990263750 (softcover)

Cover design: Kate McDonnell
Photo: An overview of the Niger delta where signs of oil spills can be seen
in the water in Port Harcourt, Nigeria. Alamy.

Library and Archives Canada Cataloguing in Publication

Title: Politics of turbulent waters : reflections on ecological, environmental and
    climate crises
 in Africa / Health of Mother Earth Foundation.
Other titles: Eco-instigator.
Names: Health of Mother Earth Foundation, issuing body.
Description: A compendium of selected articles from the Eco-instigator published
    from 2013 to 2022.
Identifiers: Canadiana 20230222250 | ISBN 9781990263750 (softcover)
Subjects: LCSH: Environmental justice—Africa. | LCSH: Climate justice—Africa. |
    LCSH: Environmental protection—Africa. | LCSH: Food sovereignty—Africa. |
    LCSH: Economic development—Africa. | LCSH: Natural resources—Africa. |
    LCSH: Africa—Environmental conditions.
Classification: LCC GE240.A35 P65 2023 | DDC 363.70096—dc23

To Earth Defenders everywhere

There is a preconception held by many people, even on the left, that imperialism made us enter history at the moment when it began its adventure in our countries. This preconception must be denounced ... The moment imperialism arrived and colonialism arrived, it made us leave our history and enter another history.

– Amilcar Cabral, *Brief Analysis of the Social Structure in Guinea*

TABLE OF CONTENTS

FOREWORD

I have been in the Niger Delta. I have been with my comrade and brother Nnimmo Bassey. Quietly and secretly, as we traversed the villages and towns, I understood what hell was. Within minutes, I was suffocating in the fumes of the gas flare rising from below the line of trees.

It's a huge ball of fire spewing its toxic elements into the atmosphere. The noise and the heat are unbearable. I felt my chest tightening. I struggled to breathe. I felt dizzy and intoxicated. All these, I felt in the village of Rumuekpe in Rivers State, Nigeria. "We have no choice," said the activists accompanying me; "These are our ancestral lands. We have nowhere to go. Our children suffer respiratory problems, skin rashes and eye irritations."

Medical specialists say that the flaring, which spews out a poisonous mixture of carbon dioxide and sulphur gases, has a massive negative health impact leading to bronchitis, silicosis, sulphur poisoning of the blood, and cardiac complications. Extreme long-term exposure can predispose one to, or cause, skin cancer. The nitrogen and sulphur oxides also mix with atmospheric moisture to send down acid rains, devastating agriculture yields.

The activists continued, "There are laws against gas flaring. It is technically illegal in Nigeria since 1984. But the government grants exemptions to oil companies burning natural gas during oil extraction. There is no political will to enforce set deadlines. Fines are nominal and the international oil companies usually buy off state officials. Profit, not health of our people or their development, is paramount in the Niger Delta."

I bear witness to this reality.

Nnimmo Bassey, executive director of Health of Mother Earth Foundation (HOMEF), an ecological think tank, and former director of Environmental Rights Action (ERA), the Nigerian chapter of Friends of the Earth International, accompanied me. He says gas flaring releases "nitrogen oxides and other substances such as benzene, toluene [and] xylene … which are known to cause cancers. The report says these pollutants can affect communities within 30 km of the flare. There are over 200 such continuous flares burning across the Niger Delta."

He adds, "And it has a huge destructive impact on agriculture, due to acid rain."

Scientists describe the Niger Delta as "one of the world's most severely petroleum-impacted ecosystems." Their report noted that the Delta is "one of the 10 most important wetlands and marine ecosystems in the world. Millions of people depend upon the Delta's natural resources for survival, including the poor in many other West African countries who rely on the migratory fish from the Delta." Of the near 27 million people living in the Niger Delta, an estimated 75 percent rely on the environment for their livelihood, often farming and fishing for market or subsistence living.

Royal Dutch Shell Nigeria's operations in the Delta have led to the deep impoverishment of the Ogoni people and surrounding communities in the Delta.

We met with Chief Eric Doo, from the Ogoni community of Goi. Previously a flourishing and vibrant community, with a bakery, fish ponds and agricultural livelihoods, Goi is now a haunted ghost village. A thick layer of crude covers the devastated terrain.

"The fishes have died. The ground water is toxic. Our cassava and yams are full of crude. This is Shell. This is their legacy, and our Hell. They have murdered our communities, killed our way of life. We have been here for generations; the remains of our ancestors now lay in this oil-soaked wastelands. And still, they refuse to acknowledge what they have done. They use the law courts, the police and corrupt public officials against us."

The chief adds with a sense of desperation:

"It's been 10 years since the oil spill. All we want is for them to apologize; to say sorry for the damage they have caused. They are one of the richest companies in the world. Surely they can compensate us for our losses, help us rehabilitate our lands and recover from this disaster."

What I saw was, Shell, a global company that "green washes" itself in the global media as a responsible company, at war with communities like Goi. They will stop at nothing to avoid liability. All that remains of the sensitive habitats here for birds and other wildlife are a toxic funeral pyres of crude soaked wood. The dreams of this community lay in shatters; the broken promises of Shell now a distant memory.

I found a group of young people bathing in the river, shimmering with a layer of crude, and asked: "These waters are toxic. Why are you swimming here?"

"We have nowhere else to go. This is where we have always swum and had fun." I asked about how they feel. "We are angry at Shell. They have made us poor, we cannot use our lands for planting. We are fishing communities, but the fish are gone because of the pollution. If they do not work with our communities we will fight them."

An estimated 1.5 million tons of oil has spilled in the Niger Delta ecosystem over the past 50 years. Many of the oil spills can be attributable to poorly maintained infrastructure such as aging pipelines.

What I saw as cleanup of oil spills in the areas I went to, is often superficial. I saw crude that is burned off and for weeks pollutes neighbouring villages with dangerous chemical fumes.

A week after visiting another polluted community, Ikarama in Bayelsa State of Nigeria, news reached me that the crude oil pool there has been set on fire and the community people are choking in toxic fumes.

United Nations Environment Programme (UNEP), in 2011, presented its report of the assessment of Ogoni environment to the then President of the Federal Republic of Nigeria, Goodluck Jonathan. The report completely confirmed the claims of the Ogoni people that "... neglectful environmental pollution laws and sub-standard inspection techniques of the Federal authorities have led to the complete degradation of the Ogoni environment, turning our homeland into an ecological disaster."

The report found that, without exception, all the water bodies in Ogoni was polluted by the activities of oil companies – Shell Petroleum Development Company (Shell) and the Nigerian National Petroleum Corporation (NNPC). Indeed, the report stated that some of what the people took as potable water had carcinogens, such as benzene, up to 900 times above World Health Organization (WHO) standards. The report also revealed that at some places in Ogoniland, the soil is polluted with hydrocarbons to a depth of five meters.

According to Nnimmo Bassey, "UNEP says that a total cleanup of Ogoni land will take a life time or about thirty years at the least. How is that a lifetime? Well, life expectancy in the Niger Delta stands at approximately forty-one years." My mind drifts back to November 10, 1995 and the execution of internationally acclaimed environmental and human rights activist Ken Saro-Wiwa and eight other Ogoni leaders. Nineteen years later, I see little public benefits that the people of the Niger Delta enjoy.

I visited the first oil well, drilled in Olobiri in 1956. There, stood a signboard announcing a museum and an Institute of Peace and Justice.

But there is neither and the signboard is overgrown with vegetation. Another dream of progress deferred.

All that is seen of the vast oil wealth is the monstrous palaces of militants, bought off in the governments Amnesty Programme and those of local political officials.

"We suffer in silence. Shell comes here and divides our communities. They accuse us of sabotage because it releases them of any responsibility for the oil spills. We have a right to life. We want the people of South Africa to know what they have done here. You must not trust them," says a resident in Ikarama community.

I have seen the scarred landscape, the trellis of oil pipelines and see a chess board of intrigue, conspiracy and violence. I wonder: Would these be tolerated in Amsterdam, Paris or New York?

This anthology of tragedy is recounted in this odyssey of grassroots stories, contained in this heroic book of heroic struggles against the abuse of global corporations who continue to pillage, rape and destroy our lands, oceans and rivers as they fuel the insane consumerism that is careening close to the precipice.

The Politics of Turbulent Waters is a must-read on how we resist this tyranny.

Jay Naidoo is Founding General Secretary
of the Congress of South African Trade Unions,
Minister in the Cabinet of President Nelson Mandela,
An Elder and Humanist

ACKNOWLEDGEMENTS

We thank the various authors whose articles are compiled in this book. We deeply appreciate their tireless efforts in using their voices and pens to fight for the rights of Mother Earth.

Our special thanks go to the HOMEF team that took care to ensure the consistent compilation, editing and quarterly release of the *Eco-Instigator* right from 2013. We acknowledge the work done in this regard by Ogechi Cookey, Stephen Oduware, Joyce Brown and Mfoniso Antia. The layout and cover designs of the *Eco-Instigator* have been handled over the period by Babawale Obayanju and Otoabasi Bassey. Our thanks also go to Kingsley Ugwuanyi for helping with copy editing of some of the issues.

The *Eco-Instigator* has been a veritable platform for our knowledge generation and sharing efforts. It is our hope that with the publication of a selection of articles in this form this heritage will be accessible in a more enduring form.

INTRODUCTION

Ogechi Cookey

For the past 10 years, the Health of Mother Earth Foundation (HOMEF) has been in the front line of the struggle for environmental justice, climate justice and food sovereignty in Africa and the globe. It has been a decade of non-stop probing of the exploitation of resources, peoples and nations which has given rise to numerous environmental and climate injustices. HOMEF has had a decennary of witnessing and standing against the injustice, the powers and structures (industries and policies) suffocating the rights of the people to a healthy environment and standing with the neglected to take charge of their once self-managed food and agricultural systems. The struggle has necessitated the reawakening of communities' consciousness to the injustices that besiege them and to their 'people power' – power to be utilized in seeking the desired change.

The book, *Politics of Turbulent Waters*, is a compendium of selected articles in the 36 issues of the *Eco-instigator* published from 2013 to 2022. The *Eco-instigator* is yet another tool used by HOMEF to pull together thoughts and reports of activities that advance environmental justice and food sovereignty. Issue by issue, these thoughts and reports flow from within HOMEF and other environmental/climate justice and food sovereignty advocates from across Africa and the globe. They form this rich assemblage (Politics of Turbulent Waters) in commemoration of HOMEF's 10th anniversary.

The title of the book is one of Nnimmo Bassey's (the director of HOMEF) numerous articles that have graced some pages of the different issues of the *Eco-instigator*. The article cum title encapsulates the messages that the book intends to convey to you, the reader. It crystallises the dire condition of Africa and its waters and the power imbalance together with the spatial disposition that plunged the continent into the calamitous environmental situation it faces. It speaks of the politics of economic development and market fundamentalism that avows to maintain the status quo in terms of destructive exploitation of Africa's marine and other natural resources.

The book itself is divided into four sections. Sections two to four each contain articles providing insight into activities and issues under HOMEF's key areas of focus – fossil politics, hunger politics and spaces for knowledge generation and sharing.

The first section begins with a riveting Covid-19 tale of lessons learnt from 'the gods of small things' – little birds nesting away in their nature-bestowed creativity as they enjoyed a climate that got a break from destructive human activities. The section is dedicated to challenges of climate change which are burning environmental issues for the world but especially for Africa which has contributed the least to the ruination of the climate but is suffering the impacts most. Laced on the pages of section one are calls for climate action as the continent and the world witnesses extreme weather events such as rising sea level, flooding, coastal erosion, desertification, heat waves, invasive pests and diseases, etc. These events come with shattering impacts on livelihoods across coastal and landlocked communities on the African continent and others.

Section two is built on articles untangling the hunger politics in Africa – centring on the issue of genetically modified organism (GMO) induced agriculture and the institutional powers destroying Africa's food heritage. HOMEF has since taken the lead in debunking the false promises made by pro-GMO groups in Africa. To put back Africa and its smallholder farmers in control of the food system, food policies and regulations including biosafety laws need to be strengthened to incorporate the rights of the smallholders. Research efforts around Africa's food systems need to be intensified. Africa must choose to stand against GMOs. Like every other system, disharmonious relationships between sub-systems, typical of the farmer-herder clash, disrupts the performance of the food system. These issues are amplified on the pages of section two.

In section three, where the subject matter is oil politics, the articles decry the despoilment of nature by the oil and gas sector. The section tackles the status quo maintained by the logic of capitalism – where the health and sustainability of nature is slaughtered on the altar of profit with accompanying environmental and social impacts being externalized to poor impacted communities as well as the already damaged Earth. The section carries messages of how institutions/engagements presumed to be working to help find more sustainable solutions to the nefarious acts of the oil and gas sector, have become part of the enablers either by sheer will or manipulation of the wirepullers.

The final section presents articles on concepts and issues interrogated in Ikike, HOMEF's learning spaces – Sustain-Ability Academy, School of Ecology and Conversations. HOMEF's knowledge spaces are arenas where learners and instigators converge to deconstruct and interrogate relevant constructs in the struggle for environmental justice, climate justice and food sovereignty. From scrutinizing the detrimental developmental role of the extractive sector to projecting uprisings that unite African struggles and, advocacies of Earth rights, section four strengthens lines of new thinking for the benefit of commons and the Earth.

SECTION 1

CLIMATE CRISES

The world continues to stand in denial of the fact that climate change is triggered mainly by society's continual reliance on fossil fuels......Weaning the world off hydrocarbons cannot be postponed forever, and it would also give us the chance to address the other major socio-economic cancers

– Excerpt from the book *To Cook a Continent* by Nnimmo Bassey

AVIAN FRIENDS, NATURECRACY AND ARTOCRACY IN THE TIME OF CORONAVIRUS

Nduka Otiono

It was yet another beautiful dawn during the novel coronavirus lockdown in Orléans, a suburb of Ottawa, Ontario, Canada. The lazy warmth of the spring sun was filtering through our window. A house wren, nesting in our backyard, a patch of land privately screened off with emerald green arborvitae trees from a popular road, was warbling joyfully again. Although, I first noticed it last spring, I did not pay much attention to the bird and its avian companions. Under COVID-19 lockdown, however, I have rediscovered my old hobby of birdwatching, making me something of an amateur ornithologist. It made a lot of difference to me that I did not have to leave our home to indulge in a childhood passion that the hustles of everyday city life in normal times had nearly torpedoed. I must confess that I have been enjoying every moment of it, happily becoming an unofficial host. From the bathroom window and the porch of my kitchen, I see them flirting and mating, twittering in their peculiar avian language, flapping their wings and as carefree as only birds can be.

As dawn flushed into daylight, the singing wren softened its songs; it sang intermittently. Going by the growing intensity of the morning sun, I must have been lost at the window for quite some time, listening to the avian minstrel. Soon, it came into view as it perched on the arched roof top extension, surveying the environment as if to confirm that it was safe enough to fly into the vent connecting its nest in the attic. At other times, its male partner accompanied this female. Most active in the early mornings and evenings, together they spend the day working and ferrying twigs and food for their chicks.

Irritated by the birds' unsightly droppings on my rooftop, the signature of their roosting in our attic, I have become hostage to the lockdown addiction, watching them come and go as they like. I have caught myself, in turn caught by my wife, staring out the window pondering, admiring and even envying the artistry, artisanal workmanship and industrious behaviour of the visiting avians. On one of my truly lucky days, different species fly in and out, fluttering and singing in the backyard: American robins, brown-headed cowbirds, Northern cardinals, house sparrows, and starlings.

Unproductive as this pastime may seem, I have come to better appreciate John Harold Johnson's philosophical declaration in his inspiring autobiography, *Succeeding Against the Odds*: "There is an advantage in every disadvantage, and a gift in every problem." Thus, a remarkable irony about the current COVID-19 pandemic is that while it has upended life as we used to know it, and continues to asphyxiate the old and young, leading to hundreds of thousands of deaths worldwide, it has also given humanity the opportunity to turn to the little but important things of life they previously overlooked. Right now, in parts of England, people are taking up gardening more passionately, nurturing home-grown tomatoes and some such veggies in their backyards. Previously uncommunicative neighbours in a country famous for its horticultural bias have been offering useful hints on how to grow aubergines, for instance, graft a twig, and even giving out seedlings for free.

In all of this, it does seem humanity is returning to nature or is it nature reclaiming the space humanity stole from it? Everywhere in the world, we have heard reports and seen pictures of indolent big cats sprawling or snoozing on major highways, primates taking over government offices, goats stretching out on tarmacs. Call it the COVID-19 Wildlife Occupy Movement (WOM) and you may not be wrong. Ever since the lockdown, there have been unusual reports of "Wild animals . . . claiming their space back as urban areas around the world are emptied due to Covid-19" [1]. The wide range of animals sighted occupying or strolling freely through deserted streets of usually bustling cities include wild goats (Wales), mountain goats (Cimesgezek, Turkey); kangaroo (Adelaide, Australia); crocodile (Toronto), monkeys (New Delhi), Coyotes (San Francisco); peacock (Dubai) deer (Paris, France; Nara, Japan; Trincomalee, Sri Lanka); wild boar (Antalya, Turkey; Haifa, Israel; France; Barcelona, Spain); buffalo (New Delhi highway) Puma (Santiago, Chile); sea lions (Mar del Plata, Argentina); wild penguins (South Africa); etc. [2]

---

1 See: LIVEKINDLY. (2020 a). Wild animals are claiming their space back as urban areas around the world are emptied due to Covid-19; Rebecca Falconer (2020). In photos: Wild animals roam in cities under coronavirus lockdown. https://www.axios.com/coronavirus-animals-roam-locked-down-areas-photos-d562784e-1a82-4b50-b4e5-4b566806944b.html. Also see TRT World. (2020), "Wild animals take over streets around the world" https://www.youtube.com/watch?v=OP3XclQXrFQ

2 LIVEKINDLY, "How NATURE Is THRIVING During COVID-19," https://www.youtube.com/watch?v=TZZVv937-D4. Also see Audrey Enjoli (2020), "14 Times Animals Reclaimed the Planet During Quarantine," https://www.livekindly.co/animals-are-reclaiming-planet-during-quarantine/

Even inside zoos and national parks and game reserves (Kruger in South Africa, Yosemite National Park, and the Hong Kong zoo), animals have been sighted taking unusual natural "vacation" as they exploit the lockdown to express their much-denied freedom. A particularly striking story is that of the pandas[3] in a Hong Kong zoo finally mating after 10 years, apparently because there were no human visitors gawking at them. In the same vein, environmentalists and nature lovers have celebrated the momentary healing of the earth due to drastic reduction in pollution because of the restrictions on nonessential automobile transportation and industrialization across the world. I call this fresh phenomenon *Naturecracy*, and by that I mean, Nature's rule over the material world ° as related to but subtly different from "ecocracy," a term that has been used by "enviromentocrats" to highlight a system of government that privileges natural order in relation to environment and development. In thinking of naturecracy in the time of COVID-19, I am re-envisioning the jubilant reign of nature, even if momentarily, as humanity retreated from the streets in compliance with governments' emergency lockdown orders to fight the super-spreading of the highly infectious virus.

There is another phenomenon that has developed in this period of coronavirus, which is Artocracy. In deploying this term, I am aligning with Nuno Sacramento and Claudia Zeiske's coinage in their 2010 book of the same title – *Artocracy* – "conceived to help structure our thinking with regard to art and society."

While naturecracy thrives and heals in a world wounded by the bureaucracy of everyday life, the pandemic has equally ushered in a reign of creativity. This creative spark among artists is visible in Africa and other parts of the world. Next to medicine and emergency medical professionals in the frontlines of the war against the pandemic, the arts and artists have become everyday consolation companion. More so, that "catchy songs,"[4] music, films, books, skits, etcetera have been weaponized to "edutain" citizens of a world stretched to the limits by a merciless scourge that has claimed over 346,000 lives worldwide. And so, while some artists are rediscovering their muses, many people have had to rely on the arts for intellectual and spiritual nourishment as well as for comic relief. What is more, as artists produce literary and fine arts, compose music,

---

3 Finally, Some Privacy: After 10 Years, Giant Pandas Mate in Shuttered Zoo. https://www.nytimes.com/2020/04/07/world/asia/panda-mating-hong-kong.html
4 Aisha Salaudeen. (March 17, 2020). *African artists are creating catchy songs to promote awareness about coronavirus.* CNN. https://edition.cnn.com/2020/03/17/africa/coronavirus-music-africa-intl/index.html

and collaboratively perform concerts remotely using ICT, the arts have proven to be a potent force that complements medical care as therapy or psychotherapy for healing an ailing world.

Given the centrality of nature and the arts to our survival of the pandemic and to post pandemic recovery, the question may be asked: How can Nigeria take advantage of the ongoing COVID-19 pandemic to rethink the role of culture and the creative industries? This question presupposes that the country has a responsive cultural bureaucracy that could re-imagine her cultural and creative landscape using the pandemic as a catalyst to create a model for the future. I am not exactly sure what kind of "model for the future" one might expect. But I would like to state my cynicism about the capacity of the traditional bureaucracy to process the challenges of cultural production in the present times towards developing a programmatic "competitive model for the future." So, if one is expecting Nigeria's government agencies to set the agenda, I am afraid, salvation will not come from that critical sector.

Therefore, we should not be looking up to government to construct any new visionary cultural architecture for the creative industries. Instead, I am confident in the capacity of independent Nigerian artists and cultural producers to further strategically entrench artocracy. This much they have been doing by establishing the country as the cultural capital of the continent as per the literary, filmic, and musical subsectors of the arts. On that note, I foresee our enterprising creative artists rising from the ravages of the pandemic to create enduring works informed by the experiences of this terrible season. But this is not to say that the government or corporate sector should withhold support from the creative industry.

It is too early, in my opinion, to see the emerging creative works in terms of a competitive model for the future. The works will speak for themselves in terms of what artistic models emerge and how competitive or not they become. The simple reason being that there is no operational school or movement at work as was the case with say, "the Zaria Rebels" of Nigeria's Independence era that sprouted in Ahmadu Bello University, Zaria. But if the pointers are to be taken seriously as evident in some recently released compositions such as Erigga's "Quarantine Cruise"[5] or Bella Shmurda's "Colodia Drive Us,"[6] then we should be expecting works hinged on humour as metaphor. Instructively, the art has gone beyond

5 https://www.youtube.com/watch?v=TDKDy5qSaC0
6 https://www.youtube.com/watch?v=aBSKuGevit0

formal artistic production. Informal memes, jokes, and online skits have become part of the daily dosage of humour. They are transmitted through WhatsApp and other social media platforms and consumed by the masses towards coping with the debilitating psycho-social consequences of the pandemic. Beyond the epicentres of the pandemic in hospital rooms, artocracy holds sway in the comfort of family homes, balconies, and social media chatrooms as evident on cable television broadcasts.

More than ever before, the new coronavirus has led me, and I believe many others, into rediscovering *the god of small things*, to appropriate the title of Arundhati Roy's popular novel. And as the Nigerian pop artist, Tekno Miles, sings in his hit single, "Rara,"[7] we should "forget about the big things oh/Say make we talk about the small things." These ostensibly "small things" include daily watching the spring birds that have made our backyard their seasonal nesting home. The god of small things is teaching us to emulate the animals roaming freely under the pandemic by not focusing on existentialism, but to take one day at a time amid an overwhelming wave of diseases and deaths encircling the world. The healing power of taking life's inscrutable experiences with equanimity is underscored by the fact that these days, "The world we wake up in" appears as "a counterfeit reality," to paraphrase Louis Netter in his fascinating article [8], "The importance of art in the time of coronavirus." And as if to further facilitate conversations on the troubled times we live in, and to foreground the primacy of naturecracy and artocracy to our survival, the speaker in Akua Lezli Hope's poem, "Arrivant," asks rhetorically: *"Why can't we see god anymore?"* And the response follows: *"because we don't bend low enough/We are being called by the little fish to save the world (Wreaths for a Wayfarer 110)."*

Indeed, it is time to start listening to the gods of small things such as the little birds building their nests at my backyard and the little fish in the river calling us to save the world.

7 https://www.youtube.com/watch?v=sZ4zMJSzd5M
8 Louis Netter. The importance of art in the time of coronavirus (April 1, 2020). https://theconversation.com/the-importance-of-art-in-the-time-of-coronavirus-135225

CIVIL DISOBEDIENCE: A KEY STRATEGY IN THE FIGHT FOR CLIMATE JUSTICE

Femke Wijdekop

On 19 December 2008, an American student, Tim DeChristopher, made a decision that would change his life. He and a group of protesters had been protesting the Bureau of Land Management's oil and gas lease auction of public land in Utah's precious red rock country, not far from the famous Grand Canyon Park. Tim managed to enter the auction hall, planning to improvise and disturb the auction in some non-violent way when to his surprise, he was asked the question: "Are you here for the auction?" "Yes" He replied, and was handed a bidder card. For a few moments, Tim contemplated the action he was about to take and its possible legal consequences. Then he started bidding on parcels of land, in total 'buying' 22,500 acres of land worth 1.8 million dollars, with no intention of paying for them.

Tim was later removed from the auction by federal agents, taken into custody and questioned. After two long years, in which hearings for his trial were postponed severally, Tim was sentenced to two years in prison. He was also fined 10,000 dollars for his act of civil disobedience. The US Department of the interior had, however, cancelled many of the oil and gas leases shortly after the auction because of insufficient environmental and scientific review of the consequences of such leases for the land in question. Tim was released on 23 April 2013 and has become a leader in the American climate justice movement, empowering American citizens to become voices for the preservation and restoration of the Earth[1].

Tim's story, told in the moving documentary Bidder 70[2], is a striking and quite dramatic example of how civil disobedience can be used as a tool to expose and challenge the fossil fuel industry's insatiable appetite for resources and land. His act of civil disobedience drew national attention to the illegal auction of public land leases, leading to the cancelation of many of them, and sparked the creation of Peaceful Uprisings – an NGO dedicated to climate justice through non-violent action.

1 Watch David Letterman's interview with Tim DeChristopher here (12m30s): https://www.youtube.com/watch?v=e_z5crtmDVg
2 Visit www.bidder70film.com to watch the documentary.

Other leaders in the climate justice movement, such as 350.org's Bill McKibben and Kumi Naidoo, director of Greenpeace International, call for civil disobedience and mass mobilization as well. The undue influence of the fossil fuel lobby on the legislator and the slow and difficult process of attaining climate justice through judicial intervention (the main problem being that the right to a clean and healthy environment is considered too 'vague' to be enforced in court), could mean that massive non-violent action by concerned citizens is the only way to protect our Earth.

This article sheds some light on the instrument of civil disobedience: its history, its characteristics and the possibilities for its application in perhaps the biggest social justice movement of the 21st century: the fight for climate justice. The aim is to inform and inspire the reader and to hopefully spark a discussion and exchange of practical ideas on the use of civil disobedience in the climate justice movement.

Civil Disobedience: A Short History

The term "civil disobedience" was first used by the American writer Henry David Thoreau in his influential 1849 essay to describe his refusal to pay the state poll tax implemented by the American government to prosecute a war in Mexico and enforce the Fugitive Slaw Law. In this essay, Thoreau argues that individuals should not permit governments to overrule their own consciences, and that they have a duty to avoid becoming agents of injustice by acquiescing to unjust governmental policies. Thoreau was a passionate abolitionist and strongly opposed to the Fugitive Slave Act of 1850 – requiring that all escaped slaves were, upon capture, to be returned to their masters and that officials and citizens of free states had to cooperate with the law. He also objected to the Mexican-American War, which he considered an act of American imperialism. In *Civil Disobedience*, he writes:

> Under a government which imprisons any unjustly, the true place for a just man is also a prison, where the State places those who are not with her, but against her, [a prison is] – the only house in a slave State in which a free man can abide with honour... Cast your whole vote, not a strip of paper merely, but your whole influence. A minority is powerless when it conforms to a majority (...) but it is irresistible when it clogs by its whole weight. If the alternative is to keep all just men in prison, or give up war and slavery, the State will not hesitate which to choose. If a thousand men were not to pay their tax bills this year, that would not be a violent and bloody measure, as it would be to pay them, and enable the State to commit violence and shed innocent blood. This is, in fact, the definition of a peaceable revolution, if any such is possible [3].

3 Henry David Thoreau, *Civil Disobedience*, Norton Critical Edition, 1966, p. 233

For his refusal to pay the state poll tax, Thoreau spent one night in jail (he was released the next day when, much to his fury, a relative paid the state poll tax for him).

Thoreau's arguments impressed and influenced some of the world's greatest leaders. Mahatma Gandhi wrote a summary of Thoreau's argument for the newspaper *Indian Opinion* in 1907, one year into his first 'Satyagraha' (nonviolent resistance based on the force of truth) campaign in South Africa. He saw Thoreau's essay as being the chief cause of the abolition of slavery in America and wrote that "both his example and writings are at present exactly applicable to the Indians in the Transvaal"[4]. Gandhi's most striking act of civil disobedience was his Salt March in 1930 in protest of Britain's Salt Acts which prohibited Indians from collecting or selling salt. Citizens were forced to buy salt from the British, who, in addition to exercising a monopoly over the manufacturing and sale of salt, also imposed a heavy salt tax. Gandhi set out from Sabarmati with 78 followers on a 241-mile march to the coastal town of Dandi on the Arabian Sea. All along the way, Gandhi addressed and attracted large crowds, and by the time they reached Dandi, he was at the head of a crowd of tens of thousands. At the beach, Gandhi picked up a small lump of natural salt out of the mud – disobeying British law – and thousands more followed his lead.

Gandhi was arrested and spent nearly a year in prison. More than 60,000 Indians were jailed in the aftermath of the Salt March while millions had started making their own salt. Inspired by the Salt March, people across India boycotted all kinds of British goods, including paper and textiles; peasants refused to pay land taxes. The Salt March raised international awareness of British injustices in India and made Mohandas Gandhi into a famous figure around the world.

Martin Luther King was also greatly influenced by Thoreau's work on civil disobedience:

> During my student days, I read Henry David Thoreau's essay on Civil Disobedience for the first time. Here, in this courageous New Englander's refusal to pay his taxes and his choice of jail rather than support a war that would spread slavery's territory into Mexico, I made my first contact with the theory of nonviolent resistance. Fascinated by the idea of refusing to cooperate with an evil system, I was so deeply moved that I reread the work several times. I became convinced that non-cooperation with evil is as much a moral obligation as is cooperation with good [5].

4 However, Gandhi felt that civil disobedience was too narrow a term to describe the whole nature of his Satyagraha movement, which had a strong spiritual component – 'love-force' or 'soul-force' – at its nucleus. Satyagraha means 'the force which is born of truth and love'.
5 King, M. L., *The Autobiography of Martin Luther King, Jr.*, Little Brown UK 2000, chapter 2. 6Ibidem.

Civil disobedience was a key element in Dr. King's campaign for equal rights for Afro-Americans:

> Whether expressed in a sit-in at lunch counters, a freedom ride into Mississippi, a peaceful protest in Albany, Georgia, a bus boycott in Montgomery, Alabama, these are outgrowths of Thoreau's insistence that evil must be resisted and that no moral man can patiently adjust to injustice[6].

A key moment in the civil rights campaign was of course Rosa Parks' act of civil disobedience by refusing to give up her seat for a white passenger on a public bus in 1955. Rosa Parks was secretary of the Montgomery NAACP chapter and had just attended a meeting on the strategy of civil disobedience. On her bus ride back home from work, she was asked to move from her seat so a white person could sit. She refused, and subsequently was arrested, tried and convicted for disorderly conduct and violating a local ordinance. After word of this incident reached the black community, 50 African-American leaders gathered and organised the Montgomery bus boycott to demand a bus system in which passengers would be treated equally. For 381 days, no African-American took any kind of public transportation in Montgomery. On 13 November 1956, the United States Supreme Court put an end to segregation on public buses.

Civil disobedience was also part of the Vietnam War protests (1965-1972). Techniques of resistance included disrupting draft board processes by raiding local branches of the Draft Board, stealing draft cards, and setting them alight in the street. It was an important element of the anti-apartheid struggle in South Africa and included clergies wedding mixed couples against the law; sit-ins at all-white canteens; mixed-race students enrolling at all-white schools, non-whites showing up at white hospitals for medical treatment and the 1989 protest march to a whites-only beach organised by Archbishop Desmond Tutu. More recently, the brave women of the Women of Liberia Mass Action for Peace used nonviolent protest – a sit-in outside of the Ghanaian presidential palace to enforce peace talks between President Charles Taylor and rebels in 2003 – in their successful campaign to end the Second Liberian Civil War.

Elements of Civil Disobedience

So, what is the definition of civil disobedience? Civil disobedience is a public, non-violent and conscientious breach of law undertaken with the aim of bringing about a change in laws or government policies. The disputed law

6 King, M. L.

or policies might have been established according to the official rules and formal requirements, yet fall short to meet the requirements of justice. The laws or policies are considered 'unjust' and the protesters feel compelled to disobey these laws in order to maintain their integrity. Following their own conscience becomes a higher, more sacred duty than following the dictates of their government.

However, those who engage in civil disobedience are willing to accept the legal consequences of their actions, even if they consider the laws unjust and their breach justified. Accepting the legal consequences is an integral part of civil disobedience. It testifies to the protester's fidelity to the rule of law and their respect for the constitutional framework within which they operate. It prevents them from being labeled (and dismissed) as 'anarchists' or 'trouble-makers'. Rather than undermining the existing political and legal system in a violent way, they seek to improve that system non-violently. They signal the existence of unjust laws that are incompatible with the principles of justice, equality and freedom upon which the legal architecture of the State should be built. As such, they give the government critical 'feedback' on the quality of their laws and policies and their compatibility with the nation's most cherished principles. One could even say that those engaged in civil disobedience act as the nation's conscience and are willing to sacrifice their own comfort for the wellbeing of the collective.

But of course, the purpose of civil disobedience is not martyrdom. The purpose is to spark a change in policy, to act as a catalyst for a more socially and environmentally just society. That is why the act of civil disobedience should be public; it should reach as many people as possible. In our age of internet and social media, this condition is easier to satisfy than ever. In order for the government to self-correct and change unjust laws into just ones, public pressure is essential. The general public has to become aware of the injustices that come masked as 'law'. The aim is to have citizens consult with their own conscience and to break the spells of indifference, ignorance or feelings of powerlessness. Especially in the West, it means to break loose from merely being a consumer and start to become a citizen again, owning our roles as 'stewards' for the wellbeing of future generations and the Earth herself.

Civil disobedience gives the public permission to think independently and critically and, to measure governmental policy on the scales of justice. In a way, it is a 'wake-up' call. Its non-violent nature and appeal to morality give it a dignified character that speaks to "the better angels of our nature". As such, it has a strong spiritual component. It is fuelled by a love for justice and a passion for freedom and equality. It is expressed in bold civic action. Perseverance, discipline, strategic thinking and solidarity are other necessary ingredients for a successful civil disobedience campaign.

Civil Disobedience and Climate Justice

Tim DeChristopher's act of civil disobedience at the gas and oil lease auction did not take place in a vacuum. For several years now, civil disobedience is employed to protest the pollution and ecocides caused by the fossil fuel industry. According to theory, civil disobedience should be used as a 'last resort' when other means of exercising influence – using your right to vote, expressing your opinion in the public debate – have failed. This point has been reached for many activists, especially those in the United States, who feel that their government is too corrupted by the fossil fuel industry lobby to truly protect the interests of its citizens to live in a healthy and clean environment. They have decided to use a more powerful yet non-violent way to communicate their concerns to the world. Some examples of 'green' civil disobedience include:

• The 'Grow Heathrow' protest against a third runway at Heathrow airport in the United Kingdom. Over the past four years, an abandoned piece of land has been transformed into a transition town and self-sufficient community, producing fruit and vegetables, relying on solar and wind energy and, offering workshops to visitors. Their aim is to "bring to light the environmental damage and misery future airport expansion at Heathrow will bring to local residents and businesses", develop and promote community and resource autonomy to support long-term community resilience[7].

• Protest vigils and sit-ins organised by Peaceful Uprising to monitor and prevent tar sand strip-mining in Utah public lands. Peaceful Uprising offers trainings to local communities on how to peacefully resist tar sand mining and uses art to educate communities and promote the campaign for climate justice. "Joy and Resolve" is their motto [8].

• Credo's pledge of resistance if the Keystone XL pipeline is not rejected by the Obama's Administration. This pipeline would run from the Alberta tar sands in Canada down to the Gulf Coast of Texas, carrying

7 https://web.facebook.com/transitionheathrow/about_details
8 www.peacefuluprising.org

tar sand oil. Almost 96,000 activists have signed this pledge: "I pledge, if necessary, to join others in my community, and engage in acts of dignified, peaceful civil disobedience that could result in my arrest in order to send the message to President Obama and his administration that they must reject the Keystone XL pipeline."[9]

- The march in Washington, in February 2013, where 35,000 people protested global warming and the construction of the Keystone XL pipeline. These protests have continued over the course of 2014. Last March, over 200 people were arrested when they strapped themselves to the White House fence as a way of peacefully protesting the pipeline9. Arrests have also been made after protesters put their bodies in the way of the construction of the pipeline as part of the so-called "Tar Sands Blockade". Canada's indigenous First Nation people play an important role in this movement[10].

- Sit-ins organised by American students and environmental activists to stop the exports of coal from ports of the American West Coast.

- The overrunning of the Gazprom oil rig in the Arctic Ocean and the subsequent arrest (and release) of Greenpeace's Arctic 30.

With the climate crisis intensifying and the prospect of more ecocides to come, civil disobedience should become increasingly important in the years to come. If the basic condition of a livable, healthy environment is no longer guaranteed by our governments, it is not fulfilling its part of the "social contract". Disobedience of unjust laws and policies is then a logical response from us, conscious citizens.

At the moment of this writing, the People's Climate March is being organised (www.peoplesclimate.org). This March will take place on 21 September 2014 during the United Nations summit on the climate crisis in New York City, led by Secretary-General Ban Ki-Moon. Tens of thousands of attendees are expected. It will be interesting to see if protesters will engage in civil disobedience (for example, ignoring a lawful order to disperse) in order to draw extra (media) attention to their message. Could a massive turn-up at the Climate March and public outrage at massive arrests put enough pressure on government leaders to abandon short term,"profit-for-the-1%" thinking for a long-term vision of environmental and social justice?

9 https://sites.miis.edu/jessygoesfarming/2013/09/24/say-no-to-keystone-nokxl-civil-disobedience-coming-to-a-corner-near-you/
10 https://www.theguardian.com/environment/2014/mar/02/keystone-xl-protesters-arrested-after-strapping-selves-to-white-house-fence

Such a turn-around would probably require a continuous application of public pressure, communicated to the world through internet and social media, backed by solid knowledge of climate change and inspired by a vision of wiser alternatives to live on this Earth. Civil disobedience could be an important strategy in this 'public pressure' campaign. It rests on a rich and tested tradition.

Conclusion

When applying civil disobedience to resist the fossil fuel industry, inspiration can be drawn from successful campaigns in other parts of the world. At the same time, the campaign should be tailored to local culture and traditions of community-based action and direct democracy for optimum effectivity. I look forward to feedback from readers on how civil disobedience could be uniquely tailored to match the needs, traditions and economic and political reality of Nigeria and hope this article sparks a broader discussion on the future of "green" civil disobedience.

BURNING THE PLANET, ONE CLIMATE COP AT A TIME

Mary Louise Malig[1]

For the third year in a row, a typhoon wreaked havoc on the Philippines during a Conference of Parties (COP) of the United Nations Framework Convention on Climate Change (UNFCCC). In 2012, during the UNFCCC COP 18 (in Doha, Qatar), Typhoon Bopha, the strongest ever to hit Mindanao, the southern area of the Philippines, left more than a thousand dead and thousands more homeless. In 2013, during the COP 19 (in Warsaw, Poland), Typhoon Haiyan, a super typhoon of levels never seen before in the Philippines, made landfall and devastated millions of families, displaced an estimated 4 million people and left in its wake at least 6,100 dead – making it the deadliest typhoon to ever hit the country. Storm surges, brought by the super typhoon, violently washed away entire communities. This year, 2014, during the COP 20 in Lima, yet again another super typhoon made its way to the Philippines. Initially, a category 5 super typhoon, Typhoon Ruby, weakened to a category 3 once it made landfall. Its path, however, included the communities still reeling from the devastation of Typhoon Haiyan the year before.

Although the Philippines is no stranger to typhoons, seeing 15-20 typhoons a year, the scale of these recent super typhoons hitting the country has inflicted damage never before seen. Scientists have been making these warnings for several years now. Warmer waters and warmer air temperatures are combining to produce more volatile and extreme weather including super typhoons of record-breaking magnitudes. One would think that, with the vivid and horrific reality of massive loss and damage in countries like the Philippines, happening exactly at the same time as representatives of 192 governments come together to discuss actions needed to address the crisis of climate change, these decision-makers would, at least, be compelled to take genuine action. Instead, it has been the complete opposite.

---

1 The article was also published here: http://peopleforestsrights.wordpress.com/2014/12/13/burning-the-planet-one-climate-cop-at-a-time/

15

From Commitments to Pledges to Contributions: Downward Spiral of Emission Cuts

Following an acknowledgement of historical responsibility for the contamination of the planet, 37 industrialized countries (known in UNFCCC parlance as Annex 1 countries) ratified the Kyoto Protocol. Here, they are legally committing to cutting emissions by at least 5 percent below 1990 levels in the commitment period, 2008 to 2012. The Kyoto Protocol, however, had flexibility mechanisms which allowed Annex 1 countries to "offset" – pay developing countries to plant trees in order for them to maintain their polluting ways, or to trade – buy and sell their polluting credits. These mechanisms have allowed Annex 1 countries to continue or even increase emissions at source.

In 2010 however, as negotiations discussed the second commitment period of the Kyoto Protocol, at the COP16 in Cancun, a new concept proposed from the COP 15 in Copenhagen was agreed to replace the legally binding commitments – pledges. Despite protests from developing countries, the Cancun Agreements, which included these new pledges, were adopted. Pledges would be voluntary and would endeavour to keep the warming of the planet below 2 degrees Celsius. Best efforts would be made to not burn the planet.

At COP17 in Durban, the following year, even more historic changes were made, breaking from the original principles of the Rio Conventions. The Durban Platform stated that the new agreement would be "applicable to all." This would begin to undermine the principle of common but differentiated responsibility to escape the historical responsibility of developed countries.

Then COP19 in Warsaw, Poland, introduced an even weaker concept replacing pledges – contributions. Technically named Intended Nationally Determined Contributions (INDC), this allows countries to decide for themselves, what they think they can contribute to keep to the global target. It did not seem possible but they found a way to commit even less.

At the COP20, it was clear beyond any doubt, that the historically responsible emitters are not interested in making any emissions cuts and the big developing countries are well on their way to competing with the industrialized countries in polluting the planet. The options laid on the table for the post 2020-agreement, are even weaker than what was "pledged" in Cancun and Copenhagen. There also seems to be attempts to change the baseline to 2010 levels instead of 1990 levels, meaning that countries will probably even increase their emissions. Furthermore, no clear legally binding mechanism to ensure that countries' contributions are actually meeting the global goal. Worse, there are even more market mechanisms proposed in addition to those that are already under the Kyoto Protocol. Amongst the proposals are, more carbon markets (including in forests and possibly even agriculture) and subnational, national and regional emissions trading schemes.

Science is very clear: to limit the increase of temperature to 1.5°C, global emissions should be less than 38 Gt of CO_2e by 2020 (44 Gt of CO_2e for 2°C). This means legally binding cuts – not pledges or contributions – with no carbon markets. At current business as usual rates, humans will reach global emissions of 57 Gt of CO_2e by 2020. Simply put, the current trajectory of the climate negotiations mean that humans will not make enough cuts in emissions before 2020 to stay on the path of keeping within the limit of the 1.5-degree centigrade ceiling. The feedback mechanism of the climate guarantees that if this decade is lost, there will be no going back from climate chaos.

Unfulfilled Promises of Finance

Following the principle of historic responsibility, developed countries should be providing finance to developing countries for adaptation and mitigation. In Cancun, long-term finance was promised along with the mechanism of the Green Climate Fund. The promise was 100 billion USD every year by 2020. That may sound like a big number but when compared to what is needed, it is meager. The UN Department of Economic and Social Affairs' 2009 UN World Economic and Social Survey estimated that 500-600 Billion USD is what is needed every year by developing countries to adapt and mitigate climate change.

The original demand of the developing countries before Copenhagen was that climate finance should be at least 1.5% of Annex 1 countries' GDP by 2020. Looking at 2009 numbers, this amount comes out to 1.5% of 39,881 billion USD, which comes out to 598 billion USD. This is a small change compared to what is spent on financial speculators and wars. According to the Stockholm International Peace Research Institute's Military Expenditure Database, the US government spent 661 billion USD in 2009 and 616 billion USD in 2008. The US government itself has spent trillions of USD in bailing out Wall Street, the speculators, and the banks.

The concept as well of "climate debt" and hence the historical responsibility to pay this debt owed to developing countries, has been completely lost. Instead, promises remain largely unfulfilled. In Lima (Peru), celebratory announcements were made of the supposedly groundbreaking achievement that they have reached a meager 10 billion USD out of the 100 billion USD originally promised.

To Reclaim the Future, We Need to Change the Present

The urgency of the climate crisis, blatantly ignored by the climate negotiations, is lived daily by social movements, indigenous peoples, and communities all living on the frontlines of climate change. In the streets of Lima, during the COP20, at least 20,000 people marched for Mother Earth, calling for a change in the system, not the climate.

It is the adherence to the capitalist system and the perpetuation of corporate profits after all that drives the climate negotiations. These negotiations promote false solutions such as: REDD (Reduction from Emissions from Deforestation and Forest Degradation) and Climate Smart Agriculture. They uphold market-based mechanisms ranging from carbon markets to techno-fixes such as geo-engineering, carbon capture and storage, industrial bio-energy and others that do further harm to the planet. One of the most crucial steps to real and deep emission cuts is to leave more than 80 percent of fossil fuels in the ground. But with the corporate capture of the negotiations by the oil and energy industry, there will never be a break from business as usual. The seeming insensitivity of the COPs to very real devastations experienced firsthand by countries like the Philippines, is intentional as governments prioritize big business over affected communities.

We need to break from the current system of over-exploitation, over-consumption, over-production and, extractivism. And in their place, flourish the many different solutions – existing methods and systemic alternatives of peasants, indigenous peoples, women and communities – such as food sovereignty, buen vivir, agroecology, community conservation, deglobalization, rights of nature and, many others. Changing the system is our only hope to reclaiming our future.

NEVER TRUST A COP

Babawale Obayanju

The temperature of 1°C is above pre-industrial levels and signifies over 50ppm increase in the number of greenhouse gases in the atmosphere above the estimated 350ppm required by science. The year 2015 (at the time of this report) was recorded as the warmest year in the history of Mother Earth (from then onwards, the world has recorded 7 top warmest years with 2016, 2019 and 2020 topping the chart at the time of this publication).

The COP has failed to take an impermeable stand on cutting emission of greenhouse gases at source, thus, downplaying real solutions. Outside the COP, different groups and peoples had consensus against false solutions such as REDD and REDD+ which are ploys whereby corporations grab productive land and forests from poor rural farmers in the name of reducing deforestation while channeling carbon to trees. Also rejected were techno-fixes, including carbon capture/storage and geoengineering favoured by corporations and their lobbyists. The peoples' climate demand was equity, which entails sharing the global carbon budget fairly.

The demand had been that the industrialized, polluting and/or developed nations pay their climate debts and cut their greenhouse gas emissions at source, as they have already used up more than their fair share of atmospheric space. They also, must support adaptation efforts by developing nations through the substantial provision of new finance and by transferring unpatented technologies at affordable prices accompanied by capacity building in a transparent manner. The demand was for system change.

It was a demand for a system where the people are put first before profit. A system where the people can access clean community-owned energy. A system where the people have a food system based on agroecology, and where communities manage their natural resources in an equitable and accountable manner that favours people and not the corporations. Sadly, the outcome of the Paris COP21 was loudly hailed in some quarters as a huge success, whereas, for the peoples of the world, it was a big hit below the belt. The outcome further confirmed our beliefs that the change we seek is to be found with us and not the COP.

The agreement at the COP had been hinged on a collection of voluntary pledges for emissions reduction with no legal obligation to keep global warming under 1.5 degrees Celsius. The parties merely agreed to "pursue efforts" to do so. There was no urgency, whatsoever, to increase action before 2020, even with the warning by scientists that urgent actions are crucial in the short term. And while there will be stock-taking in 2018 and every five years after that, there is no commitment to increase efforts based on these reviews. What hypocrisy!

The outcome of the COP might have been weak, but the resolve of the people to fight for system change has been hugely strengthened.

Until victory, Aluta must continue. We truly are unstoppable.

FIGHTING FOR CLIMATE AND ENVIRONMENTAL JUSTICE IN THE MAGHREB?

Hamza Hamouchene

It has become a tradition for me to state clearly from the outset where I stand politically and ideologically because I simply don't believe in neutral discourses. My perspective is not one of the academics and university people who choose to be neutral in the face of injustices and oppression. They justify their neutrality by saying they are objective but take such position in order to be accepted by the dominant discourses and other structures of power. My perspective is one of an activist, which I hope is progressive, radical and decolonial in the sense that it is anti-systemic and resolutely in active solidarity with the oppressed and the "wretched of the earth" in their struggles to achieve social justice.

I am going to explore three themes in this article. I will start by giving an idea about the ecological and climate crises in the Maghreb region (Algeria, Morocco and Tunisia) and then go on and illustrate how the neoliberalisation of environmental governance is being enacted there. I will end by putting forward a critique of some of the concepts of "justice" used to talk about the injustices in facing and dealing with environmental degradation and anthropogenic global warming.

The Ecological and Climate Crises in the Maghreb Region.

Anthropogenic climate change is already a reality in the Maghreb and it is undermining the socioeconomic and ecological basis of life in the region. Tunisia, Algeria and Morocco witnessed severe heat waves during the summer of 2015 and an ongoing drought this year (2016). This has been catastrophic for agriculture (particularly for small peasants in Morocco). The desert is growing, eating the land around it. This places huge pressure on already scarce water supplies. Seawater intrusion into groundwater reserves, as well as groundwater overuse, will put these countries in the category of those who suffer from absolute water poverty[1].

---

1 Hamza Hamouchene and Mika Minio-Paluello. The Coming Revolution in North Africa: The Struggle for Climate Justice (in Arabic and French), 2015. Ed. Platform, Environmental Justice North Africa, Rosa Luxemburg, and Ritimo.

The effects of climate change and the climate crisis are compounded by environmental degradation and the exhaustion of natural resources. A condition caused by a productivist model of development based on extractive industries: oil and gas in Algeria (and to a smaller extent, Tunisia), phosphate mining (in Tunisia and Morocco), other forms of mining (silver, gold and manganese in Morocco) and, the water-intensive agribusiness model paired with tourism (in Morocco and Tunisia). Alongside pollution, environmental destruction and the rising prevalence of some diseases like cancer, I saw clearly what David Harvey calls "accumulation by dispossession"[2] as well as what Samir Amin describes as "development of underdevelopment[3]. This was evident throughout my research visits to extraction sites of fossil-fuel and mining industries in the Maghreb.

It is possible to state with confidence that the poverty in these areas is related to the existence of significant natural resources. There are numerous examples: the gas and oil towns of Ain Salah and Hassi Messaoud in Algeria, the Gafsa phosphate mining basin and Gabes in Tunisia, the industrial town of Safi and the silver mining town of Imider in Morocco.

This is the paradox of extractivism under capitalism, where sacrifice zones are created in order to maintain the accumulation of capital. When I say sacrifice zones, I really mean it: Ain Salah in Algeria is one of the richest gas towns on the African continent but it is an ugly town with very poor infrastructure.

Residents call the one hospital they have the "hospital of death". Gabes in Tunisia, the only coastal Mediterranean oasis in the world, used to be called "a paradise on earth" before the installation of a chemical factory on its shores to process the mined phosphate in the 1970s. That factory has caused an ecocide in the oasis by pillaging its waters, polluting its air and sea, and killing some of its fauna and flora. Some even talk about environmental terrorism in a context of highly saturated, anti-terrorism discourse. These are just two examples amongst many, underlying some of the ills brought about by extractivism.

What do I mean by extractivism? The term refers to those activities that remove large quantities of natural resources that are not processed (or processed only to a limited degree), especially for export. Extractivism is not limited to minerals or oil. It is also present in farming, forestry, fishing and even tourism with its intensive water use. I was appalled to see the

2 David Harvey. *A Brief History of Neoliberalism.* Oxford, 2005. Oxford University Press.
3 Samir Amin. *Delinking: Towards a Polycentric World,* 1990. Zed Books

construction of golf courses in arid and semi-arid regions in Morocco. Fanon has been right all along with his critique of tourism. He saw it as a quintessential post-colonial industry where our elites have become "the organisers of parties" for their Western counterparts in the midst of overwhelming poverty.[4] The extractivist model of development has been a mechanism of colonial and neo-colonial plunder and appropriation. It has been put into practice regardless of the sustainability of extractivist projects or even the exhaustion of resources.[5]

Dependency on metropolitan centres via the extraction and export of raw materials has remained practically unaltered to this day in Maghreb countries. There has, however, been some changes to a few relevant aspects of traditional extractivism by bringing about increased state intervention into these activities. I was surprised and saddened to repeatedly hear, in Morocco, Algeria and Tunisia, statements comparing the ravages of post-colonial industries to the colonial ones. In some instances, it was even suggested that the French colonialists were more clement. To me, these comparisons speak internal colonialism, facilitated by an extractivist model of development that dispossesses populations and shifts the resulting socio-environmental costs to them.

People in these regions have long-standing grievances which sometimes burst into uprisings. Examples include: the case of Ain Salah, where people rose up massively in 2015 against plans to frack their land and pollute their waters; the emergence of an unemployed movement in 2013 in Ouragla, close to the oil wealth pole of Hassi Messaoud; the 2008 uprising of the Gafsa mining basin (met with bloody repression by Ben Ali's regime) and; the ongoing struggle of Imider communities against the royal holding silver mines that are robbing the commune's natural resources (including water) and impoverishing the area.

The Neoliberal Governance of the Environment in the Maghreb

Faced with all these injustices and destruction, who is shaping the environmental discourse and crafting a response to climate change in the Maghreb? Institutions like the World Bank, the German GIZ, and European Union agencies are ubiquitous and vocal, organising events and publishing reports throughout these three countries. They highlight some of the dangers of a warmer world and argue for urgent action, more

---

4 Franz Fanon. *The Wretched of the Earth*, 1967. Penguin Books
5 Alberto Acosta: Extractivism and Neoextractivism: two sides of the same curse. In "Beyond Development Alternative visions from Latin America", 2013. Transnational Institute / Rosa Luxemburg Foundation.

renewable energy, and adaptation plans. Given the shortage of alternatives, they seem to have comparatively radical positions when compared to that of local governments. However, these institutions are politically aligned with the powerful.

So, their analysis of climate change and the ecological crisis doesn't include questions of class, justice, power, or colonial history. The World Bank's solutions are market-based, neoliberal, and take a top-down approach. They re-empower those who have wealth, without addressing the root causes of the ecological and climate crises. Instead of promoting the necessary emissions reductions, they give polluting permits and subsidies to multinational and extractive industries. There is no reference to the historic responsibility of the industrialised West for causing climate change, of the crimes of oil companies like BP and Shell, or the climate debt owed to the Global South. The vision of the future pushed by the World Bank, GIZ, and much of the EU is marked by economies subjugated to private profit and further privatisation of water, land, and the atmosphere. The latest episode of this development includes the Public-Private Partnerships (PPPs) being implemented in every sector, including the Moroccan renewable energy plan.

These privatisations and grabs of resources fall under the rubric of "green capitalism," clearly visible in the agricultural model of these countries, especially in Morocco where water-intensive, export-oriented agribusiness dominates. The government of Morocco has the 2008 World Bank supported Plan Maroc Vert (Green Morocco Plan, PMV) which sets out the country's agricultural plan for the period between 2008–2020. Its aim is to quintuple the value of export-oriented crops by shifting land use away from staple cereal crops, promoting private investment in agriculture, and removing restrictions that stand in the way of private property rights.[6]

These hegemonic institutions have the financial and human resources to shape and co-opt local civil societies through funding and by helping to set up numerous environmental organisations. I was astonished to see the huge number of such associations and organisations that claim to be working on environmental issues in Tunisia and Morocco. To my knowledge, most of them are apolitical and seek actively, and sometimes opportunistically, EU and foreign funding. This phenomenon has

---

6 Adam Hanieh. Shifting Priorities or Business as Usual? Continuity and Change in the post-2011: IMF and World Bank Engagement with Tunisia, Morocco and Egypt, 2014. *Journal of Middle Eastern Studies*, 42:1, 119-134.

sometimes been dubbed the "NGOisation of the world." It is supposed to "empower civil society" yet, it contributes to the creation of an artificial and non-independent civil society sphere, useful only for deepening the marketisation and privatization of the social.

One example worth mentioning here is the emergence of some environmental mafias where supposedly-green organisations connected to real estate circles campaign to close down the chemical factory in Sfax, Tunisia, so the land can be developed for private profit. In a few words, the funding that comes from these neoliberal institutions won't be destined to fund progressive initiatives committed to a radical transformation of society. On the contrary, this funding is a powerful tool for continued domination.

Decolonizing Concepts of Justice: Are They Applicable to the Maghreb?

I want now to focus a little bit on the decolonial part of my work, which has involved an attempt to deconstruct some of the concepts I have been using. Based on my conversations with people in the Maghreb, the concept of "climate justice" is alien and unintelligible. This is not the result of a fault with "Orientals." The reason behind its unintelligibility lies in the fact that the concept is foreign and has no roots (at least not yet) in the region. The Arabic translation sounds odd and has no resonance with the locals. Even the larger concept of "environmental justice" is not widely used. My work in the Western NGO world introduced me to such concepts.

Beyond environmental and climate justice, we have energy justice and democracy, as well as food and trade justice. It is understandable that NGOs come up with these terms to talk about certain issues through the lens of justice and democracy, all in order to attract an audience. I feel that there are some risks involved in going down that path. The tendency to fragment such notions as justice and democracy could give the illusion that one can have justice (or democracy) in one field without the other, without putting into question the whole capitalist system that generates these interlinked injustices.

Activists, intellectuals and organisations in the Maghreb working on issues of climate change and environmental degradation generally do not use these concepts. And in the few cases where they are used, it is the exception rather than the rule. In some instances, they are imported from Europe without critical reflection and proper definitions. I strongly believe that importing and imposing concepts on populations is counter-productive. And it could end up helping to maintain some of the hegemonic structures between the North and South, as this domination can also exist discursively and epistemologically. While it is still useful to interact with and learn from movements elsewhere, we need always to contextualise our concepts and discourses and look at their history. For example, environmental justice (EJ) is born (in its sociological usage) in the United States as the result of struggles against waste dumping in North Carolina in 1982.

Since the 1980s, hundreds of reports have shown that "people of colour" and low-income populations have suffered from greater environmental harm from waste sites, refineries and transportation infrastructure than white and well-off communities have. For the people involved in this struggle, the fight against environmental injustice was equated with the fight against racism.[7] Climate justice has been introduced and developed by Environmental Justice Organisations and emerged during the early 2000s in an era of extreme, globalized state and market failure.

Climate justice only arrived on the international scene as a coherent political approach in the wake of the failure of a more collaborative strategy between major environmental NGOs and the global capitalist managerial class.[8] It was the outcome of linking social justice to geographically-specific ecological problems. The lineage of the climate justice movement includes a variety of traditions and shows that it was never separated from other struggles such as anti-racist environmentalism, the fight against Northern financial domination of the South, and the global justice movement that came to the foreground around the 1999 Seattle WTO protest. Do we then have to rely on terms such as "climate justice" to talk about the unjust politics of dealing with climate change? Or, do we need to rethink our concepts, situating them more precisely to focus on specific issues that directly affect the livelihoods of, in this case, Maghrebi people – issues such as water scarcity, drought, industrial pollution and sovereignty over resources. I am one of those who favour the latter scenario.

There is always an ecological element in the struggles I have come across. However, that dimension was secondary to more pressing issues of socio-economic rights. Rights relating to jobs, development of urban and rural infrastructure, the distribution of generated wealth and, more popular inclusion in decision-making processes. Therefore, environmental problems in the Maghreb (and elsewhere) need to be analysed in a

---

7 Joan Martinez-Alier et al. Between activism and science: grassroots concepts for sustainability coined by Environmental Justice Organizations, 2014. *Journal of Political Ecology*, Vol 21, 19-60.
8 Patrick Bond, *Politics of Climate Justice: Paralysis Above, Movement Below*, 2012. University of KwaZulu-Natal Press

comprehensive way with consideration to social justice, entitlements, and fair redistribution.

Conclusion

How can we plan for a just transition towards renewable energies and sustainable ways of producing our food and materials when our natural resources are being plundered by multinationals and when our land and water resources are taken over by agribusiness and destructive industries? We need to fight for sovereignty and democratic control over natural resources and energy and food systems. We need to fight against land and water grabs. And we must strive for more transparency against the corruption in extractive industries. Every year, the world's political leaders, advisers, and media gather for another United Nations Climate Conference of the Parties (COP). But despite the global threat, governments allow carbon emissions to rise and the crisis to escalate. Corporate power has hijacked the talks and promotes more profit-making "false solutions."

The Paris COP (COP21) in December 2015 received much attention, but the political leaders failed to deliver the necessary cuts to ensure survival. In this respect, the COP22 in Morocco (held November 2016) was bound to be no different.

In order to design and implement a just transition away from fossil fuels, we need to recapture our environment from the clutches of market mechanisms and recast the debate around issues of justice, accountability, and the collective good. We must move away from the logic of capital that compartmentalises, commodifies, and privatises our livelihoods and our lands. At the centre of this, lie meaningful and radical forms of local engagement and organising, as a counterpoint to the hegemony of those formalized international negotiations that submit to the dictates of the market.

WATCH YOUR CARBON FOOTPRINTS

Sonali Narang

Life on the earth began 4000 million years ago. Ever since, the earth has exhibited extraordinary changes in its climate as well as in the living beings inhabiting her. The earth has always witnessed strange natural phenomena. However, as time passes, it becomes more evident that the earth is being transformed not by natural events but more by anthropogenic activities. Nature, itself has taken millions of years to develop into the present outline of mountains, hills, plains, lakes, rivers, seas, beaches, air above and plants below with the living world of animals around man. Humans have plundered this beautiful inherited wealth for centuries now. Man's plundering comes in the form of acts including irresponsible cutting of forests, neglectful dumping of industrial and chemical wastes and, excessive use of fertilizers and pesticides. These have resulted in rise in the levels of carbon dioxide and other pollutants in the environment, thereby causing *global warming*" – the biggest challenge now before man. The problem of global warming which plagues all nations at the moment is a hot topic of debate at every forum. According to scientists, the root cause of global warming is the increase in the amount of carbon dioxide in the atmosphere from industries and automobile run by man.

The big question today is: How do we save our mother earth from climate change? If we think that it is only the government that has to get in the action mode to save our environment, then it is high time we changed our thinking. The government does have a major role to play, but we all, also have to do our parts with regards to saving the environment, if a safer climate and environment is the goal. We should recognise and understand the repercussions of engaging in actions that destroy the environment and must reform our acts individually and collectively, nationally and internationally.

Cutting Down Demands

Governments are designed to respond to the people's needs, and it is the people's needs that drive industry to produce a particular good. We all have to play an important role in reducing our demands for such goods which cause pollution. This would put the top polluting factories and governments out of business. Nature has more than enough resources to feed twice as many people as are currently in the world. Billions of rupees are spent on war machinery and the military, even as billions of goods and food are wasted in western societies daily. Yet, people in Iraq and of the Middle East have more weapons than they have food to eat. Many African dictators spend more than half their national income on war implements than they do in investing in their own people. Where do we place our priorities? When will we stop looking to governments and do what we can to erase this growing menace?

Nation states are trying to reach an agreement that can be helpful in the global reduction of emission of greenhouse gases. But in order to save the world from global warming, it is important for work to also be done at the personal level. There is an immediate need to change our way of living. By following some simple steps, that can easily be followed in everyday life, we can contribute in the fight against climate change. . If each man plants one little tree, it can amount to a great amount of afforestation, making the environment healthier. Increasing the use of bicycles or making a habit to walk short distances can contribute to the reduction in air pollution. In other words, it is important to minimize the use of vehicles. It is also important to pay heed to their maintenance: clean their exhaust pipes and keep the pollution they cause under strict control.

Coming to the gadgets used at home. Are all of them necessary? Are they well maintained and used efficiently? Important steps to take at home includes: turning off air conditioners, lights, fans, computers, television and radio systems when not in use. Did you know that your refrigerator and water heaters consume a lot of power? Careful use of these gadgets is a good way to save electricity. Use chlorofluorocarbons (CFCs) free products. It is said that recycling is one of the best measures of saving the environment. So, buy the products that you can reuse. Try to use renewable sources of energy. Lessen the use of rubber and plastic, instead, use paper bags and cardboard containers. Even a simple habit of buying in bulk can save a lot of packaging material, thus, contributing to saving the environment.

Preventing Wastage of Water

One of the most important constituents of the environment is water. It is very important not to pollute water bodies. Preventing the wastage of water and curbing water pollution is one of our primary duties. Turn off the taps; do not let the buckets overflow. Do not dump garbage down a storm drain.

Other Small Steps, Big Leap

When in the office, print only when it is absolutely necessary. Printing every soft copy leads to heavy wastage of paper. Avoid the excessive use of air conditioners in the office. Use emails instead of paper correspondence. Do not use disposable cups when you have the option of using ceramic ones. We all must minimize the use of animal products, which involve their killing. Animal fur and ivory are some of the excessively used products that are gradually leading to the extinction of the animals that provide them.

Small steps by each of us can make a huge leap towards saving the environment. The late Michael Jackson in his song says, "If you want to make the world a better place...just look on the man in the mirror...and make a change". Humans must take a serious look on how we use what we have. We must watch our own carbon footprints and see how much, individually, we are contributing to climate change. We must consider: where we put our rubbish; Do we recycle? How much paper do we use each day in our offices? How much electricity do we use? How often do we use the car instead of walking or taking the bus? The list goes on. If we fail to take little steps, the next generation will look back at us and scream, asking, why could you not take a step forward and do something?

We must teach our kids the importance of walking, of taking a bus instead of driving everywhere. This may not be much in the big idea of things, but it is a positive start so that their future can be filled with hope.

To conclude, "Let every individual and institutions now think and act as a responsible trustee of Earth, seeking choices in ecology, economics and ethics that will provide a sustainable future, eliminate pollution, poverty and violence, awaken the wonder of life and foster peaceful progress in the human adventure." – John McConnell, founder of International Earth Day.

DECOLONISE, REVIVE, TRANSFORM: MEET AFRICA'S FIRST EARTH JURISPRUDENCE GRADUATES

Hannibal Rhoades

At a colourful ceremony blessed by elders from the Kikuyu, Maasai and Tharaka Tribes, Africa's first ever group of Earth Jurisprudence (EJ) practitioners graduated this July (2017). Comprised of lawyers, educators, former accountants and civil society leaders from Benin, Kenya, Ethiopia, Uganda, South Africa and Zimbabwe, the group has spent the last three years engaged in an immersive 'training for transformation' in EJ.

An eco-centric philosophy of law and governance, Earth Jurisprudence recognises that humans across the planet must govern themselves according to the ecological laws and limits of the Earth system, as indigenous peoples have done for millennia. As many courts and governments fail to regulate, let alone stop, the destruction of Earth, a growing global movement is emerging. From Rights of Nature advocates to indigenous peoples, this movement is calling for a radical, Earth-centred transformation of our current anthropocentric legal and governance systems; a transformation underpinned by EJ understandings.

As a contribution to this movement, developed and led by the Gaia Foundation, the course in Earth Jurisprudence has been commended by the UN's Harmony with Nature Initiative. It supports participants to decolonise their minds, work to revive Earth-centred African knowledge systems and practices and, ultimately, contribute to the transformation of African governance from a human-centred, to an Earth-centred paradigm.

Becoming an EJ Practitioner

Blending wilderness experience and written assignments, African and western philosophical and legal traditions, advocacy strategies and practices for reviving indigenous knowledge systems, the three-year course in Earth Jurisprudence is the first of its kind.

The course places particular emphasis on the importance of experiential learning. Spending time alone in the wilderness to hone their

31

powers of observation and connect with Nature-as-teacher, each of the new graduates has embarked upon a profound personal journey 'back to roots'. Returning to their rural childhood homes, the practitioners have reconnected with their community lands, elders and bodies of traditional ecological knowledge. This process has enabled the practitioners to develop new ways of understanding their identity and some of Africa's strengths and struggles. According to Dennis Tabaro, a former accountant turned EJ practitioner from Uganda:

> The root causes of the crises facing Africa today, land grabbing and ecosystem degradation for example, date back to colonialism and are tied to the human-centred thinking that sees man as superior and having rights that override those of other beings. This course reveals Earth-centred laws and ways in which our traditional cultures recognise the rights of other beings in Nature. Human beings are part and parcel of creation. When we recognise the rights of other beings, in the web of life, to be, to enjoy their habitat and participate in evolutionary processes, then we can begin to address these crises.

EJ in Practice at the Grassroots

Putting new skills for reviving traditional knowledge and governance into the service of communities during their three-years of training, the practitioners have made great strides. Method Gundidza, for example, has been accompanying his childhood community, Bikita in Zimbabwe, to revive traditional knowledge and practices for climate-changed times. Through community dialogues, Method has helped bring together elders and youth, men and women, to discuss the problems they are facing and foster solutions rooted in their own cultures. One thing the people of Bikita have done is revive resilient local varieties of seed, including millet. They found that some elders had kept 'lost' varieties alive. According to Method:

> In the past people abandoned millet and the collective millet harvest as they were encouraged by companies and the government to use so-called improved seeds and chemical fertilizers. This made the people vulnerable. Millet is a very reliable drought crop. If the rains don't come, then at least, the millet will grow and people will have food. But in this last growing season, after a series of dialogues, the millet was in the fields again. Even when it was very dry and the other fields were brown, the millet was green. The people are also reviving their old millet seed storage system and the community harvest happened again for the first time in many years.

EJ in Practice on the World Stage

At pan-African and international levels, Africa's first Earth Jurisprudence practitioners are advocating for Earth-centred laws and policies that support communities' ecological governance systems. Earlier this year, the graduates successfully encouraged the African Commission to pass a radical new resolution calling on all African states to recognise and protect Sacred Natural Sites – places of critical ecological, cultural and spiritual importance for traditional African communities – and their related custodial governance systems. The graduates were prominent participants in the UN Harmony with Nature Initiative's 2016 global dialogue on Earth Jurisprudence. Presented at the UN General Assembly last September, this initiative is raising the profile of EJ as a paradigm that must underpin the UN Sustainable Development Goals if they are to succeed. According to Dennis Tabaro, another pressing task for the new practitioners is to play a leading role in growing and strengthening the African EJ movement.

"There is a big task ahead of this group. We are talking about nothing less than the transformation of our societies in terms of thinking and our worldview, and that means bringing many people with us", says Dennis. The practitioners will now act as mentors to the next group of EJ students. Hailing from Zimbabwe, Benin, Senegal, South Africa, Ethiopia and Uganda, the new group will now begin their EJ journey as the graduates deepen their own work for transformation.

Meet the Practitioners

At their graduation ceremony, each of the new Earth Jurisprudence practitioners shared a few thoughts on the course, traditional culture and their own commitments. Meet the practitioners here, in their own words:

Fassil Gebeyehu (Ethiopia), member of the African Biodiversity Network Secretariat: "We are all born barefoot lawyers for the Earth, but as we grow we become so consumed by the so-called modern world, by the city, that we easily forget. As Africans, many of us are born in communities that are very much embedded in nature. This course has helped me to become myself again. Now I am a barefoot lawyer by birth and by training."

Method Gundidza (South Africa and Zimbabwe), former accountant working with EarthLore Foundation: "People face many challenges in practicing traditional cultures that help conserve nature and barefoot lawyers supporting the revival of these systems face the same challenges. People say this is witchcraft, they say this is not modern. This is a big challenge we face in talking about indigenous knowledge, spirituality and how the Earth system works. But when we see nature in the way these traditions teach us, this is what is going to bring us life for future generations."

Oussou Lio Apollinaire (Benin), community leader and head of GRABE-Benin: "I am now beginning a new life with a new philosophy that orientates me to come back to the Earth and work with communities who still know how to respect the laws of nature. Our task is now to work with the new generations, to work for future generations, and stop breaking these laws."

Mersha Yilma (Ethiopia), student and long-time supporter of community knowledge revival with MELCA-Ethiopia: "The course really teaches you to look at the world differently. To learn from Nature. And when you sit and observe Nature, you learn more and more about how this world works. This is the basis of our traditional knowledge... After this course, I am ready to defend the rights of communities in my own country and the rights of our Mother Earth now. We have created a foundation and the next step is to grow from here."

Simon Mitambo (Kenya), educator and general coordinator of the African Biodiversity Network: "This course has been a great help in my work to accompany my community, who are bringing the indigenous knowledge and culture of the people back to life. We have learnt about and been able to experience the diverse cultures of Africa and to connect all of these experiences of revival together, to build our movement."

Dennis Tabaro (Uganda), former accountant and community dialogue facilitator with NAPE-Uganda: "One of the most powerful things this training has helped achieve is to give elders a space to come together and make their knowledge visible to others, especially the younger generations. Cultural leaders, community leaders and even some people in government are embracing EJ."

A FOREST IN THE CITY:
HOW CLIMATE-CONSCIOUS ARE YOU?

Ako Amadi[1]

In both scientific discourse and in conventional media communication, we are often frustrated by the interchanging usage of the closely related terms, 'global warming' and 'climate change.' The processes are complicated, but it suffices to state that global warming causes climate change. It is indeed a science to simplify science. The former results from excessive accumulation of greenhouse gases, chiefly carbon dioxide in the atmosphere; the latter is responsible for progressive environmental disasters that endanger life, property, and livelihoods. Thanks to the digital revolution, it has become easy via the ubiquitous smart phone to google up technical jargon and popular slogans anywhere and make sense of their intricate linkages.

Additionally, it is important that readers look up 'ecological footprint' and 'carbon footprint,' which actually reflect the state and modulation potential of national, group and individual contributions to global warming. In recent months, there have been massive climate protests and rallies in country capitals. Because Nigerians are not interested in such things, we wonder what the fuss is all about. In reality, climate change has become the greatest problem in the civilization of the 21st century.

If the 16-year-old Swedish girl, Greta Thunberg, has enough grasp of climate change science, so can all of us. All nations on the planet are impacted by global warming and all countries and cultures must play a role in the mitigation of global warming and adaptation to climate change. While industrialized countries should largely take greater blames for causing global warming, what should worry us more is the fact that the poorer nations will be disproportionately endangered by climate change. Global warming is the resulting distillate from a centrifuge of economic growth and reckless environmental degradation. There are apocalyptic indices. It is, in other words, a matter of life and death which we cannot leave to governments. Evidence is incontrovertible, and there is hardly

---

1 The article was also published at https://www.environewsnigeria.com/a-forest-in-the-city-how-climate-conscious-are-you/

an issue over which experts are more in agreement then climate change. Climate change doubters have now shrunk to an infinitesimal minority.

Today, climatological changes in one portion of the planet are likely to cause havoc in a distant geographic environment. A change of currents in the South Pacific could remotely trigger off temperature anomalies in West Africa that can result in heavy rainfall and floods in Nigeria. It is for this reason that the fight against global warming has progressed in joint international operations. We all have a stake in combating climate change. The attack strategy is basically two -pronged: mitigation of global warming through alternative, energy efficient, and less polluting industrialization by the rich nations targeted at reducing emissions of carbon dioxide; and adaptation by all countries to the impacts of climate change. Because plants absorb carbon dioxide in the chemistry of photosynthesis, every tree you plant or cut down has an impact on the budget of carbon dioxide in the global atmosphere.

Planting more than 500 billion trees globally could remove 25 percent of existing carbon from the atmosphere, a recent study has found. Nigerian cities must be filled with vegetation that will absorb carbon dioxide, check floods and soak up excessive rainfall and flash floods, as well as provide breeding habitats for birds and pollinating bees, beetles, and butterflies. We have no choice but to create urban forests for our own safety. And it will cost next to nothing.

Are you interested in ecological footprint in terms of the number of hours you use the air conditioner, the quantity of fuel consumed by the jeep and generating set? Are you worried about how many single-use plastic bags you take home from the supermarket? Do you talk to your children about climate change? Have you thought of replacing your well-manicured lawns with a vegetable garden? Are there trees and shrubs in your compound? Have you practiced separating domestic waste, for example separating empty bottles, plastics and paper from biologically degradable kitchen waste to enable composting of the latter? Have you thought of reducing the amount of meat you consume? This is considering the fact that compared with a 100g portion of vegetables, a 50g chunk of red meat is associated with at least 20 times as much greenhouse gas emitted and 100 times as much land use. Are you considering installing solar panels on your roof top? Any reader unable to answer 50 percent of these questions in the affirmative constitutes a climate change liability, and not the solution to the problem.

THE COMING GREEN COLONIALISM

Nnimmo Bassey[1]

The gloves are coming off. The climate crisis in the world is being approached as a mere unfolding change, as business opportunities and not as an emergency that requires drastic actions. Nations are comfortable to spend decades on talks and pretend they have ample time to procrastinate or deflect actions. However, this is not a time for propping up fictional ideas and carbon mathematics as though the cycles of Mother Earth are ordered according to some calculus or algorithms. The climate COP25 held in Madrid is drawing to a close as this is being penned. Not much progress has happened at the negotiations.

Indeed, the technocrats who are saddled with actually negotiating the various clauses of the Paris Agreement's rulebook could not conclude work on a number of articles, hence, pushed them over to be handled by the ministers who arrived in the second week of the COP. Considering that the ministers are basically politicians, their inputs tended to be weighted heavily on political considerations. Beginning from the evening of 10 December 2019, a pattern of selective consultations ensued with ministers and not with heads of delegations or negotiators. Considering that Article 6 of the Paris Agreement remains the thorny matter at this COP, observers feared that some of the ministers will be unfamiliar with the details and may indeed be unable to adequately negotiate it due to its complex and technical nature.

Issues expected to be handled by the ministers include: adaptation financing in the context of the cooperation under Article 6 and the use of the approaches for other international mitigation purposes; delivering on the overall mitigation in global emissions and; governance of the framework for non-market approaches.

There is a general tendency for nations to strenuously work towards avoiding responsibility. The current government of the USA shows clearly that nations can simply walk away from the multilateral space and allow the

1 This article was also published at https://www.environewsnigeria.com/cop25-the-coming-green-colonialism-nnimmo-bassey/

world take care of its problems. The only snag in this way of thinking is that unlike the nuclear deterrent scenario where nations hoped to beat others by arming themselves and projecting possibilities of utter destruction, the impending climate catastrophe does not offer the possibility of any nation emerging as the winner or even as a survivor. It is doubtful that anyone can survive extreme temperature increases, neither can anyone hope to survive for long under good waters. You would think that this sobering reality would force politicians to have a rethink concerning their posturing at the climate negotiations. Climate politicians are churning out new seductive words to obscure intentions and to market ideas that would help them avoid both action and responsibility. The narrative merchants bring up concepts such as nature-based solutions (NBS) which, on face value, is hard to fault. How can you reject any action that is based on nature, that respects nature and that works with and not against nature? The catch is that NBS does not mean any of that.

At the COP, there were side events that showcased how to include nature in Nationally Determined Contributions. Another one listed shell, Chevron and BP as founding members for "Natural Climate Solutions." The so-called nature-based solutions include carbon offsetting mechanisms that allow polluters to carry on polluting while claiming that their pollution or emissions are offset by mitigating activities such as tree planting or corralling forests as carbon sinks. Indeed, the NBS can be understood as the wheels of carbon stock exchanges. When nations speak of carbon neutrality, they are basically speaking of solving the climate crisis through mathematics and not through any real climate action. It does not suggest changes in modes of production and consumption. The same can be said of having Net Zero carbon emissions.

As the climate negotiation drags on, we must remind ourselves that it is essential for us to understand what we are fighting for before we can forge a real solution. The acceptance of carbon offsetting and similar notions as epitomes of carbon colonialism give reasons for worry. The burden of climate action is being forced on the victims without any regard for historical responsibilities, without regard for justice. This posture rides on the same track as slavery, colonialism, neocolonialism and their cousin, neoliberalism. Climate activists made a loud noise, outside the plenary hall on Wednesday 11 December, voicing the critical need for rich, polluting nations to remove their heads from the sands and take real climate actions. They were urged to quit their push for carbon markets and tricks to aid double counting when it comes to climate finance. They were reminded that there is a climate debt that has neither been acknowledged nor paid.

The investment of $1.9 trillion in fossil fuel projects and the expenditure of close to $2 trillion in warfare annually were held up as obscene reminders that contributing a mere $100 billion for climate finance ought not to give the world sleepless nights. That is if there is any seriousness to use the hours spent at the COP to tackle the root causes of global warming, cut emissions at source, help build resilience and pull the vulnerable from their miseries. As Asad Rehman of War on Want said at the Social Space during the COP,

> The struggle to solve the climate crisis must be tied to the struggle for economic justice and the struggles against inequality, neocolonialism and neoliberalism. The solution is not as simple as greening our economies or having more electric automobiles. It cannot be about greening the global north at the expense of the global south.

Rehman warned that anything short of the needed system change is nothing but a precursor of a new wave of green colonialism.

WANT REAL CLIMATE AMBITION?
KEEP POLLUTING INDUSTRIES OUT
AND MAKE THEM PAY

Patti Lynn, Nnimmo Bassey, and Lidy Nacpil[1]

The industries that have fueled this crisis should have no part in dictating the solutions. Rather, they should be made to pay to address the massive damage they have caused and to finance real solutions to the crisis. UN Secretary-General, António Guterres, convened a climate summit (in September 2019), hoping it would spur ambitious actions by countries around the world. The summit laudably galvanized people, organisations, and governments globally to gather in New York City. Unfortunately, Secretary-General Guterres and many others demanding urgent actions are missing critical pieces of the puzzle. No truly ambitious solutions or actions can come to fruition when fossil fuel, agri-business, and other polluting industries are at the table. The industries that have fuelled this crisis should have no part in dictating the solutions. They should be made to pay to address the massive damages they have caused and to finance real solutions to the crisis. Without these pieces of the puzzle in place, we know what we will get at this summit: proposals that will set us firmly down the path of increased global warming. For example, carbon markets and offsets are sure to play a big role. These are false solutions that enable Big Polluters to continue burning fossil fuels and devastating the earth under the guise of climate actions.

This is particularly galling as the Amazon burns and people in the Bahamas recover from the death and destruction left by Hurricane Dorian. Holding these industries liable can unlock hundreds of billions of dollars to help finance the most ambitious, most equitable and most just solutions we have. It is also exasperating because truly ambitious solutions are out there. Communities from the frontlines of climate change – those who have done the least to cause the crisis – have long proposed and advanced ambitious and equitable ways to address this crisis. Example of real solutions include:

---

1 This article was also published at https://www.commondreams.org/views/2019/09/23/want-real-climate-ambition-keep-polluting-industries-out-and-make-them-pay

keeping fossil fuels in the ground, stopping deforestation, and implementing an equitable transition to 100 percent renewable energy.

What countries need to be doing is bringing such people-driven solutions to the climate summit. Just imagine what could happen if all the power and resources gathered in New York this week were focused on the quickest and most equitable ways to end fossil fuel extraction and transition completely to renewable energy. That would be true ambition and action. This kind of ambition is exactly what people are demanding. And it will only be possible when polluting industries are not obstructing the process. For example, the International Emissions Trading Association (IETA) – one of the Big Polluters' most prominent trade groups founded by BP and includes Shell and Chevron among its members – is concurrently hosting a two-day "carbon forum" promoting "business-driven climate solutions."

If government leaders and civil society groups were truly serious about ambition, they would boycott the forum, knowing that such a forum is designed to advance false solutions leading us to a world where warming far exceeds safe limits. In reality, these polluting industries, their front groups, and the governments representing their interests (like the U.S.) have spent more than 20 years in the UN climate treaty process delaying, watering down, and blocking solutions to effectively and equitably address climate change.

So, it is no surprise that they are doing the same during the UN summit. That is why it is vital that the movement to implement a conflict-of-interest policy in the UN climate treaty succeeds. But removing the obstruction of Big Polluters and trade associations like IETA from policymaking is just the first step toward ensuring true climate solutions. Holding polluting industries liable for the damage they have caused is just as vital.

Over the past few years, media exposés have revealed that corporations like Exxon knew for decades that burning fossil fuels would lead to climate change. The fossil fuel industry then spent decades and hundreds of billions of dollars manufacturing doubt about the causes of climate change, discrediting science, and buying political influence. It ensured decades of increased emissions accompanied by stagnated climate policies. There is a groundswell of support in the US and beyond to make the fossil fuel and other polluting industries pay for the damage they have caused. Holding these industries liable can unlock hundreds of billions of dollars to help finance the most ambitious, most equitable, and most just solutions we have.

Communities in the frontlines of climate change did not cause the crisis, but they are paying the highest price. They need and are owed funding to implement real solutions that will actually turn the tide toward a just response to this global crisis. The UN Secretary-General and policymakers alike must wake up to the fact that polluting industries and their backers should no longer be allowed to obstruct climate justice. We must make them pay – and ensure those funds are used to respond to the enormous damage already done and implement the solutions we need to forge our way to a just, liveable future for all.

GREEN NEW DEAL:
A DONE DEAL OR A DOOM DEAL?

Magdalene Ime Idiang

For the past four decades, the planet has been warming up rapidly. Since 1906, the world's normal surface temperature has increased by 0.9 degrees Celsius even more in the more sensitive Polar Regions. The heat is melting glaciers, sea ice, and shifting precipitation patterns. An overwhelming scientific consensus maintains that climate change is due primarily to the human use of fossil fuels which releases carbon dioxide and other greenhouse gases into the air.

The gases trap heat within the atmosphere and the consequences on ecosystems include: rising sea levels, severe weather events, and droughts that render landscapes more susceptible to wildfires. The world is experiencing heat waves which have given rise to various changes in weather patterns. The urgency to mitigate climate change and its impacts becomes greater with each passing day. The urgency was made more obvious following the 2018 United Nations IPCC Report and the warning by scientists (in the 4th National Climate Assessment) that if global temperatures continue to rise, the world will experience intense heat waves, wildfires and droughts. Furthermore, if rapid actions are not taken, the result would be an unprecedented self-destructive climate future incomparable to whatever might have happened during all of human evolutionary history.

The United States has historically been responsible for a disproportionate amount of greenhouse gas emissions, having emitted 20 per cent of global greenhouse gases through 2014. Given its high technological capacity, the US Congress resolved that the country must take a leading role in reducing its emissions through a set of economic transformations. The Congress, through a woman representative, Alexandria Ocasio-Cortez of New York, and Senator Edward J. Markey of Massachusetts, both Democrats, set up a 14-page congressional resolution known as Green New Deal.

The resolution lays out a grand plan for tackling climate change. It contains two major ideas. First, it states what America needs to do to cut greenhouse gas emissions in order to avoid the worst consequences of climate change. And that is, to completely stop burning fossil fuel and transition totally to renewable energy. This means zero emission energy sources. Second, it shows how America will be protected during the transition, that is, a way to help the ordinary American people. This includes provision of high wage jobs, economic security for all people of the United States while also trying to fix societal problems like racial injustice. The proposal stipulates that it is the duty of the US Federal Government to create a Green New Deal to achieve net-zero greenhouse gas emissions. It also called on the Federal Government to wean the United States from fossil fuels and curb planet-warming greenhouse gas emissions across the economy while guaranteeing new high-paying jobs in clean energy industries. But what is behind the green new deal?

The green new deal was inspired by the name The New Deal (old-new deal), a set of social and economic reforms and public works projects undertaken by President Franklin D. Roosevelt in response to the Great Depression. The Green New Deal (GND) combines Roosevelt's economic approach with modern ideas such as renewable energy and resource efficiency. A study published by The Brooklyn Rail (Beyond the Green New Deal) reveals that the New Deal (old-new deal) did not end the Great Depression, that the great depression was toppled by the military-Keynesianism of World War II which brought massive employment and federal contracts.

The proposed Green New Deal has been questioned and criticized by conservative politicians in the USA who see it as a wildly unrealistic and politically untenable way to deal with climate change. The conservatives balk at the implementation cost of the GND, estimated at 93 trillion dollars and wonder how the United States government, which has 22 trillion dollars of debt, will pay for such a deal. John P. Holdren, a former science advisor to Obama, thinks the Green New Deal's 2030 goal is too optimistic, saying that 2045 or 2050 would be more realistic. Some other persons have expressed concern that setting unrealistic "aspirational" goals of 100% renewable energy could undermine "the credibility of the effort" against climate change.

The debate continues. In December 2019, the European Union presented a set of policy proposals under the name European Green Deal. The proposal was presented by the newly elected European Commission under the leadership of Von der Leyen. It had less ambitious decarbonization timeline as it targeted carbon neutrality by 2050 as against the United States' 2030 plan. The policy proposal involves every sector of the EU economy and has a plan to direct 1.2 per cent of its annual GDP to the green economy including new infrastructure, public procurement, research and development and, industrial retooling.

The policy plan also presented how the European Union Commission will make the additional investment needed to achieve the 2050 climate target, with estimates totaling 60 billion euros per year and a proposed 45 billion Euros per year from 2021 to 2027. Contributions from households, corporations, public investments and national governments are to be collected to get an additional 215 billion Euros needed to meet the target. All EU members except Poland, Czech Republic, and Hungary had signed up to the goal.

What does the Green New Deal hold for Africa? The question before us is whether a GND manufactured in the global north will be used as a prescription for the global south, as another attempt to exacerbate current suppressive, oppressive and colonial extractivist paradigms.

The GND may sound like a message of hope for its proponents. But will it hinge on the back of the poorest people in the global south and deepen foreign domination through climate initiatives that will exploit Africa's resources in terms of land grabbing and policy intrusion or compromise Africa's sovereignty? As "green industries" pile more pressure to gain access to certain minerals needed for renewable energy appliances in order to meet the needs of consumers in the global north, and as local politicians remain hooked on expected foreign exchange, what will be the fate of the fence line communities in Africa? We are talking about the large expanse of land needed to execute this plan and a significant part of the accessible land is in Africa, occupied by individuals who are least powerful, especially politically. It is a situation which can plunge these individuals into competition with powerful private interests from the world's most powerful countries, over land that provides their basic needs.

For instance, a research institute reported in 2014 that Norwegian companies' quest to buy and conserve forest land in East Africa to use as carbon offsets came at the cost of forced evictions and food scarcity for thousands of Ugandans, Mozambicans and Tanzanians. The GND could encourage exactly this kind of well-known socioeconomic and political trade-offs. Until the GND is thoroughly interrogated, especially from the perspective of those who are not on the negotiating tables but would be impacted by the deal, this might well spell doom for many and must not be seen as a done deal.

BIODIVERSITY:
KEY TO CLIMATE CHANGE, MITIGATION

Sonali Narang

The link between climate change and biodiversity has long been established and is now widely recognised. According to the Millennium Ecosystem Assessment, climate change is likely to become one of the most significant drivers of biodiversity loss by the end of the century. Climate change is affecting biodiversity by changing the timing of key life events, increasing vulnerability to pests and natural disasters, and changing habitat conditions.[1]

The climate has always changed with ecosystems and species coming and going. However, swift climate change affects the ability of ecosystems and species to adapt. Climate change is already forcing species to adapt either through shifting habitat, changing lifecycles, or the development of new physical traits. These lead to increased biodiversity loss with negative consequences for the wellbeing of humans and other species. The impact of climate change on biodiversity in the Arctic is among the most threatening. This impact is seen not just in the reduction in the amount of sea ice but in its thickness and age. Less ice means less reflective surface, meaning more rapid melting.

The loss of sea ice has implications for biodiversity loss beyond the Arctic. Less sea ice does not just lead to changes in seawater temperature and salinity, causing changes in primary productivity and species composition of plankton and fish. It also causes large-scale changes in ocean circulation, affecting biodiversity well beyond the Arctic, according to the 2010 Global Biodiversity Outlook Report. The Fifth Assessment Report (AR5) of the Intergovernmental Panel on Climate Change (IPCC) concludes that marine biodiversity and coastal ecosystems in the Arctic are especially at risk from increasing water temperatures and stratification as well as ocean acidification.

According to the AR5, the Arctic region and coral reefs are so vulnerable that risks to biodiversity emerge even with global average

---

1 https://www.millenniumassessment.org/documents/document.318.aspx.pdf

temperature increases of only 2°C. The report confirms that climate change impacts have been felt on all continents and oceans. It also considers the role of deforestation, land-use change and agriculture in the emission of greenhouse gasses which impact negatively on biodiversity and climate change adaptation. Climate change is expected to result in changes in species and ecosystem structure in the Amazon Forest, increasing risks for biodiversity.

Another disturbing aspect of climate change is its impact on cultural services. Cultural services are the non-material benefits, such as cultural identity, recreation and, mental and physical health that people gain from biodiversity and ecosystems. Climate change alters the ability of ecosystems to provide jobs, recreational opportunities and restorative experiences, which results in a decline in the mental and physical health of community people and potential losses of nature-based tourism income[2].

The UN's Global Biodiversity Outlook 3, in May 2010, summarised some concerns that climate change will have on ecosystems, thus:

> Climate change is already having an impact on biodiversity, and is projected to become a progressively more significant threat in the coming decades. Loss of Arctic Sea ice threatens biodiversity across an entire biome and beyond. The related pressure of ocean acidification, resulting from higher concentrations of carbon dioxide in the atmosphere, is also already being observed.... Ecosystems are already showing negative impacts under current levels of climate change...which is modest compared to future projected changes.... In addition to warming temperatures, more frequent extreme weather events and changing patterns of rainfall and drought can be expected to have significant impacts on biodiversity.

The AR5 highlights the threats facing biodiversity as a result of climate change and concludes that if the global average temperature reaches 4°C, climate change will likely become the dominant driver of ecosystem changes and loss. Biodiversity and ecosystems conservation are crucial because, through the ecosystem services that biodiversity supports, climate change mitigation and adaptation are advanced. Conserving natural terrestrial, freshwater and marine ecosystems and restoring degraded ecosystems (including their genetic and species diversity) are essential as ecosystems play a key role in the global carbon cycle and in adapting to climate change.

Conserved or restored habitats can remove carbon dioxide from the atmosphere, thus helping to address climate change by storing carbon. The AR5 recognises the role of mangrove, seagrass and salt marsh ecosystems

---

2 Sandifer & Sutton-Grier (2014). Connecting stressors, ocean ecosystem services, and human health., *Nat. Resour. Forum*, 38, pp. 157-167.

as important carbon stores. These ecosystems need to be protected and preserved. Moreover, conserving intact ecosystems, such as mangroves, can help to reduce the disastrous impacts of climate change, such as flooding and storm surges. This is coupled with the provision of a wide range of ecosystem services that are essential for human wellbeing.

Ecosystem-based Adaptation

Ecosystem-based adaptation includes the sustainable management, conservation and restoration of ecosystems to provide services that help people adapt to the adverse effects of climate change. Conservation and management strategies that maintain and restore biodiversity can be expected to reduce some of the negative impacts of climate change. However, there are rates and magnitude of climate change at which natural adaptation will become increasingly difficult. Options to increase the adaptive capacity of species and ecosystems in the face of accelerating climate change include reducing non climatic stressors, such as pollution, over-exploitation, habitat loss and fragmentation, and invasive alien species; wider adoption of conservation and sustainable use practices, including through the strengthening of protected area networks; and facilitating adaptive management by strengthening monitoring and evaluation systems.

Examples of ecosystem-based adaptation (EBA) activities include coastal defence through the maintenance and/or restoration of mangroves and other coastal wetlands to reduce coastal flooding and coastal erosion and the sustainable management of upland wetlands and floodplains for the maintenance of water flow and quality. Other examples relate to the conservation and restoration of forests to stabilize land slopes and regulate water flows; the establishment of diverse agroforestry systems to cope with increased risk from changed climatic conditions; and the conservation of agrobiodiversity to provide specific gene pools for crop and livestock adaptation to climate change. The wide adoption of EBA activities by the different regions in the world can help in restoring the earth's biodiversity and in ameliorating the climate situation that the world is facing today.

ACCELERATING CLIMATE ACTION BY DESIGN

Nnimmo Bassey[1]

The theme for the World Habitat Day 2021, Accelerating Urban Action for a Carbon-free World, is a strong call on architects and all practitioners involved in the design and actualisation of the built environment and related services. It is a call to them, to be conscious of the fact that climate change is an existential threat to all living beings on earth, thus, poses a fundamental problem to the present-day design industry. It is often stated that cities are responsible for some 70 percent of the global carbon dioxide emissions with transport, buildings, energy and waste management accounting for the bulk of urban greenhouse gas emissions.[2]

The process of building and delivery as well as their utilisation hugely contributes to global warming. This is because of the energy needed to extract and process building materials and to maintain habitable temperatures, as well as the general maintenance of these structures. The main global warming sources here, as you may suspect, include the emissions related to cement production and the burning of fossil fuels for energy production. In the US, buildings consume 40 percent of energy annually, and are responsible for nearly half of the carbon dioxide (CO_2) emission in the country.[3] Building materials with considerably high environmental impact include concrete, steel, wood and insulation materials.

The theme for the World Habitat Day highlights carbon-neutrality. With the just-concluded COP26[4] of the United Nations Framework Convention on Climate Change (UNFCCC), the world has been regaled with the vision of a "net-zero" carbon future. While trying not to jump into the carbon-neutral or net-zero arguments at this point, it is pertinent to state that these concepts require considerable unpacking as they centre on needed climate action and are embedded in the theme of the Day.

1 Paper presented by Nnimmo Bassey, FNIA, MFR, at the World Habitat Day celebration of the Nigerian Institute of Architects (NIA), Akwa Ibom State Chapter on 4 October 2021
2 World Habitat Day. https://urbanoctober.unhabitat.org/whd
3 Ned Cramer (2017). The Climate is Changing. So Must Architecture. https://www.architectmagazine.com/design/editorial/the-climate-is-changing-so-must-architecture_o
4 26th meeting of the Conference of Parties to the UNFCCC

Why Do We Need a Carbon-Free World?

The question is whether a carbon-free world is even possible. If the answer is in the negative, what then is the significance of considering the possibility at all? What message do we seek to convey when we prescribe the desirability of aiming for, or having a carbon-free world? A simple answer to these questions would be that we cannot have a carbon-free world but we can try to considerably reduce carbon emissions to a tolerable level. Carbon dioxide concentrations in the atmosphere have risen since the start of the industrial era from an annual average of 280 parts per million (ppm) in the late 1700s to 410 ppm in 2019. That is a hefty 46 percent increase. [5]

The tolerable level is said to be350 ppm. Besides carbon dioxide, other gases of concern in the atmosphere are methane and nitrous oxides. Ozone is also a greenhouse gas but is found mostly in the stratosphere and is useful in absorbing and preventing harmful ultraviolet radiation from the sun from reaching the earth. Global warming occurs due to increasing concentrations of greenhouse gases in the atmosphere. Heat comes from the sun in short waves, but when bounced off the earth they go up in short and long waves. Whereas the short waves pass through the atmosphere without resistance, the greenhouse gases trap some of the long waves trying to exit the atmosphere. Scientists estimate that without the greenhouse effect, the earth would be as cold as minus 18 degrees Celsius. What this tells us is that we do need greenhouse gases in the atmosphere, otherwise we would all freeze. The trouble is when the concentration of the greenhouse gases gets higher than it ought to be, we set the stage to be roasted.

Climate Change Impacts

Nigeria, like many other countries, is severely impacted by climate change. The impacts include floods, droughts, increased heat, and water stress. There is persistent land loss due to coastal erosion in the South and desertification in the North. Coastal erosion is accompanied by the salinisation of freshwater systems, thereby exacerbating species loss. Deforestation is a major contributor to global warming, with enormous impacts on food production. Unbridled flaring of associated gas poses threats to the climate, environmental/human health, and agricultural production. Oil spillages equally add to the crisis through the dumping of highly volatile hydrocarbon products into the environment. In addition to

5 EPA. Climate Change Indicators: Atmospheric Concentrations of Greenhouse Gaseshttps://www.epa.gov/climate-indicators/climate-change-indicators-atmospheric-concentrations-greenhouse-gases

desertification, water stress and the shrinkage of Lake Chad is currently affecting at least 11 states in Northern Nigeria. Gully erosion is a great menace in the Southeast and South-South regions. Lake Chad has shrunk from a size of over 25,000 square kilometres in the 1960s to a mere 2,500 square kilometres, breeding attendant social and economic upheavals in the area. Climate change has exposed over 33 million Africans (spread across Madagascar, Malawi, Mozambique, Zambia, Zimbabwe, South Sudan, Sudan, Ethiopia, Somalia, and Kenya) to food insecurity emergencies.[6]

The food crisis has been compounded by the erosion of food sovereignty due to the loss of biodiversity. Violent conflicts and poverty add another dimension to the dire situation and raise the number of the vulnerable to over 52 million. Southern Africa and some other parts of Africa warm at two times the global rate[7] and the Southern Africa region experienced two massive cyclones in March 2019 and April 2021, leading to a loss of over 1000 lives and wreaking about $2billion worth of infrastructure. Having so many strong cyclones in a short space of time is a record. The intensity and upward reach of the cyclones on the South-eastern coastline also broke the records. Cyclones Idai and Kenneth impacted close to 3 million persons. Some researchers tie the cyclones to the warming of the Indian Ocean. If this is true, we can expect more cyclones, as well as the devastation of marine ecosystems in the region, which reflects IPCC's report (2021) that the warming in this region is higher than in other parts of the world.

Will the Climate Summit Turn the Tide?

In November 2021, the world gathered in Glasgow to take stock of what has happened since the Paris Agreement of 2015. The Paris Agreement consolidated the voluntary approach to tackling climate change, which was first introduced at COP15 held in Copenhagen in 2009.

The key proposal of the Agreement is that nations would voluntarily suggest what amount of emissions reduction they would make as their contribution to tackling the climate crisis – the Nationally Determined Contributions (NDCs). Bear in mind that the Agreement also set temperature targets at 1.5 degrees Celsius or well below 2.0 degrees Celsius above preindustrial levels. By the latest submission of countries to the UNFCCC, the aggregation and analysis of NDCs show that global temperature would rise by up to 2.7 degrees Celsius.[8]

6 https://reliefweb.int/report/world/2019-natural-disasters-claim-more-1200-lives-across-east-and-southern-africa
7 IPCC.Impacts of 1.5°C of Global Warming on Natural and Human Systems. https://www.ipcc.ch/sr15/
8 UNFCCC. (2021). Full NDC Synthesis Report: Some Progress, but Still a Big Concern. https://unfccc.int/

We remind ourselves that prior to COP15, industrialised nations were required to adhere to legally binding emissions reduction targets under the Kyoto Protocol. That requirement was based on the foundational justice principle of Common But Differentiated Responsibilities (CBDRs). Today, rather than a mandatory emissions reduction, what is expected is legally binding reporting requirements. What a parody!

The voluntary emissions reduction regime is already pointing at catastrophic global warming, considering the freak weather events being experienced at the present 1.1 degrees Celsius level. Moreover, as earlier noted, parts of Africa warm at double the global average, meaning that if the global temperature lurches upwards to a 2.7C scenario, Africa will be literally uninhabitable.

An important part of the Paris Agreement is Article 6 which seeks to establish a policy foundation for a carbon emissions trading system that allows polluters to buy the license to continue polluting from less polluting nations. The fossil fuels industry and partner nations love this article because it would require nothing but a monetary exchange for their climate sins. The point is this: the polluters have the cash, and the vulnerable nations need the cash, but the planet will suffer. Science informs us that the world cannot afford to open new fossil fuel mines or fields. This sector is already responsible for about 80 percent of all carbon dioxide pumped into the atmosphere since the industrial revolution. Rather than halt the extraction of climate-harming fuels, the industry is set to invest more funds for new oil and gas projects.[9]

Net Zero Is Not Zero

Now, let us look at carbon neutrality, net zero and other concepts of their ilk. A statement issued by Oilwatch Latin America offers a good analysis of the idea behind the concept of Net Zero, which has become so popular across the world. Countries, regions, and corporations are offering to achieve Net Zero by 2050. Two things should be of concern here. The first is that net zero does not mean zero emissions. Second, 2050 may seem to be a distant date. But even if the proposed action were to be a true solution, the world cannot wait for 2050, considering the current rate and magnitude of catastrophic floods, fires, cyclones and hurricanes.

....
news/full-ndc-synthesis-report-some-progress-but-still-a-big-concern
9 Nnimmo Bassey (2016) *Ambition, Selfishness and Climate Action in Oil Politics-Echoes of Ecological Wars*, Daraja Press.

The extraction, burning, and industrial use of fossil fuels constitute the main cause of the climate crisis. Since 1830, and at an exponential rate of increase during the last two decades, the planet has warmed due to greenhouse gas emissions. Just 100 energy corporations are responsible for 71% of the emissions generated since 1988. Policies focused on monitoring and counting carbon dioxide (CO_2) molecules are a part of the problem as long as they are used to divert attention from the central issue: the continuing exploitation of coal, oil and gas under an energy-hungry, petro-dependent economic model. . Carbon accounting – the basis of most official climate policies – is all about moving molecules around, creating false equivalences, erasing emissions with a "click", and shirking responsibilities in order to carry on business as usual while covering up the roots of the climate crisis. The focus is on inventorying emissions and percentages to be reduced (or rather, to be permitted) and using the numbers to claim that the transfer of CO2 into the atmosphere can be "compensated for" by supposed future transfers out of it.

Quantifying CO_2 emissions is the smokescreen that allows the governments of the Global North to continue to finance the fossil industry in trillions of dollars, even after the signing of the 2015 Paris Agreement. Pretending that addressing climate change is a matter of measuring and managing CO_2 molecules is a way of privileging the market and subjecting traditional communities to violations of the rights of humans and nature while at the same time making global warming worse.

Examples of this farce include, proposals for "carbon neutrality" or "net zero emissions", which by assuming falsely that emissions generated in the fossil extraction chain can be offset by the carbon fixed by natural processes or geoengineering, will only exacerbate global warming. Other examples include, the Clean Development Mechanism, Reducing Emissions from Deforestation and Forest Degradation Plus (REDD+), Nature-Based Solutions, "climate-smart" agriculture and livestock-raising and, Bioenergy with Carbon Capture and Storage (BECCS). Although such proposals are usually presented as conservation programmes, they are in fact part of a speculative business model that has nothing to do with constructive responses to the climate crisis.[10]

---

10 Oilwatch Latin America. (October 2021). The Climate Debate is not About CO_2 Molecules. https://www. oilwatch.org/wp-content/uploads/2021/10/Statement_OWLA.CO2_EN.pdf

What Can Architects Do?

Architects and related designers have huge roles to play in climate-proofing our planet. Climate change does not merely threaten the planet; it threatens living beings who inhabit the planet – humans and millions of other beings. The problem is that the crisis is triggered by human beings and the economic and socio-political systems designed and built by us. It is important that architects understand these systems in order to design and deliver the built environment differently. So, what can we do as architects? Sea-level rise is already on track to continue, and this places most of Southern Nigeria at risk of going under water due to the region's low-lying nature and the fact that the geographic Niger Delta is a naturally subsiding zone. The immediate response here must include the use of flexible construction materials and designs that are responsive to the ecological peculiarities and needs of the region. Architects must pay more attention to the immediate and larger urban landscape in which their creations sit.

As architects, we are often deeply concerned about form and efficient spatiality. We work to consciously ensure that our built spaces consume as little cooling, lighting, ventilation and maintenance costs as possible. As good as these are, considering the threat of climate change, we should also be concerned about what is called embodied energy or the sum of energy required to produce goods and services. Embodied energy includes the energy utilised in mining the needed raw materials. In the building sector, this also includes the construction and replacement/demolition of our buildings, quarrying, cement production, smelting steel, baking of the bricks, transportation of materials to sites and their installation, dismantling and carting away. Did we say carting away? Let us say suitable disposing of the materials.

- Hoping that this conversation will continue beyond the symposium, let us share some ideas or actions to take on.

- Raise awareness on the risks associated with the current levels of overconsumption that is pushing beyond planetary limits and leading to dramatic biodiversity loss and climate change. We must re-examine our romance with certain climate-harming building materials, such as concrete and steel while at the same time, reducing wasteful use of materials.

- There is a real need to work with other professionals to promote the greening of our urban areas, set aside spaces for urban farming and avoid the cementification of spaces. We need to take a closer look at our traditional architecture in terms of design, materials, craftsmanship and theory, and encourage more organic approaches.

- Get involved in design for mass transit and other modes that encourage a rapid transition from dependence on fossil fuels. Integrate designs that are self-sufficient in terms of energy needs, for example, by using solar power, etc.

- Design and build multi-use spaces that are flexible and durable at the same time. Encourage the upgrading of existing buildings and retrofitting them for energy efficiency; and also design for circular use of resources and promote the recycling of wastes.

- Encourage vehicular free zones in our urban areas and encourage open meeting spaces rather than exclusive boxed-up spaces.

- In terms of theory, we should see buildings as living things that have birth, midlife and terminal points and, must be environmentally friendly with regard to materials and energy demands.

- Avoid the aping of postcard architecture; instead, we should design environmentally respectful and culturally sensitive spaces.

In conclusion, you may have heard the saying that we first shape our buildings and then the buildings shape us. This perspective should encourage and challenge architects to generate designs that not only respond to current climate challenges but lay the pathways to provoking continued robust imaginaries and actions for upcoming generations. Permit me to close with a quote that urges us to consciously ensure that our narratives capture the story of our lives as told by us and dipped in our experiences:

> ...If there is any hope for the world at all, it does not live in climate change conference rooms or in cities with tall buildings. It lives low to the ground, with its arms around the people who go to battle every day to protect their forests, their mountains and their rivers because they know that the forests, the mountains and the rivers protect them. The first step toward re-imagining a world gone terribly wrong would be to stop the annihilation of those who have a different imagination – an imagination that is outside capitalism as well as communism. An imagination which has an altogether different understanding of what constitutes happiness and fulfilment.[11]

11 Arundhati Roy. (2013). Decolonize the Consumerist Wasteland: Re-imagining a World Beyond Capitalism and Communism. Accessed at http: https://www.commondreams.org/views/2013/02/19/decolonize-consumerist-wasteland-re-imagining-world-beyond-capitalism-and-communism

TIME FOR A PEOPLE'S COP

Nnimmo Bassey

The 26th Conference of Parties (COP26) to the United Nations Framework Convention on Climate Change (UNFCCC) took place from 31 October to 13 November 2021 and had a loud but uncertain achievement. It was not just about the Glasgow Climate Pact which highlighted the phasing down of coal. The COP itself was the phasing down of the victims of climate change who are fighting a tough battle against a crisis to which they did not contribute. It was a COP that left its justice foundation on life support and offloaded the burden of climate action unto generations yet to be born.

While COP26 went on, there was a parallel COP26 Coalition People's Summit which centred on forging real climate action rather than being driven by vested fossil interests. The urgency shown by the popular People's Summit exposed COP26 as a Conference of Polluters, Conference of Profiteers and Conference of Procrastinators.

The badge of procrastination in the face of an emergency was displayed in the emblematic Net Zero pledges of the parties. The net zero concept was so pervasive that posters with elephants and whales were displayed at train stations and other public spaces in Glasgow to celebrate it and perhaps, to announce expanded threats that could emerge with big animals being designated as carbon sinks.

COP26 was an avenue for world leaders to showcase their ambition towards tackling the climate menace. The reality was that all they could display was their voluntary pledges to cut emissions, capped with pledges of when they would attain net zero carbon emissions. The voluntary suggestions on what levels of reduction countries would take are the linchpin of the Paris Agreement. Nations were excited to endorse and celebrate the Agreement with its Nationally Determined Contributions (NDC) because it afforded the big polluters the opportunity to avoid making emissions cut based on science and historical responsibility.

The Paris Agreement set paradoxical temperature targets that were considered ambitious and chose the voluntary pathway to achieve it. This was a paradox that attempted to seal the Pandora box. Looked at more critically, the temperature targets set in the Paris Agreement can be seen as being purposely ambiguous rather than ambitious. As was noted by the Prime Minister of Barbados during the COP, it is unlikely that NDCs can solve a global problem. The truth in this position has become evident by the projected outcome of the NDCs and Net Zero pledges. The best possible outcome of the present pledges is given as a 2.4C average temperature increase above preindustrial levels. That average stands beyond 1.5C and well below 2.0C which are the targets of the Paris Agreement. We note the apparent contradiction in those targets when we realize that anything that is "well below" 2.0C should be less than 1.5C. The question arising from this is whether an upper limit can be lower than the lower target? For regions like Africa that have temperatures about 50 percent above global averages, a 2.4C global average possibility translates to an incinerating 3.6C average. It beats the imagination that anyone from these vulnerable regions would accept that possibility as a laudable target.

There was a loud debunking of the concept of net zero before and during COP26. It was shown that net zero is not zero and does not herald the stoppage of emissions. It merely projects some mythical action whereas it means a continuation of business as usual. It orchestrates a continuation of burning fossil fuels and stoking the atmosphere with carbon while proposing carbon capture, carbon removals or some measures of solar radiation management as remedies. Net zero has also been shown to be a glorified name for carbon trading which helped to portray COP26 as a carbon trade fair. While nations trade in hot air and negotiate inaction, children and youths are becoming more strident in their denunciation of the procrastinating leaders. They see the pledge to achieve arithmetic net zero by 2050 or 2060 or 2070 as a blatant insult and an attempt to deny them a future.

For the youths, the struggle is about justice today and not a promissory note that may not ever be fulfilled, or that would be of no consequence by 2050 should the planet have already stepped into catastrophic climate change by that time. The unwillingness to follow the principle of common but differentiated responsibilities (CBDR) was also manifested in the way the issues of climate finance and that of loss and damage were handled. When it comes to climate finance, the Glasgow Climate Pact sounds as if it were a draft or recommendation for people other than parties to implement. It "Notes with deep regret that the goal of developed country

Parties, to mobilize jointly USD 100 billion per year by 2020 in the context of meaningful mitigation actions and transparency on implementation, has not yet been met, and welcomes the increased pledges made by many developed country Parties and the Climate Finance Delivery Plan: Meeting the US$100 Billion Goal and the collective actions contained therein." This may sound like excellent diplomatic phraseology but should be seen as unbecoming in an emergency. A section was also allocated to platitudes on the matter of loss and damage. If the UNFCCC had listened to the call for the recognition and payment of a climate debt accumulated over centuries of rapacious exploitation of peoples and colonial plundering of nature, there would be no debate over climate finance.

The COP26 outcome could not call for a phasing out of fossil fuels even though science clearly shows that it is their burning that is roasting the planet. And this is because of the undue influence of the fossil fuel industry. Rather than stop funding fossil fuels, the industry is set to pump more finances into the dying sector. In Oil Change International's report, Sky's Limit Africa, we learn that the fossil fuel industry plans to sink USD $230 billion into the development of new extraction projects in Africa in the next decade and up to USD $1.4 trillion by 2050. Tone-deaf? The COP could not make any move that would hinder the plans of the fossil fuel sector. This is because, with 503 delegates from 100 fossil fuel companies at the conference, and being part of 27 national delegations, such a suggestion was dead on arrival. The industry had more delegates than Brazil who, with 479 delegates, had the largest national delegation at the COP.

The choice of words in the climate pact is incommodious. A critical example is with reference to climate justice. The pact says, "Noting the importance of ensuring the integrity of all ecosystems, including in forests, the ocean and the cryosphere, and the protection of biodiversity, recognized by some cultures as Mother Earth, and also noting the importance for some of the concept of 'climate justice', when taking action to address climate change." How on earth can a framework ostensibly predicated on justice, state that climate Justice is only important "for some"?

Given the outcome of the COPs, we conclude that it is time to replace the COP with a Climate Change Conference of Peoples. When Copenhagen flopped, Bolivia convened the Peoples Summit on Climate Change and the Rights of Mother Earth in Cochabamba in April 2010. With more than 30,000 delegates from over 100 countries, the peoples of the world came out with a clear roadmap for climate action as well as the

Declaration of the Rights of Mother Earth. It is time to denounce net zero myths and demand real zero emissions. It is time to echo the truth that climate change is a global problem that must be tackled not by xenophobic nationalist self-interest tagged NDCs but by binding emissions cut based on CBDR.

SECTION 2

HUNGER POLITICS

The language of hunger is universal, but what is less universal is the questioning of why people are hungry ... Hunger has become a political tool for manipulation of peoples and nations, with specially devastating impacts on the poor....

– Nnimmo Bassey

GMOS FOR FOOD AND NUTRITION SECURITY: A COSTLY DISTRACTION

Hans R. Herren

In the aftermath of the food crises of 2008 and 2010, policymakers across the world called for an increase in investments in agricultural research. Increasing agricultural growth, especially in Africa where majority of the population depends on agriculture as its key income source, is expected to not only yield high returns but also pro-poor growth [1]. This strategy is supported by African governments with a commitment to increase investments in agriculture to 10% of GDP. The International Assessment of Agricultural Science & Technology for Development (IAASTD) 2009[2] and UNEP's 2011[3] Green Economy reports noted the high returns from an increase in public agricultural research investments.

For a number of economic as well as ecological reasons, the Green Revolution (GR) has largely sidestepped African farmers, while most agricultural research and extension investments went into cash crops. Food needs on the other hand, were satisfied with cheap imports. Combined with increase in population growth, decline in soil fertility, and impacts of global climate change, the continent has failed to increase its productivity over the last decade according to World Bank 2007[4] report. Although public investments are now growing again, these are not necessarily flowing into supporting the transition from traditional agriculture to agroecology and organic. Instead, they try yet again to implement the flawed GR despite all that is known about its shortcomings.

In line with the GR approach to achieve agricultural growth in Africa, the genetic modification (GM) of crops has risen to the forefront and been heralded as a viable alternative technological and reductionist solution to the current traditional agriculture methods. While some of its most vocal

---

1 World Bank (2007). *Agriculture for development.* World Development Report 2008.
2 IAASTD (2009). International Assessment of Agricultural Knowledge, Science and Technology for Development: Global Report., Island Press.: Washington DC – http://www.agassessment.org/reports/IAASTD/EN/Agriculture%20at%20a%20Crossroads_Global%20Report%20(English).pdf
3 UNEP (2011). *Towards a green economy: pathways to sustainable development and poverty eradication.* http://www.unep.org/greeneconomy/Portals/88/documents/ger/ger_final_dec_2011/Green%20EconomyReport_Final_Dec2011.pdf
4 World Bank (2007).

proponents[5] contend that biotechnology is currently kept out of African countries at the cost of starving and poor farmers, we argue that numerous and scientifically backed up agro-ecological alternatives exist to increase productivity – sustainably and with a proven track record[6] – to the benefit of the small-scale farmers in sub-Saharan Africa. Our position is based on a review of existing studies evaluating the effective and potential benefits from GM technology vs. alternatives in the economic, environmental and social dimensions, with a focus on African farmers.

While Africa has traditional herbicide and pest tolerant varieties, GM technologies developed for African farmers come with newer generation varieties. One example is a drought-tolerant variety – Water Efficient Maize for Africa (WEMA) – managed by the African Agricultural Technology Foundation (AATF). Although it has stimulated high hopes, to this date, however, AATF is yet to release yield-results from its ongoing trials. Since yield increases from similar genetic modifications were limited in the US[7], it is very likely that the drought-tolerant varieties supplied to AATF actually might yield worse results.

Advancements in seed technologies and sustainable agricultural methods implemented by thousands of East African farmers are effective in not only substantially increasing yields, but also in improving soil fertility and abilities to retain moisture, prevent soil erosion, reduce carbon emission and increase biodiversity among other benefits[8].

FAO as well as UNEP and UNCTAD[9] report in 2007 and 2008, respectively, that in an African low-input environment, sustainable

5 Collier, P. (2011). *The plundered planet: why we must – and how we can – manage nature for global prosperity.* Oxford University Press; Paarlberg, R. (2008). *Starved for science: how biotechnology is being kept out of Africa.* Harvard University Press.

6 For a general overview, see long-term evidence by Mäder P., Fliessbach A., Dubois D., Gunst L., Fried P., Niggli U. (2002). Soil fertility and biodiversity in organic farming. Science, 1694-1697; or Rodale Institute (2011). *The Farming systems trial: celebrating 30 years.* http://www.rodaleinstitute.org/files/FSTbookletFINAL. pdf.. See also latest results to be published by FiBL (2011). Farming system comparisons in the tropics. http://www.systems-comparison.fibl.org/

7 In the United States, although yield increases were above the 6 to 10 percent expected (Monsanto 2009), in an African environment numerous alternatives exist for obtaining similar increases; Monsanto (2009) 'Monsanto, BASF Scientists Disclose Discovery of Gene Conferring Drought Tolerance in Corn Plants', Monsanto Press Release June 9, 2009

8 Niggli, U., Fliessbach, A., Hepperly, P. & Scialabba, N. (2009) *Low greenhouse gas agriculture: mitigation and adaptation potential of sustainable farming systems.* FAO, April 2009; UNEP (2011). *Towards a green economy: pathways to sustainable development and poverty eradication.* http://www.unep.org/greeneconomy/Portals/88/ documents/ger/ger_final_dec_2011/Green%20EconomyReport_Final_Dec2011.pdf; Khan, Z. R., Midega, C. A. O., Njuguna, E. M., Amudavi, D. M., Wanyama, J. M., & Pickett, J.A. (2008a). Economic performance of the push-pull" technology for stemborer and Striga control in smallholder farming systems in western Kenya. Crop Protection, 27(7), 1084-1097; Khan, Z. R., Midega, C. A. O., Amudavi, D. M., Hassanali, A., & Pickett, J. A. (2008b). On-farm evaluation of the "push-pull" technology for the control of stemborers and striga weed on maize in western Kenya. Field Crops Research, 106(3), 224-233.

9 UNEP and UNCTAD (2008). *Organic agriculture and food security in Africa.* United Nations: New York and Geneva. http://www.unctad.org/en/docs/ditcted200715_en.pdf

agricultural practices reduce costs of synthetic inputs (i.e. pesticides replaced by push-pull methods), increase yields, enhance economic diversification and strengthen households' self-sufficiency and food securities. Furthermore, smallholder farmers can take advantage of both domestic and international markets for organic and other products derived from such productions. These multipronged efforts aim at improving the livelihoods of farmers across the scales – moving from soil and the seed to the crop and animals, and finally to the household and the social, economic and ecological sustainability of the region as a whole.

While genetically modified seeds may have the potential to save input costs (such as labour) or under optimal conditions, increase yields[10], these solutions do not pay off for the smallholder farmer, as they often demand additional fertilizer use and access to irrigation. Furthermore, the economic costs of potential contaminations[11] are too large given the numerous alternatives that can improve livelihoods. When considering the need for more resilience at the system level in the face of climate change, the solution lies in more system and crop diversity, which go against the use of a few GMO varieties in mono-cropping and rotation systems.

It is in this context that an eco-social intensification of the traditional agriculture, based on both a scientific foundation[12] and farmers' knowledge, offer solutions that are specifically benefiting African smallholders. Given its low demand for capital, the strengthening of continued participatory research in sustainable agriculture – a knowledge-intensive practice – can have a strong benefit for the farmers[13]. It should be the governments and development partners' goal to not only disseminate but also support the development of innovative solution to the agricultural production challenges through participatory agro-ecological research and extension.

Given the key issues in raising and maintaining higher agricultural productivity as well as assuring the restoration and maintenance of the key ecosystem services in the face of the combined challenges of climate change, growing demand for quality and quantity of nutrition by an

10 One key question is furthermore whether this yield increases actually translate into proportional increases in nutritional content, and to what extent they are sustainable with the onset of yield drags when double-stacking genetic traits (HRH, pers. comm.)

11 And for some crops potential ecological genes escape via gene flow into natural populations of wild relatives. The potential for contamination is also larger in African environments given the weak institutional framework. As already shown in the Indian case studies of Bt cotton, farmers have difficulties in applying an effective pest resistance management strategy (i.e. using border crops)

12 See for example Long-Term System Comparison undertaken under the coordination of FiBL (2011) in FiBL (2011) 'Farming System Comparisons in the Tropics', http://www.systems-comparison.fibl.org/

13 See for example the development of push-pull methods in East Africa that control both pests and weeds, resulting in significantly higher yields and income (Khan etal. 2008a, 2008b).

increasing population, the solutions need to address the causes of today's problems. The time for the implementation of the IAASTD recommended new paradigm is now. The paradigm places soil fertility restoration and maintenance, as well as, the crop, animal and production system diversity up-front. Complex problems as outlined above need complex solution instead of the reductionist ones presented by the promoters of GMOs, pesticides, herbicides and synthetic fertilizers. Agro-ecology provides a safer, more ecologically, socially and economically sound alternative for African smallholders as well as all other farmers that care for their land and customers.

A SECOND LOOK AT GMO FOOD POLICIES IN NIGERIA

Oluwafunmilayo Oyatogun

Nigeria makes for excellent study in several areas of policy, economics and socio-culture. However, one aspect stands out – biosafety concerns, including especially, genetically modified organisms (GMOs). Nigeria has a population of approximately 178 million people, which is about 2.5 per cent of the world's population. Nigeria's Lagos is one of the world's megacities. Nigeria is already Africa's most populated nation by a long shot. It is primly located between latitudes 4° and 14°N, and longitudes 2° and 15°E, offers savannahs, mangrove swamps, tropical rainforests, and dense centres of agricultural productivity.

GMOs in Nigeria are increasingly being portrayed as the solution to the poverty and hunger entrenched in Nigeria's large population. The country's underperforming agriculture is often cited as a result of lack of modern technologies and high-yielding crop varieties, among other barriers. Historically, crop production was increased in Nigeria by expanding the land under cultivation, mostly for cash crops destined for foreign markets. However, the current focus has been on improving yields per plot of land. It is no surprise, therefore, that Nigeria is increasingly field-testing a variety of GMO crops with a plan to commercialize them. While the government has shown strong support for introducing GM technology in the Nigerian market, there is a strong resistance to the move and debate on the risks of GM crops to human health and the local environment.

Some international policies on food have an eye on sub-Saharan Africa because of the reported over 180million undernourished people in the region. There are also issues of land degradation and unsustainable farming practices, which put a strain on the agricultural system of the continent. These internationally derived conclusions are used as constructs to put pressure on countries like Nigeria to embrace modern biotechnology on the premise that this would minimize the land intensity and improve yields per plot.

The Convention on Biological Diversity is the only significant set of guidelines by which the entry of GMOs into Nigeria may be controlled.

However, with the generic one-size-fits-all model of many international agreements, the CBD does not address Nigeria's most fundamental agricultural constraints. In fact, in a HOMEF workshop in 2013, some smallholder farmers decried the Convention as "too technical to be relevant to those who are most stricken by adversity as a result of GMOs."

A Nigerian National Biosafety Bill before the National Assembly defines bio-safety as "the range of measures, policies and procedures for minimizing potential risks that modern biotechnology may pose to the environment and human health" (Biosafety Bill 2010). In the case of Nigeria, the modern biotechnological products of concern are GMO foods. One critical concern of environmentalists towards the bill is the lack of provision for public consultation. According to the bill, Part viii, section 6, makes provisions for the public display of applications from individuals or corporations intending to import or introduce GMOs into the country. However, section 6(2) of the bill indicates that the announcement of the display of such applications is not mandatory.

Also, even though the bill makes provision for fines of up to 5 million Naira ($28,000), it does not measure up compared to potential damage. While several proponents of the bill argue that it will close the gaps currently penetrated by multinational agencies, opponents are wary of the effectiveness of a "substandard" Biosafety bill. It is typical for the large corporations and developers of GMOs, such as Monsanto, DuPont, Dow Chemical and Bayer Crop Science, to be actively lobbying for GMO approval. Opponents to GMOs argue that genetic engineering does not respect the rights of nature as genetically wholesome entities. Rather, it is an experimentation to facilitate capitalist and supposedly modern ideas of agricultural development.

The reductionist principles of GMOs are not compatible with the objectives of sustainable agriculture. Industrialization and globalization of agriculture are at the root of GMO technology, especially in the current Nigerian context. In portraying inconclusive technologies as a solution, GMOs attempt to solve the problems of agriculture with the same kind of thinking that caused these problems. Ecological "modernization" does not tackle mainstream modernity enough to oppose it; it merely adjusts the rules to accommodate ecological considerations. Some, such as Marteen Hajer have described it as a "new form of cultural politics, representing the greening of modernity". John Barry and Oluf Langhelle have condemned it as a paradoxical attempt to 'green capitalism' or 'deradicalize sustainable development', respectively.

Unfortunately, a key flaw with the ecological modernization of agricultural systems is the explicit ignoring of growth limits. To what extent can genetic material of food be tampered with in order to achieve efficiency? Does genetic modification of natural organisms alter the ecosystem enough to negate any environmental gains it creates from reduced fertilizers and pesticides? Another flaw with ecological modernization is that it maintains a myopic view of environment. For example, GMOs have ripple effects by altering ecosystem cycles. It is well known that adopting GMOs leads to decreased plant biodiversity and this affects the sustainability of ecosystems. Invasive species become increasingly problematic when GMOs lead to new weeds and pests with heightened resistance to pesticides. Moreover, GMOs represent liberalism principles of modernization theories on a micro-scale.

With seeds, as with markets, there are no boundaries; therefore, open pollination of GMO seeds can lead to the wide unintentional spread of new genes. Ecological experts fear that this spread could lead to the catastrophic persistence of transgenes within the local agricultural web in Nigeria. The impending Biosafety Bill ignores the Precautionary Principle of the Cartagena Protocol on Biosafety. The 'proceed with caution' principle was included to protect environments, agricultural and food systems – especially in African countries. However, Nigeria is playing 'catch-up' with other nations based on incompetent knowledge of GMOs. GMOs are a problematic solution as they do not consider the holistic nature of the natural food cycles and are an extension of neoliberal principles to ecological spaces.

ON MONSANTO'S CLAIMS
THAT GMOS ARE SAFE

Nnimmo Bassey, Mariann Bassey Orovwuje
and Gbadebo Rhodes-Vivour

We have read with interest the response from Monsanto to Premium Time's report of National Biotechnology Development Agency's surreptitious granting to permit for Monsanto to bring GMOs into Nigeria. We restate here that Monsanto's applications were approved without due diligence and that the law setting up National Biotechnology Development Agency (NBDA) is extremely flawed in that it gives individuals in the agency the latitude to toy with the health of Nigerians, our environment and food systems. Monsanto argues that their GMOs and their weed killers are safe. The truth is that the company is good at avoiding liability while exploiting the agencies that ought to regulate them. They claim, "A big part of that confidence comes from knowing that independent experts who've looked at GMOs have concluded that they're as safe as other foods. That includes groups like the American Medical Association and the World Health Organization, as well as government agencies like the FDA."

This is an interesting argument. We quote two statements[1], one from Monsanto and the other from FDA and leave the public to read between the lines.

Philip Angell, a Monsanto director of corporate communications said: "Monsanto should not have to vouchsafe the safety of biotech food. Our interest is in selling as much of it as possible. Assuring its safety is the FDA's job."

For the US Food and Drug Administration (FDA) "Ultimately, it is the food producer who is responsible for assuring safety."

When Monsanto and FDA make statements like these, the reading is that consumers are left to literally stew in their soups. In the words of David Schubert, Professor and Head of Cellular Neurobiology Laboratory at the Salk Institute of Biological Studies, La Jolla, California:

---

1 http://www.gmwatch.org/articles/gm-quotes/16079-regulatory-breakdown

> One thing that surprised us is that US regulators rely almost exclusively on information provided by the biotech crop developer, and those data are not published in journals or subjected to peer review... The picture that emerges from our study of US regulation of GM foods is a rubber-stamp 'approval process' designed to increase public confidence in, but not ensure the safety of, genetically engineered foods.

This is exactly what is happening in Nigeria today, unfortunately. We have an agency that disrespects the voices of the people, ignores national interests, and blatantly promotes the interests of biotech corporations. The relationship between National Biosafety Management Agency (NBMA), National Biotechnology Development Agency (NABDA), and Monsanto is rife with conflicts of interest against the Nigerian people. How is it that the regulation is so influential on the regulator? The evidence in leaked WikiLeaks cables is clear.

How can we have NABDA sit on the Board of NBDA, be a co-applicant with Monsanto and then sit to approve the application? This should fit into the definition of corruption in this season of Change. Monsanto has been desperate to tell the world that their weed killer, laced with the ingredient known as glyphosate, is safe. The debate about the safety of glyphosate has been interesting with Monsanto in their response to Premium Times claiming that "glyphosate poses no unreasonable risks to humans or the environment when used according to label instructions." The above claim says two or more things. First, that glyphosate poses risks. Second, this risk can be tolerated when the chemical is used according to label instructions. Third, when something goes wrong, Monsanto will absolve itself of culpability by claiming that the chemical was not used "according to label instructions."

The scientific debate over whether glyphosate causes cancer continues. But based on research, several countries have banned the use of the chemical. The very fact that there is no consensus on the safety of glyphosate is the reason why Nigeria must apply the precautionary principle. It is interesting that Monsanto accuses International Agency for Research on Cancer (IARC) of selective interpretation of scientific data. This is a case of a kettle calling a pot black. We doubt if there is any other corporation that engages in selective interpretation of data more than Monsanto.

There was a time when scientists insisted that cigarettes do not cause cancer. Today, that has been exposed as a lie. Monsanto claims that their liability over polychlorinated biphenyl (PCB) is over an historical misdemeanor. This is another problem with Nigeria's Biosafety Act. If problems emerge in future over toxic chemicals introduced into the Nigerian environment today, Monsanto will go free because the law does not have provisions for strict liability. Meanwhile, we remind ourselves that if toxic PCB is in history, so is Monsanto's Agent Orange, the defoliant used in the Vietnam War and the toxic template on which the company continues the business of killing biodiversity.

GMOs are basically regulated because their safety is in doubt. The approval granted Monsanto to conduct field trials of genetically modified maize requires that these crops should keep a distance of 20m from non-GMO farms. That is absolute nonsense and is designed to ensure that our natural maize varieties are contaminated. It is known that pollen grains travel several kilometres. Contamination has been one key tool used by Monsanto in countries like USA and Canada to chase after non-GMO farmers that actually are the victims of these companies polluting activities.

Our agricultural systems, eating habits and cultural requirements are not the same as those of Americans, for example, and bringing these crops into our country will expose us to unimaginable health impacts. We would also be closing markets against ourselves. A case in point is a recent refusal of Brazil to buy corn from the USA due to GMO concerns[2], even in the face of shortage of corn needed for chicken feed. Note that Brazil is a country already with other varieties of GMOs!

Finally, we ask, are we so stupid that a genetically modified crop, Bt Cotton, that just failed in neighbouring Burkina Faso, (and the farmers are making claims from Monsanto) is what we are glibly opening our country to? Are we having regulators or GMO traders making decisions over our destiny? We restate our stand that the so-called permit issued to Monsanto to introduce GMOs into Nigeria should be overturned and the Biosafety law itself should be repealed. We also call on the National Assembly to urgently investigate the process leading to the granting of the permit on Sunday, 1t May 2016, to assure Nigerians that we are not pawns in a commercial game.

---

2 http://www.bloomberg.com/news/articles/2016-06-08/gmo-concerns-stop-brazil-chicken-producers-buying-u-s-corn

EAT AND QUENCH: LET'S LISTEN TO WHAT OUR FOOD IS TELLING US

Jibrin Ibrahim

There have been mixed reactions about the introduction of GMO crops into the Nigerian agricultural system and market. Most anti-GMOs insist that its introduction will do more harm than good in all areas. They state that GMOs will destroy biodiversity, give rise to super-weeds in the farm, pollute other non-GMO crops in nearby farms; that its chemical content (for example, Glyphosate) is known to be carcinogenic, etc. This article discourages GMO crops deployment to Nigeria, while emphasizing that our traditional and local varieties are still the best and can feed us as a nation. One author had written that:

> Our food is normally composed of a lot of dirt; poison, dangerous chemicals, GMOs, and we are all rapidly eating ourselves to death. The easiest way of demonstrating this is to refer to research by the European Union on what they found in the food we sent them to eat. They discovered that the items from Nigeria contained glass fragments, rodent excreta, and dead insects. They also found high levels of chemicals like dichlorvos, diometrate and trichlorphon in the products.

Some of the above-mentioned chemicals were used in the planting process, others in preservation. The poisonous chemicals did not serve their purpose because microbes such as salmonella, aflatoxins and mold had contaminated the food. Nigeria does not meet basic standards of food hygiene in the planting, growing, preservation and transportation of its food. I remember the shock of a Kenyan colleague who saw meat being carried in the open boot of a rusted taxi and shortly after, a man on a motorcycle carrying the leg of a cow on his head without any covering. He asked me if we have any organisations that set and monitor standards and I confirmed that we had but as always, they do not do the work they are paid to do.

It was not surprising that the EU was categorical in its decision in 2015 and 2016 to formally declare that the 42 food items exported from Nigeria were not fit for human consumption. The items include beans, melon seeds, palm oil, bitter leaf, pumpkin, shelled groundnut and live snails. In other words, the things we eat every day that we were trying to sell to our compatriots in Europe. It might well be that the exporters had actually chosen the best from our markets to export to Europe. But the reality is that our best is not good enough for human consumption. Had the food items passed the sanitation test, then issues of not having labels, improper packaging, lack of health certificates, and other entry documents would have arisen? After the incident, Audu Ogbeh, the Minister of Agriculture and Rural Development, warned that Nigerians might be killing themselves in instalments through the food that they eat. Ogbeh listed several of such poisonous foods, including moi-moi (bean cake) wrapped with cellophane (nylon) and cooked in a manner that transfers dangerous chemicals into the beans. Another dangerous habit of millions of us is consuming sachet water that has been exposed to the sun at over 30 degrees Celsius to multiply the number of liver and kidney failures in our society.

Currently, there is panic in informed circles that the massive quantities of tilapia fish and frozen chicken consumed in Nigeria have been preserved with chemicals normally used for embalming dead bodies and that is why they never go bad. Not only are we all accelerating our movement to our deaths, we are already embalming our bodies before time. Talking of meat that never goes bad, I have always wondered what gala which we are told is a sausage is made of. Every other type of sausage I know of, goes bad after some time but not gala.

This week, the Nigerian Stored Products Research Institute (NSPRI) revealed that Nigerian peasant farmers spend $400 million annually on the purchase of pesticides. They say that we use them in an improper manner and millions of Nigerians are falling sick due to pesticide poisoning. This information is from the Executive Director of the institute, Professor Olufemi Peters. He lamented that rather than continue to kill ourselves with these chemicals, there are cheaper and healthier forms of storage such as the inert atmosphere silos for grain storage. Sadly, public health was one of the first victims of the collapse of governance in the country. One of the most serious threats to public health in the country is the grand entry and dangerous plot, to take over our agriculture, by Monsanto the chemical company that produces genetically modified organisms (GMO) and calls their dangerous products, food. The Nigerian government has given approval for GMOs to be grown on our land. The National Biosafety Management Agency (NBMA), into which Monsanto has been pumping dollars, has become the advocacy agency for promoting their GMOs and chemicals. Our own governmental institutions are mortgaging our future.

The first major Monsanto project in Nigeria is to grow glyphosate-infused maize. Recent studies have linked glyphosate to health effects such as, degeneration of the liver and kidney, and non-Hodgkin lymphoma. It is unfortunate that Bill Gates, with his America First mentality, is sponsoring Monsanto's Water Efficient Maize for Africa, a five-year development project led by the Kenyan-based African Agricultural Technology Foundation, which aims to develop a variety of drought-tolerant maize seeds. Why will he not invest in the Institute of Agricultural Research project in Ahmadu Bello University that is developing draught resistant maize that does not have the dangers of what Monsanto is doing? My fear now is that Aliko Dangote who is planning to invest billions of dollars into Nigerian agricultural production is now sucked into this Monsanto project. There are reports that some of the food aid being currently imported into Nigeria is GMO.

As a first step, the Ministers of Agriculture and the Environment should call the NBMA to order and make them withdraw the authorisation issued for the production of GMO crops. Given our fragile ecosystems and stressed environment, we must take our biosafety seriously and avoid the path of introducing crops that are dangerous to the health of our people and our environment. Nineteen European countries that care about the health of their people have completely banned genetically modified crops. Even the Russian State, Duma, recently passed a bill banning all import and production of GMOs in the country. We must not allow Nigeria to be turned into a dumping ground for what sensible countries have rejected. Sincere scientists have shown evidence that Monsanto's crops are genetically enhanced to tolerate the use of the herbicide, glyphosate, which was declared as a possible carcinogen by the World Health Organisation's International Agency for Research on Cancer (IARC).

Every day, more and more Nigerians are falling sick and dying and as we weep for them, we often wonder why so many young people are going. Maybe the question we should be posing is: How come some Nigerians are still alive given the intense and systematic way we are poisoning ourselves.

NIGERIA DESERVES AN UNBIASED BIOSAFETY REGULATORY SYSTEM

Mariann Bassey-Orovwuje

It has become the norm for the Nigerian biosafety chief, Dr Rufus Egbeda, to rise to the defense of genetically modified organisms (GMOs). This was my response to some participants (not Nigerians), at a high-profile meeting, who saw my article, "Nigeria bio-safety chief defends GMOs", published in Premium Times, on 9 October 2017, and were visibly alarmed that a regulatory officer would be promoting GMOs, when he should be the umpire. In fact, one said: "This couldn't happen in my country." I am taken aback by some of the biosafety chief's statements such as, "Genetically modified organisms are not different from their conventional counterparts." If this was true, why would GM promoters or scientists go into so much trouble of inserting activated toxin genes from the soil-living bacterium Bacillus thuringiensi (Bt) into some crops? When the NBMA boss admits that the crops are "modified," how can these "modified" crops be the same with their natural, untainted, conventional counterpart?

Monsanto adduced the same arguments in their application to bring in their GM Maize to Nigeria. They asserted that their maize is equivalent to conventional maize. As we have said in many quarters, and we will say it again, the theory of "equivalence" is a worn-out argument that has been discredited by independent science, including in a joint South Africa-Norway Biosafety project published in 2011. Monsanto's Maize application to NBMA was accompanied with a cocktail of chemicals – glyphosate formulations which will be applied to MON 89034 and NK603 (Maize). Contrary to Monsanto's claims of its safety, the International Agency for Research on Cancer (IARC), a sub-unit of WHO, concluded that there was strong evidence of genotoxicity and oxidative stress for glyphosate according to publicly available research; this is in addition to findings of DNA damage in the peripheral blood of exposed humans. In a nutshell, the agency said glyphosate is likely to cause cancer.

On 19 October 2017, against all odds and despite industry scaremongering and pressure, the proposal to fully ban glyphosate by 2020 went through EU Parliament Environment committee. That means the EU Parliament environment committee supports glyphosate ban by 2020. Let us be reminded that BT cotton, another of Monsanto's application, had been rejected in Burkina Faso for failure to deliver good quality yield, one of the hyped promises from Monsanto. It was that same failed variety that was recycled and submitted here in Nigeria, and was approved by NBMA, possibly to mark its first year of existence. Many reports of this Bt cotton's abysmal failure abound. In the words of Parshuram Ghagi, from Yavatmal district in India, whose relative died of pesticide poisoning, "Bt Cotton resistance claims have proven hollow."

Dr. Sharad Nimbalkar, former Vice-Chancellor of Dr Panjabrao Deshmukh Krishi Vidyapeeth, states unequivocally, "Bt Cotton variety in use has lost its potency. Besides, pests become resistant to even the pesticides over a period of time. As a result, the number of sprayings required to save the crop has increased." A new peer reviewed analysis, *GMO Bt toxins: Safe for people and environment or super toxins?*, systematically compares GMO and natural Bt proteins. It shows that GMO developers, in the process of inserting Bt toxins into crops, have removed many of the elements contributing to this narrow toxicity.

Thus, developers have made GMO insecticides that, in the words of one Monsanto patent, are "super toxins". The authors of this review additionally concluded that references to any GMO Bt toxins being "natural" are incorrect and scientifically unsupportable. It is worrisome to read that the Biosafety Chief said "that cowpea and sorghum were presently being tried at the Institute of Agricultural Research in Zaria... also another product under trial called the 'newest rice' by the National Cereal Research Institute, Badegi." Is this for real? There have been applications for Bt Cotton (MON 15985) and Confined Trial (1) NK603 AND (2) MON89034 X NK603 Maize, and most recently the AMY3 RNAi Transgenic Lines (transgenic Cassava Clones) by International Institute for Tropical Agriculture (IITA) and ETHZ Biotechnology Lab in Zurich, as was announced by NBMA. Aside this announcement, there is no clarity on how other staples, cowpea (beans), sorghum, rice, all major Nigerian stable food, are being genetically modified and on field trials in Nigeria.

When did the trials for cowpea, rice and Sorghum begin? Which institution(s) or corporation(s)/companies, or laboratories are collaborating with the said institutions doing the trials? Under what laws were these trials authorised? How come it was not subjected to public comments like the case of the cotton, maize and cassava as provided by section 25(1) of the NBMA Act 2015 which states:

> The Agency shall upon the receipt of the application and the accompanying information under section 23 of this Act, display copies of such application and relevant information at such places and for such period as the Agency may, from time to time determine to enable the general public and relevant government ministries and agencies study and make comments on the application and relevant information within 21 days.

The director-general had urged citizens to view genetically modified organisms from a knowledge angle and ignore statements that paint it as harmful." Earnestly, is Nigeria's chief biosafety regulatory officer saying that GMOs pose no harm or risks? GMOs are basically regulated because their safety is in doubt. If indeed GMOs are safe, why should we have a regulatory agency? Why do we need a Biosafety Management Agency? The Agency was established to provide regulatory framework, for safety measures to check the adverse effects that GMOs would have on human health, animals, plants and the environment. If indeed GMOs were safe, NBMA should be disbanded and the staff redeployed to line agencies. Staff promoting GMOs can be sent to the National Biotechnology Development Agency (NABDA), the agency mandated to promote GMOs. That is where they would be a perfect fit.

In 2010, the American Academy of Environmental Medicine warned that evidence that GMOs directly cause health harm is strong enough to warrant warning people to avoid eating them. The academy noted that numerous studies and incidents have suggested that GMOs can cause problems including: immune dysfunction, insulin disorders and, damage to organs and the reproductive system. Also, in the earlier peer review studies, *GMO Bt toxins: Safe for people and environment or super toxins?*, the authors said, "Ciba-Geigy measured its Bt 176 toxins to be 5-10 times more toxicologically active when inserted into plants. Monsanto patented a series of novel Bt toxins with up to 7.9-fold enhanced activity and called these 'super toxins' having 'the combined advantages of increased insecticidal activity and concomitant broad-spectrum activity'. The most powerful of these is now found in commercial MON863 corn."

I dare to say that agroecology is the bold future for farming in Nigeria and Africa as a whole. Let us keep those toxic chemicals, pesticides and insecticides and, all those imported solutions out of our food and agricultural systems and out of our plates.

Nigeria deserves a biosafety regulatory system that is unbiased, pro-environment, and pro-people. I am afraid that NBMA, as presently set up and run, is skewed in favour of GMOs. Going by the incessant statements of the Director-General, the NBMA cannot be an unbiased referee, as it is clear, it is already flying the colours of the pro-GMO train.

RAGING CATTLE COLONIES DEBATE

Oduware Stephen

CSOs and individual stakeholders have continued to express their concerns about the proposed cattle colonies, stating that it is not the solution to the perennial herdsmen-farmers clashes across the country. There has been mixed reactions as the minister of Agriculture, Audu Ogbeh claimed that the idea of cattle colonies was meant to put an end to the incessant herdsmen-farmers clashes across the country. It is really worrisome and disheartening to see the spate of conflicts between herders and farmers and how it has degenerated into full-fledged war. With the rate of killings and destruction of properties coupled with the incubation of reprisal attacks, the impending consequences would be grave – one that should best be imagined – if not checked.

Many well-meaning Nigerians are perturbed by the unmanaged conflicts between the herders and farmers in several states. Some stakeholders believe that the issue has a political undertone. They ask that the government show more commitment, secure the lives of people and take necessary unbiased steps to quell the clashes and bring all perpetrators to book. Furthermore, the stakeholders argued that rearing cattle like other livestock is a private business. Thus, owners of cattle rearing businesses should be able to create an enabling environment for their business to thrive subject to the local regulations governing their business area without the meddling and unwarranted intervention of the national government.

The director of Health of Mother Earth Foundation (HOMEF), Nnimmo Bassey, in his blog post (Earthly Tales) said: "the idea of creating grazing or cattle colonies[1] across the nation as announced by the Minister of Agriculture sounds rather bizarre and raises a number of concerns." In the post, Mr. Bassey affirmed that "top on the list of concerns is the undertone of the word colony. For most Nigerians, the idea of a colony would be one defined as a country or area under full or partial political control by another, often a distant country." Though it could be said that

---

1 https://www.premiumtimesng.com/regional/north-central/255261-nigerian-govt-gives-reason-proposing-cattle-colonies.html

the minister used the term in the sense sometimes used to describe animals of the same breed staying together in a closed structure, "the imagery requires further interrogation" Mr. Bassey stated. He further explained that the distrust in the polity could heighten the wrong signals associated with the perceived meaning of colony. Colonialism was entrenched by the power of the gun. Thus, the blog espoused that it is very unlikely that colonizing any territory, for any purpose, at a period of heated conflict and distrust, will be the way to resolve the conflicts.

According to Mr. Bassey, the way to go is to rebuild the environment; fight desertification; improve on the fertility of the soils, thus, stimulating higher farm yields; increase agricultural extension services and; create linkages to markets. Another solution suggested is that the 'Great Green Wall Programme', aimed at combating desertification amplified by climate change through improved use of land and water resources, should incorporate pastoralists in their fodder production scheme for sustainable development. Nigeria could take a cue for effective environmental management from the much greener southern Niger Republic.[2] According to Mr. Bassey who is an environmentalist, restoring the environment is a practical measure to restoring and building peace. This, he believes should be the direction of government and indeed the political agenda of any people-oriented party.

Independent Newspaper reported that Adeola Elliott, the immediate past chairman of Agric and Agro-Allied Group of Lagos Chambers of Commerce and Industry (LCCI), emphasized that cattle rearing is an agricultural business and wondered why the government had interest in the matter. The former chairman submitted that the herdsmen should not have problems negotiating land usage with the landowners if truly they are sheep or cow herders or breeders. He views the colony idea as suspicious as the herdsmen have been found to carry weapons like guns. Dr. Jide Johnson has also criticized the use of the word colony, saying that it sends wrong impression and sounds like a warning. It signals colonization of other people's territory by herdsmen. He expressed his dismay at how the Federal Government is unable to propose a colony for mass education and housing but is proposing one for cattle rearing – saying that the proposed colony for cattle is absurd. He advised the government to borrow a leaf from the Botswana and Ghana experience, stressing that if colonies are created for the herdsmen, government must also do same for fishermen in Nigeria, on the international waters, and other farmers across the country.

2 https://www.indexmundi.com/factbook/compare/niger.nigeria

Dr. Johnson further stated that there are laws that govern businesses and the government should not be directly involved in the matter. Proffering a solution to the issue, he said the herders should rear their cattle in open lands and not encroach on other people's land. According to him, "When you graze your cattle on other peoples' farmland it will create a problem and I think one of the solutions people have suggested is that it is unhealthy for cattle to travel long distance – that is where the colony comes in so that they are limited to a particular place, let each farmer take responsibility for his cattle, approach the indigene, buy your land and then rear your cattle within the perimeter of the land."

The President, Federated FADAMA Community Association, Oyelekan Muftau, said Nigeria should have outlived cattle roaming and take lessons from other countries. According to him: "If you want to raise an animal you have to be ready to raise the animal. It is not about being nomadic. What if all poultry farmers and livestock farmers want their livestock to be roaming the street to eat; what do you think will happen?" Furthermore, he noted that as other livestock farmers are taking care of their livestock, the herdsmen too should find means to feed their cattle and stop moving them around. Joseph Ojeyemi, General Secretary Federated FADAMA Community Association, advised stakeholders to work together to find lasting solutions to the current challenge. He said, "it would not be out of place for the country to take lessons from other countries and replicate same for peace and growth". He emphasized that there can be symbiotic relationship between farmers and herders. He cited Kenya where he said "their cattle do not graze around" and the maize and guinea corn farmers sell their produce to the cattle keepers and make money in return.

The cattle colonies issue is one that requires urgent attention and should be addressed without ethnic, political or religious undertones. The root cause should be isolated and treated without bias. Cattle colonies is not the solution to the herder-farmer conflict because it is like robbing Peter to pay Paul.

EATING GENETICALLY ENGINEERED INSECTICIDES

Nnimmo Bassey

All through the ages, in the development of agriculture, humans have selected and cultivated crops and animals that thrive in their environments and are good for their health. Some of the factors that determine what we love as food are highly sensory and include texture, taste, colour and smell. Taste, for example, can drive people to eat things they know are not good for their health. Besides, people may tilt to a food product due to the appeal used in advertising it on the mass media. Communities and nations make regulations and laws to govern what their people eat, how they are produced and sometimes what is forbidden. One reason why care is taken in this regard, is the close links between crops and ecological health and, between food and human health.

When we say that we are what we eat, we are not far from the truth. Apart from the fact that the statement emphasizes the impact of food on our health and wellbeing, it also talks about our culture, spirituality and socio-economic relationships. Food plays a key part in our cultural activities. Without food, our celebrations and festivities are not complete. Food is so much expected at social events that by simply mentioning "item 7" everyone knows that you are referring to food and refreshments. It will be hard to find any religion that does not have food as a major aspect of some of its rituals. Agriculture is key in any economy.

Food can be an instrument of control and power. Weather variations and extreme weather events can bring communities and nations to their knees. Violent conflicts and wars can also render people hungry and expose them to the need to receive or purchase food aid. Yes, some food aids are paid for and are not exactly humanitarian. One nation that stood her grounds and insisted on what sort of food aid was acceptable is Zambia. They rejected the genetically engineered grains that were extended to them as food aid in 2002. And although much political pressure was piled on the nation, they did not starve but transited to bountiful harvest the following year. In the case of Nigeria, after the devastation of the agriculture of the

North East, we have received tones of seeds without verifying if they were genetically modified or not. That is how much food aid can trump caution.

What do consumers look for when they go shopping for groceries? Research has shown that consumers that care to read the labels on the food products they buy prefer to buy those that are pesticide free and are not genetically modified. Generally, buyers prefer fresh, clean and natural products. Unfortunately, many of our foods in Nigeria are sold in measures using cups and basins. Foods such as beans, garri, corn, amala, and the like are often neither packaged nor labeled. You simply have to trust your eyes to tell you whether what you are buying is wholesome or not. And, our people hardly read the labels on the packaged products on the market shelves. They may read the brand names and pay less attention to the contents. Agencies saddled with policing our borders against entry of unauthorized foods, such as the ones that are made of genetically engineered materials, appear overwhelmed by the influx of these products. Products are imported mostly with the assumption that whatever is presented as food is safe. It is as if it is assumed that because a thing was made in the United States of America, for instance, then it must be good for our consumption. We simply do not know what we are eating.

However, we should care to know as our health depends on that knowledge and our choice. Regulators and promoters of genetically engineered crops and foods in Nigeria accuse those that question the technology of being fear mongers or anti-science. This may be dismissed as a hollow accusation. But, when they make such arguments frequently, the real fear is that they may believe themselves. Besides, they also believe that they are running the best biosafety system in Africa. They boast that other countries such as Burkina Faso who junked genetically engineered cotton, cannot be compared to the supposed high skills and facilities Nigeria boasts of. This arrogant posturing is extremely dangerous.

Food is not all about science. Even if it were reduced to that, any science that is not in the interest of society is to be treated with extreme caution. Poisons are produced by scientists. Cigarettes are designed and promoted by scientists. Atomic bombs, biological weapons and diverse weapons of mass destruction, are all made by scientists. Can anyone claim that such inventions and productions should not be questioned or restricted? When scientists produce genetically engineered beans (cow pea), do they consider the fact that the insecticidal beans could also kill non-target organisms and that even the target pests could develop resistance?

When crops are genetically engineered to withstand herbicides, do they consider that they kill other plants and not merely weeds? And what about the soil microorganisms they kill, thereby, disrupting the webs of life in the ecosystems?

Working beneath the supervisory radar, the promoters of these technologies are set to erode our biodiversity and set the stage for ecological harms. Nigeria has quickly become the testing ground for novel and risky technologies, exposing citizens to higher levels of danger. With regard to the recently approved genetically engineered beans, we note that this beans variety, with the transgene Cry1Ab used in its transformation, has not been approved anywhere else in the world. The International Institute of Tropical Agriculture (IITA) may have concluded field trials for a cassava variety that has never been planted anywhere else in the world. That cassava was engineered to produce starch that would last longer than normal before degrading. Right now, there is another application for a new cassava variety engineered to have more starch than normal.

All these genetically engineered events are prepared overseas and brought for testing in Nigeria. Yet, we boast that we are so equipped and innovative in the sector. Even the genetically engineered cow pea is originally a Monsanto product given to Africans on humanitarian grounds. Humanitarian grounds indeed!

Fellow compatriots, if anyone tells you that the producers of genetically engineered crops and foods are cocksure of their products, ask them why they fight against nations having strict liability clauses in their Biosafety laws. Uganda just inserted such a clause in their genetic engineering regulatory law, ensuring that makers of GMOs will be held liable for any harm that may come from cultivation or consumption of their products at any time, even if such effects come years down the road.

FOOD SOVEREIGNTY AND MATTERS ARISING

Benita Siloko

In recent years, there has been an increasing interest in food sovereignty. Food sovereignty is people having right to food that is culturally appropriate, produced through sustainable methods and to define their own food and agriculture system. Despite its importance, there have been some controversies over the issue of food sovereignty. Advocates of food sovereignty have said that food should not be traded like other commodities. For example, in the statement of the World Forum on Food Sovereignty, "food is not just another merchandise and the food system cannot be viewed solely according to market logic"[1]. A community's need for safe and culturally appropriate food must be the main driver of agricultural policy. The profit motives of speculators and transnational agricultural companies fail to respond to the food needs of local communities. It has been said that food security is best considered in food sovereignty. We have to focus on food produced by the people and that are healthy and, respond to the needs of the people appropriately.

The availability of food does not automatically address the issue of food sovereignty if the people are compelled to eat what they would rather not eat. In other words, the decisions about food and its production should be hinged on the priorities of local producers, distributors and consumers, not on the preferences of "powerful corporations or geopolitically dominant governments." Local control helps protect small-scale agrarian communities from any possible destructive effects of market fluctuation and rapid changes in the prices of foodstuffs. It also enjoys knowledge of place and benefits from traditional wisdom to make informed decisions about production of appropriate food.

It is becoming increasingly difficult to ignore that industrial agriculture is one of the main source of GHG emissions and highest degree of landscapes specialization means that both agro-inputs and outputs frequently travel over long distances. The distance that food moves from farm to mouth has climate change implications. However, labour intensive

---

1 http://www.ukabc.org/wfs5+.htm

and biodiverse small farms are more likely to reduce GHG emissions in production, increase capacity for carbon sequestration and reduce the distance from which food is transported.

Beyond the compound and contextually diverse struggles for agrarian reform lies a rank of other hurdles to greater food self-sufficiency.

Dependence on industrial food surpluses has dampened smallholder earnings in local markets. In the long term, this has served to undermine the viability of small-scale farming. Where agro-export-oriented wide range holdings keep commanding notable portions of the best arable land, redistributive land reform continues to remain a priority in efforts to control food deficits and move in the direction of greater self-sufficiency. One of the most captivating features of food sovereignty is the thought of strengthening direct solidarity-based relationships between producers and consumers.

Another facet of localization that needs to be considered originates from the reality that urban and peri-urban places are not only areas of consumption but are also increasingly major sites of food production.

With the ongoing migrations of the rural poor to urban-slums, the significance of urban agriculture will continue to increase. Urban food production is difficult to quantify, since it stems mainly from independent livelihood initiated by individuals or groups who produce food for consumption and for the market.

Food sovereignty is fundamentally a multidimensional idea. The only way to be food sovereign is to grow systems of aggregation, processing, commercialization and distribution that are connected to other sectors of the economy. Food sovereignty discourses have frequently concentrated closely on food and farmers. But if food producers and consumers are to be truly sovereign, then both will have to be supported by and incorporated into a variety of social, economic and political fora that go well beyond food itself. In other words, food sovereignty requires a healthy, sustainable and diverse economy that goes well beyond food production.

On a final note, as Nigerians, we must be mindful of what we buy, cultivate or eat. This caution is tied to the issue of GMOs. We can bet that no one will knowingly eat an insecticide. But that is what we do if we eat any crop genetically engineered to be insecticidal. Some African countries have enacted strict laws to protect themselves from GMOs. An example is Uganda where, since the law was enacted, their President Museveni and the Ugandan parliament have been branded as being anti-science.

Should good genetic engineering science leave room for doubt only so that when harms manifest, the producers would not be held strictly liable? Responding in the affirmative makes nonsense the Precautionary Principle which should be the bedrock of Biosafety regulation. It simply means that where there is doubt, we should be cautious. The speed with which Nigeria is permitting GMOs is highly suspicious and offers no assurance that the government is concerned about food safety and the preservation of our biodiversity.

FARMER-HERDER CLASH:
BEYOND ETHNIC AND RELIGIOUS LABELS

Mfoniso Antia

Nigeria is a country endowed with human, socio-cultural and natural resources. The country has in the past few years experienced a strain on its resources due partly to poor management of some resources (as seen in the extractive sector) and partly to total negligence of other important economic sectors (e.g. agriculture). Nigeria's six geopolitical zones (North Central, North-West, North East, South-South, South-East and South West) are known for different but interrelating occupations, which cut across farming (crops and livestock) and trading.

Pastoralism is predominant in the Northern region of the country while crop farming and trading cut across all zones. However, there are peculiarities with regards to farming, depending on what thrives in a particular zone. In the past decade, Nigeria has battled with both political agitators and the terrorist group, Boko Haram. The activities of these groups have led to destruction of lives and property. Herders' conflict with their crop producing counterparts over land space for feeding of cattle and cropping respectively, has increased the death tolls. A lot of speculations and assumptions have been going on while trying to trace the root cause of the farmer-herder incessant clashes. There are bits of varying opinions and undertones to the conflicts but one must put sentiments aside to be able to critically look into and find out the real reason for these crises. This opinion piece is in no way justifying the horrendous killings perpetuated by the herders but is merely trying to direct the readers to view these conflicts from the lens of an environmental scientist. The writer believes that it is only when the reason behind the conflicts is found that proper solutions can be proffered.

With increase in global temperature comes a handful of attendant impacts, one of such impacts is drought and desertification which have dried up natural water sources and degraded pastures in Northern Nigeria. Fertile lands have dwindled due to these impacts of changing climate. Combined with population boom, these impacts are fuelling conflicts as herders are forced to migrate down South in search of fodder for their livestock. The noticeable increase in population would imply that there are more people to feed which in turn mean more agricultural settlements and less available land and water for herders. All of these tend to trigger more and more disputes between the farmers and herders. Man has always adopted migration as a strategy to cope with his existential vicissitudes as life's difficulties force him to move from one place to another in search of better opportunities to meet his needs.

In a 2017 paper titled 'Climate change, pastoral migration, resource governance and security: the Grazing Bill solution to farmer-herder conflict in Nigeria', Lere Amusan stated:

> While many factors shape human's decision on migration, the compelling roles of environmental factors have gained increasing attention in recent years. Man's decision to move and his choice of destination are often informed by his goals and experience in one environment, either by virtue of the limitations, which it imposes or the opportunities that abound elsewhere.

In the case of the herders from Northern Nigeria, their decision to move down south is informed by drought and desertification which has resulted in scarcity of fodder for their livestock and, their sole decision to feed their flocks at all cost. As the herders move southward, their cattle eat and destroy plants and crops (which are sources of livelihood for others) on their way. There are communities in which the herders have settled in during the course of their nomadic sojourn. These communities, mostly made up of a farming population, have their own experience of strain on natural resources like water and lands. In responding to these strains, other attending implications of migration and also in a bid to protect their sources of livelihood, the farmers have reacted by asking the herders out of their communities. This has resulted in the incessant clashes which have claimed thousands of lives.

Conflicts between farmers and nomadic herders have become a national security issue in recent times, owing largely to its plurality and ethnic undertone. Environment-induced migration, such as that of the herders, creates volatile contact and competition between groups having highly conflicting natural resource-dependent livelihood systems. In the case of farmers and pastoral herders, it further strains already fragile national fault-lines and fuels insecurity. A problem created as a result of an environmental imbalance would need an environmental approach to tackle it. Tagging the clashes as merely religious or ethnic problems is a grave error as it blinds the eyes of the people to the root cause – the changing climate and its impacts.

Nnimmo Bassey, Director of Health of Mother Earth Foundation, stated that to proffer a lasting solution to these crises, we need to interrogate the causative factors propelling this unwholesome development. He said this in his welcome words at the organisation's Sustainability Academy co-hosted with the Confederation of Traditional Herders Organizations in Africa (CORET) on October 18, 2017 at the International Conference Centre, Abuja. In his closing remarks, he challenged participants at the event to ponder on certain questions that would shape their views about the conflict in an attempt to resolve it. The questions are:

What are the economic roots and what role does careless relationship with the Earth play, especially with regard to the preservation of our forests and grasslands?

a. Why are we not utilizing the symbiotic relationship of animal husbandry and farming, where animals help fertilize the soils of fallow lands that also serve as pasture?

b. If climate change escalates the movement of herders, is migration the only way to mitigate the impacts?

c. Would better soil and water management mitigate the rate of desertification in Nigeria?

d. If the Great Green Wall project restores its area of focus, would that reverse the migration and conflicts?

e. Are there cultural practices and political factors that lock in the crises?

Recommendations proffering solutions to end the clashes can be found on HOMEF's website[1]. To tackle the farmer-herder clashes, there is need to look beyond political, ethnic and religious inclinations and see them for what they are, environmental wars, which need environmental approaches and solutions.

Several Nigerians tend to see climate change as a mere political ploy used by some to request and squander funds. It is hoped, however, that with the daily experienced droughts, desert encroachment, flooding, etc. we would be able to accept or agree that climate change is real and its impacts are already here.

---

1 https://homef.org/2017/10/20/climate-change-pastoralism-land-and-conflicts/

GMOS DON'T INCREASE CROP YIELD

Joyce Ebebeinwe

Claims that genetically modified organisms (GMOs) will be the main way to feed the world are mere propaganda. Nnimmo Bassey, Director of the Health of Mother Health Foundation (HOMEF), made this submission during an event held July 25, 2019 in Benin City, Edo State. The event was the 'Dialogue on Food and Farming System in Nigeria' that brought together officials of civil society organisations (CSOs). Bassey said in his welcome address that in reality GMOs do not necessarily increase yield or solve the problems of pests and diseases. He informed that according to research at present, enough food to feed almost double of the current population is already being produced. However, most of the food produced is used for industrial purposes, for animal feed or is simply wasted due to poor storage and processing facilities and, lack of access to markets. He underscored the right to question the attempt to overturn the food systems, promote monocropping and project toxic chemicals as safe. "We must consistently defend our food sovereignty which ensures our right and access to safe, nutritious, healthy and culturally appropriate food at all times," Bassey stated.

Speaking at the Dialogue, Daniel Olorunfemi, Professor of Genetic Toxicology in the University of Benin, explained the process of genetic modification and how it affects human and environmental health. He listed the health impacts of GMOs to include immune disorders, cancer, reproductive defects and infant mortality. He adding that, one of the environmental impacts of GMOs is that they present risks of horizontal gene transfer and unintended harm to non-target organisms. "We do not need GMOs. We have the landmass, rich soils and good climate conditions that can ensure food productivity." Olorunfemi asserted. Speaking on the cultural, political and economic perspective of GMOs, Bassey pointed out that GMOs erode local knowledge and destroy the resilience of natural ecosystems which is based on biodiversity.

Mr. Bassey attested that "real solutions exist" and are contained in the United Nations-World Bank sponsored International Assessment of Agricultural Knowledge, Science and Technology for Development (IAASTD) research. The research which was carried out by 400 development experts for a period of three years recommended that nations must urgently revitalise public sector agricultural research, invest in smallholder farmer-oriented, low-input, agroecology farming systems and reform unfair trade-related rules.

Discussions on the viable alternative to GMOs which was led by HOMEF's Biosafety Project Officer, Joyce Ebebeinwe revealed that Agroecology presents a holistic approach to the challenges of agricultural productivity and in addition, climate change. Agroecology is a knowledge intensive system that manages ecosystems by replacing external inputs with natural processes, ensures quantity and quality production and, preserves the soil for future generations. Some of the innovations of agroecology highlighted include biological pest control, the push and pull method, participatory plant breeding and agroforestry.

The dialogue closed with group discussions on the way forward for Nigeria and the following resolutions were reached by all the participants:

The government of Nigeria should:

- ban GMOs now and begin to invest in agroecological farming systems.

- critically review the National Biosafety Management Agency Act, 2015 to close loopholes that allow for the unchecked infiltration of GMOs and ensure that regulators consider environmental and human health on a case-by-case basis as they entertain applications.

- increase support for farmers in terms of infrastructure, extension services, access to land and loans and to markets.

- include agroecology in her National Climate Change Adaptation Plan and increase funding for research in its principles and practice. create a database to reach and sustain contact with real farmers and avoid working with "ghost or absentee farmers".

- establish seed banks to preserve indigenous seed varieties and promote seed fairs to facilitate learning/exchange among farmers.

Civil society organisations should:

- carry out more awareness to drive the message of the impacts of GMOs to the farmers at the grassroots.

- engage more with the media especially by using social media for a wider coverage.

Farmers should:

- question and reject seedlings suspected to be genetically modified.
- form clusters to advocate against GMOs and synergise with CSOs to engage the government.

Consumers should:

- insist on their right to safe and nutritious foods.
- reject GMOs and carefully scrutinise labels before making purchases.

It was also recommended that state and local governments should urgently declare their states and local government areas GMO-free as a way of encouraging the Federal Government to take similar steps.

AGRA ISN'T THE FACE OF AGRICULTURE

Nnimmo Bassey[1]

The announcement of the nomination of the President of the Alliance for a Green Revolution in Africa (AGRA), Agnes Kalibata, as the Special Envoy of the UN Secretary-General to the 2021 UN Food Summit is very troubling. It is not a shock because of the person of Kalibata but because of her connection to AGRA. It is a shock because AGRA stands in stark contradistinction to some fundamental positions of UN agencies such as the FAO. The FAO leans toward the promotion of agricultural systems that are in harmony with Nature as opposed to systems that erode biodiversity and force farmers to depend on artificial and chemical inputs. For example, the FAO launched an initiative to scale up agroecology as a key pathway to supporting the SDGs.

An important International Symposium on Agroecology organised by the FAO in 2014 was attended by six UN organisations, 700 participants from 72 countries and, 350 civil society organisations and NGOs. The symposium considered diverse ways by which agroecology can be enhanced around the world to contribute to realizing the SDGs. The benefits of agroecology were pointed out as including food security and nutrition, resilience, promoting health, protecting biodiversity and soil fertility and, mitigating climate change. During the symposium, FAO Director-General, Graziano da Silva noted that it strengthens "the role of family and small scale farmers, fisherfolk, pastoralists, women and youth." At the end of the symposium, the participants endorsed the launch of the Scaling up Agroecology Initiative and demanded that the FAO develop a ten-year plan for its implementation.

After over 10 years of the existence of AGRA, it is hard to find any evidence that a so-called green revolution is happening in Africa. According to Timothy Wise, "AGRA's stated goals are to double yields and incomes for 30 million farming households by 2020." Wise noted that:

1 This article was also published at https://www.environewsnigeria.com/agra-is-not-the-face-of-agriculture-nnimmo-bassey/

Despite millions of dollars spent by AGRA since 2006, few comprehensive evaluations of AGRA have been made available. An additional USD 30 billion was recently pledged at the African Green Revolution Forum to continue AGRA's work and help launch the organisation's new strategic vision, without a clear understanding of how effective AGRA has been in increasing agricultural productivity, adopting green revolution technologies and reducing poverty and malnutrition in the countries over the past decade.

Critics see AGRA as a body that deploys all the right language in framing its work as supporting small-scale farmers whereas the reality is that its approaches promote the strategies of big business and the promoters of genetic engineering.

AGRA has not categorically denied leaning on genetic engineering but, like the International Institute for Tropical Agriculture (IITA), they would claim that they don not rule out technologies. This is duplicity of focus – posing as a supporter of small-scale farmers working with Nature while in reality working with systems that fight Nature and undercut the resilience of local ecosystems. This is why the elevation of the President of AGRA as the Special Envoy of the Secretary-General of the UN to the UN Food Summit is a loud endorsement of genetic engineering in agriculture, which comes with a stab of worry. The move is rightly seen by critics as a route to taking control of the agenda and muffing the voices of African farmers and environmentalists while promoting the profits of agri-business.

Unfortunately, big capital, such as that wielded by the Bill and Melinda Gates Foundation, the parent of AGRA, has shut the ears and hearts and, governments from paying attention to the people. They promote environmentally harmful agribusiness, negate local knowledge and food systems and, promote systems that are ultimately inimical to the best needs of local farmers. We are convinced that the UN Secretary-General can better be represented by persons and organisations whose fundamental ideologies promote agroecology and systems that would protect global biodiversity, tackle hunger and fight global warming. At this point in time, a Special Envoy should be someone that would clearly show support for the implementation of the International Assessment of Agricultural Knowledge, Science and Technology for Development (IAASTD).

The findings of IAASTD were captured in the 2008 report titled Agriculture at the Crossroads. The report clearly showed that the future of food supply in the world will depend on the production from small-scale farmers as opposed to industrial agriculture and those applying genetically engineered organisms (GMOs). A special envoy of the UN Secretary-General should be someone who would demand that African governments implement the decisions of The African Union's (AU) Maputo Declaration, better known as CAADP. That Declaration was officially adopted by member states in 2003 with the requirement that each country should allocate at least 10% of their annual budgets to agriculture by 2015. Only a handful of African countries have met this target with the continental average standing at about 5%. AGRA is not the face of agriculture in Africa and cannot speak in our name or represent us in any way.

HUNGER: THE NEW PHASE OF CLIMATE CHANGE IN AFRICA

Cadmus Atake-Enade

Climate change is transforming the planet's ecosystems and threatening the well-being of current and future generations. It is increasing the rate of food shortages resulting from impacts such as droughts and high temperatures globally. Since the first climate talks in Geneva in 1979, there have been series of climate talks, yet no profound solutions have been adopted. Several world leaders and scientists have been busy postulating false solutions to climate change and rapidly driving the world into hunger due to food shortages. It is estimated that about 870 million people, or one in eight persons, suffer from chronic undernourishment and hunger.

Among the vast majority of the undernourished and hungry people, about 852 million people, that is nearly 98%, live in the global south, while 16 million people, less than 3%, are in the global north. Among these undernourished and hungry people, Africa has been the only region where the number of hungry people has consistently increased, with nearly 20 million added in the last decade.[1] In Africa, the modest progress achieved in recent years up to 2007 was reversed, with hunger rising 2 per cent per year since then. Analysts say that the increasing hunger can be traced to increase in droughts, increase in temperature, monoculture and land grabbing resulting from false solutions postulated by some climate scientists supporting polluting entities in their bid to maintain the status quo.

Food availability and access to adequate food constitute one of the most basic and essential requirements for maintaining a healthy and productive life. Presently, hunger and malnutrition comprise the major threats to human health, and climate change will continue to affect all aspects of food security globally. Food insecurity and shortage are likely to pose a major challenge for countries that are vulnerable to extreme weather events and those that have low income and a high incidence of hunger and poverty. Inhabitants of affected nations are already at risk and will find it very difficult to overcome food production and income losses

---

1 https://news.un.org/en/story/2012/10/423022

resulting from extreme weather events. This situation could mean short-term and long-term setbacks in food availability and access. Short-term infrastructural damage from extreme weather events of growing intensity will also add to making food distribution difficult.

In rural Africa, groundwater and rainfall are essential inputs for food production and are the main sources of potable water. The rural areas of Africa are where more than half of the region's young people live. Climate change impacts on water resources directly affect the availability of water for agricultural and domestic use. One area currently experiencing serious water deficit is the Sahel region where longer and more intense droughts constitute one of the most dramatic climatic change impacts recorded in any region. This situation is expected to worsen in the coming years, affecting more than 60 million young women and men. Outside the Sahel, groundwater supplies are expected to decrease by as much as 10 per cent, with a 10C increase in temperature. And the world's temperature is expected to increase above pre-industrial level.

The threat to agriculture is global and not restricted to one region. In northern Australia and the southern United States, for example, food production could decline as a result of drier surface conditions. The production of biofuels and other forms of bioenergy presents serious challenges also. Bioenergy is the largest new source of agricultural demand in recent years, and this has important implications for food production and availability in areas where agricultural capacity is diminishing. It takes a lot more grain to power the world than to feed it.

The corn equivalent of the energy used for a few minutes of driving would feed a person for an entire day, and that same person could be fed for a year with the equivalent energy burned from a full tank of ethanol in a four wheel-drive sports utility vehicle. REDD+, a carbon offset mechanism, is also another major challenge in this regard – a process whereby industrialized countries in the global north present forest, agriculture, soils, and even water as sponges for their pollution instead of reducing greenhouse gas emissions at the source. This has led to land grabbing, thereby reducing land space for agriculture and food production which in turn leads to food shortage and hunger.

As dire as the situation may seem, there are local knowledge systems and agricultural practices that support resilient food production in the context of food sovereignty. Analyses that promote false solutions to climate change are simply tools of neo-colonialism aimed at force feeding Africans with genetically engineered crops and foods touted as the only solution to supposedly burgeoning populations. The solutions remain simple: keep fossil fuels in the ground, cut emissions at source, avoid food wastage, support agroecology and equip smallholder farmers with essential tools and natural inputs.

AFRICA CAN NOURISH HERSELF

Fidelis Allen

The 7th Public Lecture of the Right Livelihood College Campus at the University of Port Harcourt, Nigeria, co-hosted by Health of Mother Earth Foundation (HOMEF), was held on 25 June 2021 with Professor Hans Harren speaking on the topic *Africa Can Nourish Itself*. The lecture, which was held virtually for the second time since it started in 2015, was attended by students, civil society actors, community folks, management and staff members of the University of Port Harcourt, and friends of the College in different locations of the world. These lectures are part of the Port Harcourt College Campus' efforts at realizing the vision of linking those who have been at the forefront of change-making concerning key global problems with the academic community, for the sharing of experiences and knowledge, for the common good. This informed the initiative at the Right Livelihood Award Foundation in Sweden several years ago. All previous and future speakers in the annual public lectures on the campus were/will be laureates of the Right Livelihood Award Foundation awarded for their change-making role in society. The story of these lectures and the rich profile of the speaker for this year was highlighted in the preliminaries by Fidelis Allen and Nnimmo Bassey.

Nnimmo himself and the late Ogoni environmental rights activist, Kenule Saro-Wiwa, have been the only recipients of the Right Livelihood Award Foundation from Nigeria to date. Professor Prince C. Mmom, who represented the Vice-Chancellor of the University of Port Harcourt, had expressed the university's pleasure regarding the collaboration with the Health of Mother Earth Foundation and the Rights Livelihood Award Foundation. The overriding theme of food security under which the topic of this year's lecture was presented is of great concern to many today. Policymakers, civil society and multilateral organisations, including the World Food Programme, are worried about the state of food security. Africa is expected to double its current population by 2050. With 1,340,598,147 in 2020, Africa already accounts for 18.2% of the global population. Nigeria, in particular, is expected to reach the same population level as

China by 2050. Worse, rising insecurity due to the activities of kidnappers, killers, bandits and terrorists in the country, is threatening the ability of households in urban and rural communities to access adequate nutritional food. Africa as a whole is facing a grave crisis in its agricultural systems and socio-economic and political conditions, with enormous implications for the availability of peace and, affordable and nutritious food.

These contexts were mainly the motivation for the choice of subject for this year's public lecture. Hans began the lecture with a context that includes his vast experience of almost thirty years working in Africa, as well as the time he spent in Nigeria. His extensive knowledge of agriculture and food systems during these years has benefited students, teachers and policymakers in Africa, including Nigeria, Kenya and Togo, to name a few. Hans had received the Right Livelihood Award in 2013 for his contribution to change in society through his exploits in the use of knowledge for the transformation and empowerment of students and practitioners, although he expressed misgivings about the sustainability of those efforts since his leaving Africa. He founded several organisations and directed research centres that have contributed greatly to practice and scholarship, including the International Institute of Tropical Agriculture of Nigeria in Jos. "I am very pleased to be back in Nigeria, even though virtually. I enjoyed my time in Nigeria with the farmers," Hans stated as he began the lecture. He immediately explained the correction he made on the topic, from 'Africa can feed itself' to 'Africa can nourish itself'. The sense here, according to him, is that feeding is associated with animals, whereas nourishment pertains to human beings.

This conceptual distinction seems cultural as he explains that in Europe, people are nourished, in contrast to the idea of the feeding of animals or nonhuman life. He then took the whole issue of whether Africa can nourish itself in the context of the Sustainable Development Goals. He saw these goals as an important framework for the realization of food security in Africa. As he argued, "the SDGs offer the transformative path suggested by the International Assessment on Agriculture, Science, Technology and Development (IAASTD) Report signed by 18 African countries." The objectives of the IAASTD Report and the SDGs are consistent with the capacity to assist countries in making progress on food security and food justice. His diagnosis of food systems in Africa which has worsened with the outbreak of Covid-19, was insightful. He insisted that agroecology was the way out. Such a model for building food systems addresses the issue of food security that also focuses on nutrition and the question of food sovereignty from the three-dimensional fronts of environment, society, and economy.

All three have been missing in the present character of food systems in Africa. The overproduction of food crops, such as cassava and corn, to the detriment of vegetables and other green crops, was mentioned as inimical to the health of people. The need for a balance between basic foods and vegetables in Africa, he said, will help solve the problem of diabetes and obesity. So far, the food systems in Africa do not promote this balance, something the lecturer believes must change. Other problems with Africa's current food systems include, insensitivity to climate change which the existing model significantly contributes to. He talked about the need for system change through system-thinking, which allows the connection of food systems to every other aspect of life. This, for him, should be integrated into the training of students in universities, a role he believes universities can play conveniently and for which he would be willing to offer more help. He also highlighted the fact that the dietary choices of consumers tend to shape farmers' choices. In other words, farmers respond to the food choices made by consumers.

Another problem also resides in the move away from food systems based on ecosystem services, to systems that promote the production of cheap food without nutrients just to make a profit. Hans again proposed agroecology as the solution. He argued for the need for subsistence farming to integrate agroecology which he believes is the way to sustainable agriculture and food security. The model takes into consideration the need to protect the ecology, society and the economy of the people. This three-dimensional feature of the model agrees with the concept of sustainable development. It will check the over-production of a few crops to the detriment of the others. There are over 3,000 crops that can be farmed, but farmers have concentrated on a few, merely six or so in Africa, according to Hans. His critique of the food systems in Africa is based on this. This has promoted diseases, which he argues governments have continued to spend a lot of money on through their annual budgets.

This needs to change through the balance that an agroecological model brings. It can begin with a change in diet from the present mono-food diet to a green diet. This is one way in which agroecological farming, in contrast to conventional farming, supports the environment, society and the economy. It feeds the soil so that the soil can feed plants. Africa can nourish itself if its leaders take the steps laid out in the agroecological model, among which is to break away from monocultural farming and from the use of dangerous pesticides, which have long been banned in Europe and several other regions of the world. Africa should discourage agricultural systems that destroy ecosystem services and biodiversity, and promote policies that favour local farmers.

In addition, the opportunity for the continent to nourish itself exists with the availability of land. Thus, leaders should stop selling off the land to foreigners and multinational corporations. Already nearly 50% of the available land has been sold off. This should be stopped so that farmers can be given more access to the land. Furthermore, the importation of food should be discouraged. This is a political issue with a lot of external political pressure, which has to be tackled.

FIDDLING IN NAIROBI
WHILE AFRICA GOES HUNGRY

Timothy A. Wise[1]

In light of the United Nations' Food I Systems Summit on 23 September 2021, the urgent need for structural changes in how we grow, harvest, distribute and consume food has never been more apparent. According to the U.N. Food and Agricultural Organisation's (FAO) annual hunger report[2] released on 12 July 2021, the world experienced an unprecedented rise in severe hunger for nearly one year (from 2019 to 2020). The agency's annual estimate of "undernourishment" showed an increase of up to 25% in 2019, rising to between 720 and 811 million people in 2020. Sub-Saharan Africa saw as many as 44 million more people suffer severe undernourishment, with 30% of the continent's residents struggling to feed their families. A stunning 66% of the continent faced "moderate or severe food insecurity" in 2020, according to FAO estimates, up from 51% in 2014. That is an increase of 244 million food-insecure people in just six years.

The Alliance for a Green Revolution in Africa (AGRA), in its 2020 Annual Report[3] released the same day as the FAO, sounded its alarms. After noting the challenges of COVID-19 and climate change, AGRA's report gushes about the "evidence of improved productivity, better crop quality, higher incomes, and more months of food from [farmers'] surplus." In stark contrast to the well-researched data from the FAO, AGRA's "evidence" was a sloppy set of hastily compiled data presented with examples carefully chosen to show progress (See my analysis of AGRA's report here[4].) AGRA seems to be living in a world different from that of the poor, rural Africans, which makes them oblivious to the documented shortcomings of its technology-focused approach to agricultural development. AGRA leaders and donors seem unaware that the number of severely undernourished people in Sub-Saharan Africa has risen nearly 50% since AGRA was founded in 2006. That is why African farmers, faith, and community

1 This article was also published at http://www.ipsnews.net/2021/08/fiddling-nairobi-africa-goes-hungry/
2 https://www.fao.org/3/cb4474en/cb4474en.pdf
3 https://agra.org/wp-content/uploads/2021/07/AGRA-Annual-Report-2020.pdf
4 https://www.iatp.org/sites/default/files/2021-07/New%20AGRA%20Reports%20Offer%20Little%20Evidence%20to%20Justify%20Continued%20Donor%20Support_1.pdf

organisations are now challenging AGRA's failing model[5], calling on donor agencies and foundations to stop funding the 15-year-old initiative.

Business as usual at the Food Systems Summit

The COVID-19 pandemic was, of course, largely to blame for the steep rise in hunger in 2020, but climate change and conflict also contributed. So did mis-guided agricultural policies. It was the sixth straight year of increases in undernourishment, a trend that last year prompted U.N. Secretary-General Antonio Guterres to call for this year's Food Systems Summit. The world was clearly not on track to achieve the core Sustainable Development Goal of eliminating severe hunger by 2030. The Summit has been mired in controversy from the outset. Guterres was widely criticized for his partnership with the World Economic Forum, the corporate elite who gather each year in Davos to discuss the poor world's problems, side-lining the Rome-based U.N. agencies that generally take the lead on such matters. He compounded the legitimacy crisis by naming AGRA President, Agnes Kalibata, as Special Envoy to lead the Summit.

Major civil society networks and organisations boycotted the summit preparations[6], which were denounced for favouring technological solutions offered by corporations while failing to put the right to food – and COVID and climate change – at the centre of the agenda. The U.N. Special Rapporteur on the Right to Food, Michael Fakhri, recently issued a blistering critique of the Summit. The business-as-usual approach to the summit, with its Nairobi based staff (of AGRA) organising virtual "dialogues" and vetting "game-changing solutions" to food systems failures, seemed deaf to the loud alarms from the FAO. The worst hunger remains in rural areas in developing countries.

Africa's failing Green Revolution

For the last 15 years, the Green Revolution has been the dominant approach in Africa. AGRA has led the charge from its Nairobi headquarters, with overwhelming $1 billion funding from the Bill and Melinda Gates Foundation, but also with support from the Rockefeller Foundation and a small number of bilateral donors. African governments have chipped in with waves of subsidies to farmers – as much as $1 billion per year altogether – to purchase the Green Revolution's products: commercial seeds, fertilizers and other inputs.

5 https://afsafrica.org/afsa-news-advisory-press-conference-2-september/
6 https://www.csm4cfs.org/hundreds-of-grassroots-organizations-to-oppose-the-un-food-systems-summit/

The Green Revolution's "theory of change" is as simplistic as it is flawed: put seeds and fertilizers in the hands of small-scale farmers; they will see their yields double, so too their incomes from the sales of surplus crops and; they will become food secure from the food they grow and can now afford to buy. Evidence suggests that none of that has come to pass. Adoption rates for the expensive new seeds and fertilizers remain low, even with governments subsidizing farmers' purchases. Many of those who adopt have not achieved large yield increases, even in favoured crops such as maize. Only a few have seen rising incomes from sales of growing surpluses; some have ended up in debt after a bad harvest. And food insecurity has grown from its already alarming levels. This is less a theory of change than a proven route to continued hunger.

Fiddling in Nairobi

AGRA is set to unveil what it will no doubt present as a bold new strategy. But it will likely do little more than fiddle with its current strategy, just as it has done before. The failing premise that commercial seeds and fertilizers can dramatically reduce hunger and poverty in rural Africa through a productivity revolution, remains unchanged. Emperor Nero infamously fiddled while Rome burned. AGRA should stop fiddling in Nairobi while more Africans are going hungry. And donors should listen to African civil society leaders and say no when AGRA claims to speak for Africans as a ploy to ask for millions of more dollars for its failing strategy.

SECTION 3

OIL POLITICS

While the price of crude oil increases and yields more revenue to both the government and the oil companies, the environmental and social impacts are still externalized to the poor communities. To ensure that oil must flow at all costs, it does not appear to matter how much human bloodletting happens in the process.

— Excerpt from the book *Oil Politics – Echoes of Ecological Wars* by Nnimmo Bassey

POLITICS OF ECOLOGICAL DEFENCE

Nnimmo Bassey

It cannot be denied that the multiple crises currently confronting humankind are intimately linked to man's perception of nature's resources and to how this perception drives the manner by which the resources are exploited and utilized. The last century has been driven by the mind-set that man can extract whatever is needed and if anything gets broken such can be easily fixed. This has been the path of limitless exploitation, limitless growth and limitless power. Unfortunately, this exploitative system chooses to forget that Planet Earth is finite and that most of what is being exploited are non-renewable. The path of limitless exploitation has led mankind into the fetters of limited thinking.

For one, our concept of energy has been so shrunk that what comes to mind when we think of energy is either electricity or the power to move objects and human beings. The movement of objects and beings, gives man a sense of satisfaction, achievement and even pleasure but many a times, is devoid of a sense of care. The development and ultimate unravelling of capitalism can be understood in its overall view of nature as something to be exploited and not to be nurtured, respected and protected. This mind-set requires examination so that we see clearly that the nature-society dialectic that is generating and compounding the unfolding ecological crises is not accidental.

Literature abound to show the origins of reckless despoliation of the environment due to mankind's ambition to accumulate by cornering common goods for private enjoyment. A review of the literature shows a trend – of careless exploitation – that was visible even at the transition from feudalism to industrialization in Europe. The reality is simply getting worse across the world today. And in some quarters, technology has been blamed. But some commentators point out that technology is not the primary driver of man's antagonistic relationship with nature 'but rather the nature and logic of capitalism as a specific mode of production'. The concept of disaster capitalism has been well defined by writers like Naomi Klein; the world is truly, increasingly faced with situations where catastrophes are seen as opportunities for business. When floods, earthquakes or tsunamis level the properties of the weak in society, the power brokers sweep in, demolish what may be left standing and then appropriate everything without any sense of accountability or responsibility. Some of these disasters have been termed 'natural disasters' whereas they are clearly the result of the activities of humans.

Someone was quoted as saying that oil spills make economic sense in that they could generate new businesses for those who would handle the clean-ups. In fact this "witness" at a hearing even went as far as insisting that where fishermen are displaced from their trade they would have an opportunity of staring a new line of work perhaps with any compensations they may be paid. It may sound crude, but this captures the basic sense in the drive for disposition, acquisition and accumulation for profit. In this context there is pretty little economic difference between activities that maintain the integrity of natural ecosystems and those that destroy people and their environment. The narrow pursuit of profit makes it impossible to see into the future, as whatever can be grabbed now is fair game. The environment is the theatre of life. We are part of it and not apart from it. We do not own it and cannot reasonably appropriate it as private property. This is why continued colonization of the atmosphere through unmitigated pumping of greenhouse gases is unreasonable and utterly unacceptable. Defending the environment is an unavoidable political duty.

As the exploitation of nature draws to the zenith of unreasonableness, merchants begin to see nature as an object for speculation and wholesale commodification. Good concepts such as sustainable development are being turned on their heads. The concept of green economy, on which even the brownest sectors cling, turns out to be a platform insisting that nature cannot be defended except it is assigned a monetary value – absolutely ignoring the intrinsic value of nature. On the whole, the expansion of capital conveniently overlooks the ruination of nature. This is why the Nigerian environment, from the South to the North, has been so utterly abused and ignored. We are confronted with situations where land is grabbed with brute force, forests are chopped down, pollution is rife and wastes are not adequately taken care of. The sorry state of the Nigerian environment is best seen through the lens of the impacts of the oil and gas sector.

The United Nations Environmental Programme's (UNEP) assessment of the Ogoni environment shows the level of ecocide inflicted by over five decades of reckless exploitation. UNEP surmises that it would require about 30 years of work to detoxify the Ogoni environment where active oil extraction was shut down in 1993. Almost two years after the presentation of that report to the government of Nigeria, little has been seen by way of responses to the clear situation of environmental emergency the report announces. The system of nature is circular and things remain in a state of recycling and replenishing until man interferes with them. Current dominant production systems are linear and overload natural systems with excessive amounts of waste products. The governing creed appears to be that the more polluting the actions, the more profitable they are. And, in a twisted sense, that is right because it extends to the doctrine of pillage and brigandage in which environmental costs are externalised to the poor and to nature. Transnational corporations are in the vanguard of the unrelenting assault on nature. By their mode of operation, they are forever seeking ways to block the doors of justice and not to do what is right. State companies driven by similar neoliberal principles are just as bad.

LIVES AND WATER RESOURCES AT RISK IN NAMIBIA AND BOTSWANA

Ogechi Okanya Cookey

Following the licensing of more than 13,600 square miles of land in the Okavango wilderness region of Namibia and Botswana for oil and gas exploitation by ReconAfrica, life can never be the same for the human and wildlife population in the region. Even the region's scant water resources face threats of pollution and further shortage. According to Jeffrey Barbee and Laurel Neme's report in National Geographic, "The company's licensed region ... is home to some 200,000 people and abundant wildlife, including important migratory routes for the world's largest remaining elephant population." The region houses "the largest herd of African elephants left on Earth and myriad other animals – African wild dogs, lions, leopards, giraffes, amphibians and reptiles, birds – and rare flora." The waters in the region are home to hippos, sitatungas, or African fish eagles.

The Okavango River is particularly "the lifeblood of the region," the report reads. It is an important water resource for not only Namibia and Botswana but Angola as well. Conservationists and community leaders in the region have already raised an alarm over the threat that the proposed oil and gas exploitation and production activities would pose to their water resources and already endangered wildlife. The wildlife reported to be under threat include the endangered grey crowned crane, African wild dog, black rhinoceros and white-backed vulture as well as 20 other vulnerable species (like martial eagle and Temminck's pangolin).

Communities in the region, especially those that are far from the town, depend on their rivers for drinking water. Some get their drinking water from hand pumps and wells that are hand-dug. According to two community members quoted in the report, "if these people [ReconAfrica] come with a system that will damage the water, this is life-threatening to us."

"What happens if the company drops the groundwater table and people who live there can no longer access the water they have relied upon for generations?" Barbee and Neme had asked in their report.

ReconAfrica, which is a petroleum exploration company head-quartered in Canada, believes that the region also referred to as Kavango Basin may house about 31 billion barrels of crude oil. Plans to drill test wells to ascertain the presence of exploitable oil and gas in the northeast of Namibia has already been approved by the government while drilling permit in Botswana is in the works. Once oil is found, drilling of hundreds of wells in the area is bound to begin as ReconAfrica's plan revealed. Aside from this, it is feared that some of the wells will be opened using modern frac stimulations. This entails fracking which is a contentious practice whereby underground shale is injected with high-pressure fluid to crack open the rock and release more oil and gas.

Studies have shown that fracking leads to groundwater contamination, use of large amounts of water which has terrible effects in water-deficient areas, exposure to toxic chemicals. It also leads to the release of greenhouse gases (e.g. methane), general air pollution, blowouts due to gas explosion, earthquakes, infrastructure degradation, food-chain poisoning, congenital disabilities, illnesses like cancer, habitat destruction, mass fish death, and the death of other marine species. The activity of fracking raises concerns for workplace safety, community loss of land and water, and in broader terms, contributes greatly to climate change.

Besides the ruinous impacts of fracking, the construction and installation of oil and gas infrastructure such as roads to oil fields, pipelines, drilling platforms and other buildings have their devastating effects on the environment. Noise from oil exploration sites can change the living pattern of animals in the area from diurnal to nocturnal. This is the case of forest elephants in Central Africa, according to the report. The elephants no longer come out in the day time. In the report of Jeffrey Barbee and Laurel Neme, it was noted that oil and gas infrastructure can negatively impact animal habitat, migratory pathways and biodiversity. This is the experience in Nigeria's Niger Delta region where Shell's roads and other oil and gas infrastructure have led to the destruction of water bodies and forests.

According to the National Geographic contributors, "if the broader interconnected region is pocked with oil wells and associated roads, infrastructure, and workers' camps, habitat inevitably will be degraded and fragmented."

Environmental devastation is not all that awaits the Okavango region if oil and gas exploitation and production kick off; social disintegration is also a consequence. A predicted social outcome is that: with the arrival of oil and gas workers with huge remuneration, there is bound to be a high inflow of alcohol and sprouting of joints that market them, more roads and pollutions. The traditional way of life of the indigenous people in the region will begin to erode.

Another possible negative outcome of the influx of oil workers is poaching for high-value animals like lions, primates and elephants. Other normal-value species are equally unsafe as there may be an untenable demand for then as meat – what is called bush meat in the local Nigerian parlance.

The above effects should be captured in the Environmental Impact Assessment (EIA) of oil and gas exploitation plans. Nevertheless, the EIA of ReconAfrica's exploration plan in the Okavango region has been faulted by expert reviewers. Knowing the limited available water resources in the region, experts who reviewed the EIA expected to see a detailed assessment of the company's water usage for the test drilling, which is suspected to include fracking. Information in the public domain shows that the amount of water expended on fracking now is 28 times more than what was used about 15 years ago. This development is dangerous for arid regions.

There are alternatives to fracking. Experts quoted in the National Geographic report criticized the failure of ReconAfrica's EIA to capture the possibility of using solar and wind power which are sustainable renewable alternatives to fracking. It is in the character of big polluters – oil and gas multinationals – not to go for sustainable alternatives. They are yet to be innovative enough to seek out ways of doing business within the ecosystems' limits. Advocates of alternative and sustainable approaches are sidelined and often silenced. Take as an example, the case of Ken Saro-Wiwa and the other eight Ogoni environmental activists whose wrongful execution was masterminded by Shell and the dictatorial government of late Sani Abacha.

With all the looming consequences of ReconAfrica's plan in the Okavango region, the company's EIA did not include the assessments of interested and impacted stakeholders. It is, thus, not surprising that a vast majority of the people in the Okavango region are mostly unaware of the oil and gas exploitation plan in their own region. The National Geographic report has it that "even many who live in the affected region were unaware."

The chairperson of George Mukoya Conservancy was quoted to have said that he did not know there was any company coming to drill oil in the region. George Mukoya Conservancy, which generates revenue from tourists and through sustainable hunting, is one of the sites that will be impacted negatively by the proposed oil and gas plan. This conservancy is 50 miles away from one of the test well sites.

According to Barbee and Neme's report, the law in Namibia supports the involvement of interested and affected stakeholders (including people, organisations and agencies) in the EIA of projects of the oil and gas nature. This notwithstanding, ReconAfrica's EIA has failed to uphold the provisions of the law, yet ReconAfrica claims it follows the regulations and policies of Namibia as well as international best practices.

This is a clear indication of the double standards displayed by oil and gas multinationals, which environmental activists in Nigeria's Niger Delta have decried for decades. They keep to best practices in more advanced regions and implement worst practices in Africa.

If the Namibian test wells prove productive, ReconAfrica's plan is to strike a deal with oil and gas multinationals like Exxon, Total, and so on. The company is confident that it will cut a deal with the multinationals.

The ominous question is: Will the Okavango region become like or come next to Nigeria's Niger Delta region with regard to environmental degradation resulting from oil and gas exploitation and exploration if ReconAfrica succeeds? It is hoped that the Okavango region will not suffer the pains of Nigeria's Niger Delta – a fate that should not be wished even for an enemy zone.

A CRITIQUE OF THE
IUCN-NIGER DELTA PANEL FINAL REPORT

Richard Steiner[1]

In July 2013, there was a release of the International Union for Conservation of Nature (IUCN)-Niger Delta Panel (NDP) final report titled 'Sustainable Remediation and Rehabilitation of Biodiversity and Habitats of Oil Spill Sites in the Niger Delta'. The main report including its recommendations for the future, fails to meet its professed objectives, presents little new information, contains inaccuracies, represents a flawed process, and seriously undermines the credibility of IUCN. The following are preliminary comments on the released final report, given that the report's 11 Annexes were not included and were, thus, unavailable for review. Upon review of the Annexes, there may be more comments to offer.

Background

The IUCN Secretariat has had a "partnership" with Shell for several years. In January 2011, Shell apparently approached IUCN proposing the Niger Delta Panel (NDP) process. The internal discussion between Shell and IUCN was concealed at the time from those associated with IUCN and have experience in oil spill issues of the Niger Delta. When in September 2011 people became aware of the secret internal discussions between Shell and IUCN regarding the Niger Delta issues, some person raised concerns about the underlying premise for the NDP process, the Terms of Reference (TORs) for the project, and the secretive internal discussions from which it derived. In a September 11, 2011 email to IUCN Director General, IUCN President, and the Head of the IUCN Business and Biodiversity Program, I wrote the following:

- I was, thus, dismayed to learn a few days ago that IUCN had entered into an agreement with Shell to convene a panel on oil spill restoration in the Niger Delta, and that there appears to have been a deliberate attempt by the Secretariat, Council, CEESP Chair, *et al.,* to conceal

1 This report was first published by the author on 1 September 2013.

this project from those of us associated with the Union who had most experience with this issue.

- I read through the TORs for the project, and with respect to whoever drafted them, this is simply one of the most uninformed documents I have read on the Delta, and I have read many such things.

They reflect a profound misunderstanding of what is actually occurring in the Delta, and a part-and-parcel of Shell's fiction about the issue. Further, it is difficult to believe that a company that needs over $100 billion in after tax profits over the past 4 years does not know what it should be doing to behave responsibly in the Niger Delta – they do, but they just make too much money not doing so. I am concerned that Shell is simply wanting green validation from IUCN for their irresponsible activities in the Delta, and it most certainly does not deserve such. And, it seems evident that, through projects such as this, Shell is attempting to continue delaying responsible action in the Delta. Shell used the 4-year UNEP Ogoniland study to successfully delay action, and now are looking to use IUCN for another few years delay. I informed a wider audience of these internal discussions between Shell and IUCN, and was accused by IUCN of committing an "ethical breach" in doing so.

My 9-11-11 email to IUCN Secretariat closed with the following:

> I respectfully ask that you contract an independent investigator to look objectively into how this project was conceived and developed, the deliberate attempt to conceal the project from those involved with the Union who are most knowledgeable on these issues, and to recommend ways to prevent a repeat of this sort of episode in the future. As well, and most importantly, I respectfully urge you to terminate the Shell/IUCN Niger Delta Panel project, and to terminate the Shell/IUCN partnership agreement as it clearly does not, and cannot, lead to constructive conservation action.

However, IUCN elected to proceed with the NDP process. In January 2013, IUCN released an Executive Summary of the Final Report, but oddly not the Final Report. I asked in April 2013 for the Final Report, and was told it would be available in May. The final report, dated July 2013, was finally made available to me at the end of August.

The Final Report does not include the 11 Annexes, to which it repeatedly refers. Thus, it is difficult to review the report in total. I have asked for the annexes. And the final report does not include a list of the panel members (which are found only on a FAQs link), and even that list, if made available, would not provide sufficient detail to substantiate the claims of the panel's oil spill expertise as made by the report.

I asked IUCN via email to disclose how much money Shell has paid it for the NDP process, but IUCN replied that it was confidential and would not disclose the information. One of my primary objections regarding the IUCN-NDP process was/is that Shell has been required by Nigerian Law for decades to respond to and restore damage from oil spills (see discussion below). Yet, through this IUCN-NDP process, Shell is asserting that it does not know how to comply with the law, and that it has not been in compliance with these Nigerian legal requirements.

The IUCN-NDP process was initiated exactly when the 4-year UNEP study of oil contamination in Ogoniland was completed. This supports the suspicion that Shell is using such studies as a convenient excuse, a cover, to delay taking necessary steps to improve its performance in the Niger Delta. It is a simple delay tactic, and all that this tactic requires is willing collaborators, which Shell has apparently found in UNEP and IUCN. This may be why IUCN concealed this process as long as possible from those who might object. Then, last month, Shell announced its long anticipated exit from most of the onshore regions of the Niger Delta. Below is part of the August 2, 2013 news story in Dutch News.

Shell to pull out of Niger Delta Friday, August 2, 2013

Anglo-Dutch oil giant Shell is to pull out of its oil activities in Niger Delta, its managing director in the country told the NRC in an interview on Friday. "We are leaving," Mutiu Sunmonu told the paper. The "recklessness" and size of theft are forcing Shell to halve its activities in the country. On Thursday, CEO Peter Voser talked of "divestment" in Nigeria during the presentation of the company's second quarter results. He gave the "challenges" in Nigeria as one reason why Shell booked disappointing results.

In summary, Shell has:

- received $ billions in profits from its oil operations in the Niger Delta,

- been required to conduct its business there with the highest international technical standards,

- not re-invested sufficiently in its onshore infrastructure to make it safe

- continued to operate in the Niger Delta knowingly, with substandard infrastructure and operational ideals,

- commissioned studies by UNEP and IUCN for a few $ million to present the appearance of propriety, all the while simply delaying for over 6 years the necessary reinvestment in the onshore infrastructure to comply with Nigerian law,

- thus, subsequently announced that it is leaving the onshore area.

So, for a few million dollars paid to UNEP and IUCN over the past 6 years, Shell has knowingly continued to operate a substandard oil production and transportation system in the Niger Delta, earned $ billions, re-invested little, and is now "leaving." And that is Shell's "sustainable business model" in Nigeria. It is clear that Nigerian law requires Shell/SPDC to employ the highest international standards in its operations in Nigeria, and it is equally clear that these legally required standards have not been met by Shell/SPDC. In addition, it is apparent that Shell/SPDC either knew, or should have known, that it has been consistently out of compliance with Nigerian federal law. Such willful neglect should be considered as evidence of gross negligence on the part of SPDC. Fundamental in this is that if a company cannot conduct its business safely (e.g. protect against the illegal activities repeatedly cited by the company and the IUCN-NDP report), then it should not operate in the region unless and until it can.

Preliminary Conclusion

In a normal client/contractor relationship, a client would likely conclude that the final report of the contractor – IUCN-NDP - was not fit-for-purpose, and either request substantial amendment with more detail, or request its money back. However, as discussed in the Background section above, this is not a normal client/contractor process. Shell received precisely what it wanted from this process – a few more years to make $ billions from oil in the Niger Delta; not having to upgrade its oil infrastructure to international standards and to correct its irresponsible business practices; and now will be leaving the area. This was my concern before the project was initiated, and remains my unfortunate conclusion now. That IUCN participated willingly in this corporate deception, allowing environmental harm to continue unabated in a biodiversity hot spot, calls into serious question the credibility of IUCN.

RESISTING SHALE GAS IN SHALA, ALGERIA

Hocine Malti[1]

A law enacted in 2012 and endorsed by the Algerian Parliament in 2013 has authorized the production of shale gas. The situation in Algeria is unique in the sense that only the national hydrocarbons company, Sonatrach, has started some activity for shale gas. For various reasons, foreign companies are not yet interested there. TOTAL was associated with Sonatrach on the Ahnet permit located in the In Salah region but had said it is no more present with ambiguous explanations that are however, not convincing. Sonatrach should have drilled to date about ten shale gas wells. I say "should" because the most total Omerta prevails in this area, two of them (Sonatrach and Omerta) having permit to operate.

Anti-shale gas movement/protest began to take shape as soon as the law became known in 2012 with the first provisions of the law taking momentum after its promulgation. It was at In Salah that the protest was and is still most powerful; there was created in the course of 2014, a collective anti shale gas protest. Since 1 January 2015, the entire population of this small town, in the heart of the Sahara, is manifesting daily its anger in the central square of the city which was renamed *Sahat Essoumoud* (Place of resistance). This population has already suffered other injuries in the past, including the French nuclear tests in the 1960s and the sequestration of carbon dioxide in the gas field Krechba, where leaks extremely dangerous to humans, environment and promoting global warming, are taking place.

Two statements made in 2014 by the Prime Minister and the Minister of Energy contributed to pouring more oil in the fire. The Prime Minister said that the chemicals used in hydraulic fracking are not more harmful than those that soaked baby diapers. And according to the energy minister, the people of In Salah want to hurt their country and seek to lead Algeria into the situation in Iraq or Libya by their demonstration of rejection of the government's project. This protest is unprecedented in Algeria for several reasons. First, it is indeed the first citizens' revolt that has lasted so long. Although it has recently abated because of Ramadan (that had just ended)

1 This paper was presented at Summer University of ATTAC – Marseille – August 27, 2015

and the scorching temperatures that prevail at this time of the year, the anger continues to rumble at In Salah.

Second, contrary to what has happened in the past, these people do not express any political claims, nor financial. Third, this is the first protest in which we see almost as many men as women in street demonstration. In the first quarter of 2015, there were collective protests, like the one in In Salah, all over the country – the people gathered to say, "No to shale gas" and put forward, on February 23, a request for a moratorium to the President of the Republic.

Highlighted in the arguments accompanying the request, were all dangers for man, fauna and flora that hydraulic fracking – the technique used to extract the gas from the mother-rock – presented. There was also mention of the huge quantities of water – a precious commodity in the desert zone – consumed in each well (15 to 20 million litres). It was also stated that the production of shale gas is not a profitable activity in Algeria, given the enormous capital it requires and because Algerians have no mastery of the necessary technology. Reference was equally made to the risk of pollution of soil, subsoil, air and underground water layers that come from fracking.

The greatest danger is the possible contamination of the Albian layer that contains tens of trillions of cubic metres of water from rains that fell over the Atlas Mountains situated in the north of the country – a water that has been accumulated in this geological layer. If such an event were ever to occur, the life of generations of North Africans would be endangered. Pollution is already there – from industry used water in ponds dug in the sand and covered with plastic to ensure relative tightness. These waters, containing all kinds of extremely hazardous chemicals, eventually seep into the ground.

Furthermore, being exposed to air and sunlight, this water pollutes the atmosphere during evaporation by the fumes they give off, and the land by the residues that they generate. In fact, the In Salah people found out that since these two wells were drilled in the immediate vicinity of the city, pigeons, hawks and flocks of migrating storks have been dying. They asked the local authorities to look into the phenomenon and determine the causes of such carnage and the national hydrocarbons company to install devices for measuring the toxicity of the air in the region. These requests have been ignored for the moment. However, by its resolute approach, the population seems to have won the bale, since Sonatrach, with the agreement of the State certainly, seems to have abandoned the drilling of a third well that was programmed on the permit.

Why such a Sustained Pressure from the State?

Two reasons explain the stubbornness of the regime which wants to exploit shale gas at all costs: alignment with U S policy in the matter and the panic that reigns in the ranks of power since the drastic fall in the oil revenue of the country was recorded.

On the first reason: when they called Abdelaziz Bout eflika and elected him President in April 1999, the army and the security services, which are the backbone of the regime, have made him understand that he could not exercise his powers beyond red lines. They have drummed this into his ears from the outset. In order to escape this tutelage and not be a 3/4 president as he often said himself, and in the hope that he will gain respect of the army generals who had settled him in the chair of the president of the Republic, he sought support from abroad, especially that of the U S president. In two meetings with George W. Bush in October and November 2001, he made a deal with him. One, Algeria will immediately adopt the new U S doctrine on energy – the result being a disguised sale of the Algerian oil wealth to U S companies. Two, his government will make available to U S security services, the huge amount of information on Al Qaeda that it then held. In return, the U S would provide to the men of the regime and to him personally, support and protection.

The most controversial provisions of the law on hydrocarbons which was then adopted – a 100% copy of the doctrine of the administration of George W. Bush on the matter – were finally cancelled at the end of a saga that lasted 5 years. But the commitment of Bout eflika to intensive exploitation of Algeria's oil resources to meet the needs and wishes of the Americans, was maintained. It is in this frame work that the Ministry of Energy made, in the course of the years 2010 and 2011, secret contacts with multinational oil companies, leading to the enactment in 2013 of the new law authorizing the exploitation of shale gas. The alignment of Algeria to U S policy in this area has come to light in the first quarter of this year (2015). Being afraid that the virus of anti-shale gas dispute will reach the management of the national company of hydrocarbons, the government appealed, in February of this year, for the services of a "specialist" Mr. Thomas Murphy. Mr. Thomas who is the director of a research centre in charge of monitoring the operations on the Marcellus gas field in Pennsylvania, was invited to Algiers with a purpose to "preach" the good word to the senior managers of Sonatrach. Knowing that the financing and management of the centre that Mr. Murphy runs are provided by some 300 companies involved, in varying degrees, in the exploitation of shale gas in this field, we can easily imagine what Mr. Murphy did say to the executives of Sonatrach.

We noticed, as well, in March of this year, the declaration of the Under Secretary of State for Economic Affairs, Mr. Rivkin, during his visit to Algeria. He said during the press conference held at the U S embassy, that he had no advice for Algerians. But he informed them nonetheless that the exploitation of this gas created jobs in his country, that the technique of hydro cracking was safe and without hazards and that the United States were willing to provide them the necessary technical assistance, if they wished.

The second reason why the regime has decided to enforce shale gas exploitation began to take shape in 2011, when it suddenly realized the shortness of oil and gas fields where production took place, leading to the continues drop in revenue. Also, the price of oil began a nosedive. That became even a more important force since November 2014.

The problem is that hydrocarbons provide 98% of the foreign currencies of Algeria and the country imports almost everything it consumes. Since nothing was done by the president to prepare for what he calls "the post-oil era" (a matter he has been on since the last fifteen years at least), he finds himself panicking due to his carelessness. The president is aware that any decline in these revenues will directly affect the daily lives of citizens, whose rude awakening he fears. Moreover, and most importantly, this hydrocarbon annuity is the foundation of the regime as it is deployed for buying consciences and support inside and outside the country and also for buying social peace by means of distributing the money as grants and loans which are never refunded, etc. These are done in order to extinguish the numerous hotbeds of tension that are prevalent around the country. The regime amass oil revenues that allow it to strengthen and perpetuate its power. These revenues also allow the barons of the regime to swell their bank accounts by the huge commissions they receive from oil companies operating in the country, and also those they receive from sales of Sonatrach oil and from almost all its contracts of supply of equipment and services. These are then the reasons why the government in place in Algiers has adopted a scorched earth policy, replacing an annuity (a grant) with another, while it allows the unconventional exploitation of hydrocarbons, although it is aware of the dangers to the population.

All these notwithstanding, I am convinced that the mobilization of the In Salah population has managed to sow doubt in the minds of Algerian politicians. This is a fact unprecedented in Algeria. At all times and on all occasions, the regime considered itself alone as the possessor of the truth, thinking that citizens were minors incapable of any thought. It, therefore, did not have to discuss or negotiate anything with the citizens and could manipulate them at will. But here for the first time, we really feel the regime hesitates. That is why our support to Algerian anti-shale gas militants and the residents of In Salah in particular, is important and will certainly help to overcome the regime's reluctance and to impose the desired policy change.

THEY DON'T CARE IF WE EXIST –
CRUDE OIL SPILL IMPACTS AT FORCADOS

Nnimmo Bassey

The 14th of February was celebrated as Lover's Day across the world, but in parts of the creeks of the Niger Delta it turned out to be a tragic day. While lovers dressed with a touch of red, Forcados communities were braced for the unknown with the threat of having their water ways coated with crude oil rose by the hour. On that day, Shell Petroleum Development Company (SPDC or Shell) announced that there was an oil spill from their 1.2 metres (48 inches) export line and that they were investigating the cause. The point of leak lies under 4.5 metres of water. To be sure that the right thing was done, that the environment was protected and that communities were not left in limbo, the Minister of Environment, Amina Mohammed and the Minister of State for Environment, IBRAHIM Usman JIBRIL, visited the Forcados Terminal to see things for themselves. They forsook the luxury of getting there on a chopper and took to the boats to get there through the choppy, and at times, treacherous waves. Their move sent a strong signal that the business of ecological defence in these parts was taking a necessary curve.

We should also say here that since taking office, these ministers have toured the environmental crisis hotspots in Nigeria – including areas polluted by oil and industrial activities, impacted by desertification and loss of wetlands and, facing the menace of gully erosion. They have also been in constant consultations to ensure that the implementation of the UNEP report on Ogoni environment is not only implemented but that other parts of the Niger Delta would not be left in the lurch.

Forcados in Burutu Local Government Area of Delta State, Nigeria, hosts the second oil export terminal in the country besides the one at Bonny in Rivers State. There was no media announcement and no paparazzi on the Forcados visit. Government officials on the visit were John Nani, the Commissioner for Environment, Delta State and Dan Yingi, Chairman of the Environment Committee of the Delta State House of Assembly. The other officials were Mrs Akutu, the Permanent Secretary in the Ministry and Idris Musa of the National Oil Spill Detection and Response Agency (NOSDRA). And then there were three of us from the environmental justice constituency: Emem Okon, Monday Itoghor and yours truly, Nnimmo Bassey.

Arrival at Forcados Terminal was an hour's bounce on the waves in a convoy of military boats. On the way we passed solitary boats with stoic fisher women and men hoping for a catch, and obviously at home with the boisterous waves around them. On arrival at the Terminal, the visiting team was given a presentation on the incident by Shell officials. Before zeroing in on the incident, they went on a history tour of developments on the Terminal as well as on past incidents.

Spills Remembered

The terminal commenced operations 1971, that is 45 years ago and had a major upgrade in 1998. Shell noted that the incident of 14 February 2016 occurred almost on the 10th anniversary of an 18th February 2006 militant attack on the pipeline. They also mentioned an attack on their 36 inches produced water pipelines in 2006. Produced water is dumped into the creeks and rivers of the Niger Delta after treatment by the production companies. The company provides constant electricity from gas turbines to the two major communities in Forcados, Ogulagha and Odimodi. Shell has 36 power generating turbines in the vicinity and only needs two to power their operations at the Terminal. Since they shutdown, power is supplied from diesel run electricity generators. This may soon be rationed as supply runs low.

Shell also informed that on 4 March 2014, there was a third-party interference on their export line at a depth of 8 metres and that this was through a sophisticated theft point that only professionals could have been able to manoeuvre. The current spill happened 5km off the coast and led to loss of 300,000 barrels of crude oil from government owned Shell, Nigerian Petroleum Development Company (NPDC) and Seplat Petroleum Development Company (a Nigerian company).

Chronology of a Spill and Response

The loading of a vessel, MT Yamuna Spirit, commenced from 10:00 am on 12 February 2016. Loading was suspended at 0:20 am on 14 February when the spill was noticed. Seplat and NPDC were informed to stop pumping crude oil to the Terminal at 5:41 pm on 14 February.

Shell deployed booms at 9:35 am on 15 February to curtail the spread of the crude and a specialised surveillance aircraft arrived from Ghana at 10:30 am on 17 February to join the effort. By the time of the visit, they had deployed 27 skimmers and plastic tanks for collection of recovered crude. They also stated that community people were recruited to join the clean-up effort. When the Minister asked what actions had been taken to protect and assist the impacted communities, Shell officials informed that so far, they had recovered 25 barrels of crude and had mobilised relief materials such as rice, beans, vegetable oil and water to the major communities. Tellingly, Shell would not disclose how many barrels of crude oil has been dumped into the sea, creeks and the lands from this incident.

Cause of Incident

Although investigations by the Joint Inspection Team – made up of company and government officials, as well as community representatives – have not been concluded, Shell insisted that the spill was caused by a third-party interference. How are they so sure of this? They displayed thick concrete pieces collected from the sea bed at the point of leakage. The pipe is protected by being encased in concrete reinforced with wire mesh. The second point that they claimed provided irrefutable proof was that some community people informed them that they heard a big bang at a time that coincided with when the spill occurred. On being questioned by the Minister of Environment, they agreed that they would have to wait for the conclusion of the investigations and further expert examination, before drawing any conclusions about the cause of the spill. My note here was that even if the exact time of the rupture of the pipe was known, hearing a loud noise from the community could not rigidly prove that a third-party interference had occurred on the pipeline at a point that is 5 km out at sea. That sounds like one "hearsay" taken too far!

The Minister of Environment appreciated that Shell notified the ministry of the spill on 15 February. She told them that President Buhari is determined to ensure a clean-up of Ogoni land as well as the entire Niger Delta. She noted that whether the present incident was caused by equipment failure or by third party action, the government was concerned that the communities, the environment and the economy should not suffer.

They Do Not Care if We Exist

After the official presentation, it was time to visit some of the impacted communities. We headed towards the open sea, but after about 15 minutes in choppy waves and heavy salt water sprays, it was obvious that it was not the right time to proceed in that direction using the boats we had. So back to the Terminal, we returned. From here we went to Oseigbene village (also called Okutu), right at the edge of the Terminal, to see things for ourselves. Shell had tried to say that the spill was being contained and kept from hitting the shoreline, but the visit to this village showed very extensive crude oil pollution of the community, especially their creek, the major source of potable water. There were booms and skimmers deployed by Shell here, but these were clearly rudimentary and ineffective. The crude oil simply coursed beyond the feeble booms while the skimmers whirled and skimmed what they could.

The mangrove forests were heavily impacted. Dead crabs and fish littered the shoreline at the village. It was a river of oil as far as we could see. The effort to put up a clean-up show for the visiting Minister did not quite pan out as they may have expected. Community women spoke up. They told the Minister that Shell does not appear to care whether they existed or not, that no one cared if they were humans. They had no road, no electricity and no water. They had no jobs and were not engaged in the clean-up processes. They had also not received any relief materials. Their children were sick as a result of the spill and some were in hospitals receiving treatment. After the visit, the oil company officials said they were not aware of any illnesses arising from the spill. The Minister assured the community that her visit was to ensure that their situation was handled properly and that their environment would be cleaned up. She also noted that the women and children bore special impacts from incidents like the present one and that something would be done to assist them.

A short helicopter overflight around the spill point showed efforts being made to curtail the spread of the spill. Again, the booms deployed out there did not appear to be doing any better than the ones seen at Oseigbene. This is the story of oil and the Niger Delta.

SECTION 4

KNOWLEDGE SPACE

...the first step towards reimagining a world gone terribly wrong would be to stop the annihilation of those who have a different imagination- an imagination that is outside capitalism as well as communism. An imagination which has an altogether different understanding of what constitutes happiness and fulfillment.

Excerpt from 'Walking with the Comrades' by Arundhati Roy

WE SHALL NOT BE SILENT

Nnimmo Bassey[1]

When Ken Saro-Wiwa wrote that silence was tantamount to treason, he knew what he was saying. When he declared in the dock that we all stand before history, he was as prescient as any prophet could be. Today, we see clearly that keeping silent in the face of ecological destruction is treason. Keeping silent while the environment and the people die is not just being callous but is plain treason. He knew the vision of the Ogoni people and had no doubts about his mission. He endured personal insults, attacks and pains. He took all that because he desired to see a democratic Nigerian nation where no group or individual is marginalised and where everyone lives in dignity in an environment that is safe and supportive of livelihoods.

Ken Saro-Wiwa, although not a president of a nation, sits well alongside great visionary African leaders in the pantheon of great African and global leaders. He was a man of many dreams. He was murdered, but as is universally accepted, even if you kill the messenger, you cannot kill the dream.

As the turmoil in Africa is interrogated, there is need to make efforts towards finding out what the roots are and whether there are common factors connecting them. People should ask the questions: when, where and why did the rain begin to drench us? How could storm clouds gather and yet we say there would be no rain? One of the regrets of Ken Saro-Wiwa was that he and the Ogoni leaders in the struggle in the early 1990s had not invested enough in training up cadres and upcoming leaders. He stated this in a number of ways in the communications he was able to smuggle out of prison. The regret was clear in the very last letter he wrote while in detention and which is included in *Silence Would Be Treason – The Last Writings of Ken Saro-Wiwa*. Part of the letter read:

> One source of worry is what will happen to our struggle when Ledum and I are put away. We had not had enough to train the cadres or put alternative leaderships in place. And putting members of the Steering

1 Presented by Nnimmo Bassey at HOMEF's third Sustain-Ability Academy with the theme, 'Turmoil in Africa: Uprising or Chaos?' and with Firoze Manji, director of the Pan African Institute of Thought Works, as the Instigator.

Committee on the police wanted list has deprived us of a lot of hands. I have been able to direct things and even contribute to the publicity war from detention. I don't know if I'll be able to do so from prison. We have no funds, not even a bank account. Everything had hinged so much upon my resources that my absence will cause a lot of problems. We'll have to get around that somehow.

It is inspiring to see that the seeds sown by the martyrs of the Ogoni struggle continue to fire the imaginations of the marginalised peoples of the world and all those carrying the epic bales of ecological sanity. Saro-Wiwa was an apostle of peaceful resistance. Like others before him, the arrows aimed at him by agents of multinational corporations and the governments that polish their bloody shoes, did not cow him. His vision of an Ogoni ethnic nation of proud and dignified people lives on. Today, everyone sees the Ogoni people and marvel at the tenacity with which they are committed to peaceful resistance in the face of ecological provocations and extreme pressures including those of land grabbing and outright violence.

It is heart-warming that the Movement for the Survival of the Ogoni People (MOSOP) continues to hold up the banner announcing the possibilities of a restored Ogoni environment, attainment of political and economic emancipation and securing the collective dignity of the people. Other organisations are also working towards the same ends in Ogoni and in other parts of the Niger Delta and the entire Nigerian nation. With this, there is hope that the labour of our heroes past will never be in vain indeed.

August 4, 2014 made it three years since the United Nations Environment Programme (UNEP) issued its critical report on the state of the Ogoni environment. The report uncovered that the Ogoni environment has been so damaged that rather than support lives and livelihoods, it was killing the Ogoni people. The UNEP report confirmed the alarming fact that all the water bodies in Ogoni are polluted with hydrocarbons and a variety of deadly elements including carcinogens. The pollution is so deep that it would require twenty-five years of work to decontaminate the waters so that people can safely drink and use the resources found in them. The report also revealed that the land in Ogoni is polluted to a depth of five metres in several places and would require five years to clean up before the waters can be cleaned.

Ken Saro-Wiwa declared that what was happening in Ogoni was an ecological war. That may have appeared as a very strong way to describe the situation, but one thing is clear, he has been vindicated. That war is not over. It will not be over until the children in the land can safely swim again in the rivers and creeks. It will not be over until the people can fish, collect crabs, periwinkles and other seafood, and eat them with assurance of nourishment and not death by instalment. The ecological war will not be over until the farmers can plant and harvest yams and cassavas that are safe to eat and are not covered in hydrocarbon pollutants. The ecological war in still on! It must stop!

The ecological war rages as the days go by and the UNEP report remains unimplemented in a real sense. Erecting signposts reminding the people that the communities are polluted does not say where the people should relocate to or whether the contaminants are being cleared. Surely, three years is enough for any serious work to have commenced on the detoxification of Ogoni environment. The UNEP report was an alarm bell signifying that the petroleum sector's footprint in the Niger Delta is deadly and cannot be ignored. The harm done cannot be wished away. It must be confronted and dealt with. The ecological war in still on! It can be stopped!

The same can be said of the polluting extractive activities in other parts of Nigeria and indeed Africa. The mines of Plateau State were abandoned without decommissioning. The environment remains toxic and over 1100 sinkholes there continue to pose grave danger to man and beasts. The environment of the coalmines of Enugu and Kogi States begs for restoration. The same is the situation with the gold mines of Obuasi, Ghana, the coal mines of Witbank in South Africa and the diamond mines of Kono in Sierra Leone, to mention a few.

Many of the conflicts in Africa do not happen because Africans are bloodthirsty tribal peoples that are always at conflict with ourselves. No! Many are proxy wars fought on behalf of agents of resource expropriation and transnational resource thieves. Outright wars and terror across the continent are fought so that arms merchants can ply their bloody trade. Then, the manipulated persons wave weapons produced by the merchants of death who laugh all the way to the bank while the swayed abduct young girls, kill children in their sleep, burn down villages and soak in the blood of children, mothers and fathers.

DEVELOPMENT OR AMPUTATION? THE ROLE OF EXTRACTIVE INDUSTRIES

Firoze Manji

We hear so much nowadays about the contribution made, or that could be made, to 'development', by transnational extractive corporations operating in Africa. There is no doubt that resource extraction is a critical sector within African national economies. But what is its real contribution to development? Extraction of non-renewable resources should be considered as being equivalent to amputation. Africa is said to have 10 percent of the world's reserves of oil, 40 percent of its gold, and nearly 90 percent of the chromium and the platinum metal group, with probably much more yet to be discovered. Natural resource extraction contributes more than 30 percent of Africa's GDP. According to a McKinsey report, resource extractive industries "will continue to profit from rising global demand for oil, natural gas, minerals, food, arable land, and the like..." The annual flow of foreign direct investment into Africa increased from $9 billion in 2000 to $62 billion in 2008 – relative to GDP, almost as large as the flow into China", most of it into the extractive industries.

However, according to Carlos Lopes, the executive secretary of United Nations Economic Commission for Africa (ECA), "Average net profits for the top 40 mining companies grew by 156% in 2010 whereas the take for governments grew by only 60%, most of which was accounted for by Australia and Canada." He points out that the profit made by the same set of mining companies in 2010 was $110 billion, which was equivalent to the merchandise exports of all African Least developed countries (LDCs) in the same year. "It is fair to say, therefore, that the resource-to-development model puts raw materials' suppliers at a significant disadvantage. The conclusion that can then be drawn from this situation is that the current resource-for-development model is not working to bring about equity or boost development.

Nevertheless, the belief that with proper management African countries could still benefit from opening their territories to the extractive industries endures. For example, Lebogang Motlana, the Director of UNDP's

Addis Ababa-based Regional Service Centre for Africa, claims that "The extractive sector is expected to play an important role for development in many African countries, triggering growth in new and dynamic economic sectors and industries, as well as investments in jobs, infrastructure and basic social services. ...The sector provides huge opportunities for sustainable development and poverty reduction if properly managed with the right mix of policies and enforcement systems in place.

The contribution of extractive industries to environmental destruction and to climate change has been well documented elsewhere. The apparent profitability of these industries is due to the fact that they externalize those detrimental effects; they do not take account of the costs associated with environmental damage. But there is a fundamental dimension about natural resource extraction that has been ignored both by the proponents and opponents of the extractive industries. In (almost) every instance of resource extraction, we are dealing with extraction of non-renewable resources. In such cases, the word 'extraction' is really a euphemism for amputation. As any dentist knows, once one 'extracts' a permanent tooth, there is no natural replacement. It is an amputation.

Now consider an economy in which more than 30% of the GDP is attributable to resource extraction, or more accurately, resource amputation. This is like saying: "we are going to amputate a third of your body. Sure, we will pay you for cutting off parts of your body and selling these in the market. Of course, we will make profits from this investment, but you will benefit because we will compensate you with a nominal amount that will contribute to development and poverty alleviation (provided you do not tax us too much)".

When expressed in such terms, it sounds absurd, ludicrous. Yet, isn't that fundamentally what is going on? Whatever euphemisms might be used for extraction of non-renewable natural resources, the fact remains that it is a form of amputation. It is hard to accept the argument, therefore, that such amputation leads to development. Let me cut off your leg so you can walk better? It is high time extractive industries started being described as what they really are – amputative industries. By this, it becomes clear the extent to which the future is being sold out. Looked at from this perspective, it is hard not to agree with Nnimmo Bassey's famous saying: "Leave the oil in the soil, the coal in the hole and the tar sands in the land!"

Experts looking at the amputative economy might argue that the problem is that there is need to, as Carlos Lopes puts it, "rectify some of the initial problems that have continued to plague the management of the continent's natural resources. At the fore of this endeavour is the capacity of governments to get the best deals for their countries during contract negotiations." In other words, Africa needs to be strong enough to argue for a greater share of the profits arising from amputations. Given how much has already been mined from Africa and how much is stockpiled outside the continent, there is, perhaps, a case for ceasing further exploitation of Africa's natural resources.

Real development will only be possible if these amputative industries are controlled not by transnational corporations and speculators on the stock exchanges but by citizens, for these natural resources belong to the commons. The income derived from controlled and limited exploitation can then be invested in sovereign value-adding manufacturing and services sectors that are geared to meeting the needs of the majority. Amputation cannot be taken lightly. Sacrifices of this kind should be made only where there are demonstrable and significant benefits that materially contribute to breaking Africa's dependency on the North and breaking its position as exporter of primary products for satisfying the need for super-profits of international corporations and financial institutions.

HOW ECONOMIC GROWTH
HAS BECOME ANTI-LIFE

Vandana Shiva[1]

An obsession with growth has eclipsed man's concern for sustainability, justice and human dignity. But people are not disposable – the value of life lies outside economic development. Limitless growth is the fantasy of economists, businesses and politicians. It is seen as a measure of progress. As a result, gross domestic product (GDP), which is supposed to measure the wealth of nations, has emerged as both the most powerful number and dominant concept in this age. However, economic growth hides the poverty it creates through the destruction of nature, which in turn vitiates communities' capacity to provide for themselves.

The concept of growth was put forward as a measure to mobilise resources during the Second World War. GDP is based on creating an artificial and fictitious boundary, assuming that if one produces what one consumes, one does not produce. In effect, "growth" measures the conversion of nature into cash and commons into commodities. Thus, nature's amazing cycles of renewal of water and nutrients are defined as nonproduction. The peasants of the world, who provide 72% of the food, do not produce; women who farm or do most of the housework do not fit this paradigm of growth either. A living forest does not contribute to growth, but when trees are cut down and sold as timber, there is growth. Healthy societies and communities do not contribute to growth, but disease creates growth through, for example, the sale of patented medicine.

Water which is available as a common that is shared freely and protected by all, and provides for all, however, does not create growth. But when Coca-Cola sets up a plant, mines the water and fills plastic bottles with it, the economy grows. But this growth is based on creating poverty – for nature and local communities. Water extracted beyond nature's capacity to renew and recharge creates a water famine. Women are forced to walk longer distances looking for drinking water. In the village of Plachimada

1 This article was also published at http://www.theguardian.com/commentisfree/2013/nov/01/how-economic-growth-has-become-anti-life

in Kerala, India, when the walk for water became 10 km long, local tribal woman Mayilamma said "enough is enough. We cannot walk further; the Coca-Cola plant must be shut down." The movement that the women started eventually led to the closure of the plant.

In the same vein, evolution has gifted man the seed and farmers have selected, bred and diversified it. This is the basis of food production. A seed that renews itself and multiplies, produces seeds for the next season, as well as food. However, farmer-bred and farmer-saved seeds are not seen as contributing to growth. The process creates and renews life, but it does not lead to profits.

Rather, growth begins when seeds are modified, patented and genetically locked, leading to farmers being forced to buy more every season. Nature is impoverished, biodiversity is eroded and a free, open resource is transformed into a patented commodity. Buying seeds every year is a recipe for debt for India's poor peasants. And ever since seed monopolies have been established, farmers' debts have increased. More than 270,000 farmers caught in a debt trap in India have committed suicide since 1995. Poverty is also further spread when public systems are privatised. The privatisation of water, electricity, health, and education does generate growth through profits. But it also generates poverty by forcing people to spend large amounts of money on what was available at affordable costs as a common good. When every aspect of life is commercialised and commoditised, living becomes more costly, and people become poorer. It is imperative to note that both ecology and economics emerged from the same roots –"oikos", the Greek word for household.

As long as economics was focused on the household – its root – it recognised and respected its basis in natural resources and the limits of ecological renewal. It was focused on providing for basic human needs within these limits. Economics as based on the household was also women-centered. Today, economics is separated from and opposed to both ecological processes and basic needs. While the destruction of nature has been justified on grounds of creating growth, poverty and dispossession have increased. This is non-sustainable as well aseconomically unjust. The dominant model of economic development has in fact become anti-life. When economies are measured only in terms of money flow, the rich get richer and the poor get poorer. And the rich might be rich in monetary terms –but they too are poor in the wider context of what being human means. Meanwhile, the demands of the current model of the economy are leading to resource wars oil wars, water wars, food wars and all sort of wars.

There are three levels of violence involved in non-sustainable development. The first is the violence against the earth, which is expressed as the ecological crisis. The second is the violence against people, which is expressed as poverty, destitution and displacement. The third is the violence of war and conflict, as the powerful reach for the resources that lie in other communities and countries for their limitless appetites. Increase of money flow through GDP has become disassociated from real value. Those who accumulate financial resources can then stake claim on the real resources of people –their land and water, their forests and seeds. This thirst leads to them predating on the last drop of water and last inch of land on the planet. This is not an end to poverty. It is an end to human rights and justice.

Nobel-prize winning economists, Joseph Stiglitz and Amartya Sen, have admitted that GDP does not capture the human condition and urged the creation of different tools to gauge the wellbeing of nations. This is why countries like Bhutan have adopted the gross national happiness in place of gross domestic product to calculate progress. There is need to create measures beyond GDP and economies beyond the global supermarket, to rejuvenate real wealth. There is need to remember that the real currency of life is life itself.

GLOBAL BLACKNESS

Hakima Abbas[1]

A message to the Black grassroots (in the U.S), shared with the hope that it reaches Black people on a move. Black people everywhere, see you and are with you in the struggle. It has been, for Africans outside of the U.S., significant and joyful to see the movement for Black life and dignity take hold, grow and capture the imagination in this moment there.

The most recent uprisings and mass actions across the U.S. is the culmination of mobilisations and organising that have been ongoing for decades – that were visible from response to the lack of government action to the devastation of Hurricane Katrina, down to the case of the Jena 6, of Troy Davis, of Trayvon Marn, and now of Michael Brown and Eric Garner; as well as in the attempts to build viable alternatives as in Cooperation Jackson. This moment in the movement has been triggered by the revolts in Ferguson but the movement is one for Black lives, Black life, Black dignity and Black self-determination, going on in the tradition of Black liberation struggles. Understood in this continuum, it has been wonderful to hear Assata Shakur present in the chants in Ferguson: "It is our duty to fight for our freedom, it is our duty to win." Indeed in this movement, it is paramount to call out the names and organise to secure the freedom of the political prisoners that remain captive in U.S. prisons for also demanding and defending Black life and dignity: Sundiata Acoli, Mutulu Shakur, Robert Seth Hayes, Albert Woodfox, Mumia Abu Jamal, Herman Bell, among many others.

There has been an outpouring of global solidarity for the Black movement in the U.S. by Black people in, to name but a few, South Africa, Kenya, Zimbabwe, Colombia, Brazil, the UK, France and by non-Black people fighting against imperialism the world over, including in Palestine where the historic solidarity between African and Palestinian peoples continues. Black people globally are claiming 'we are Ferguson' as an understanding of the linked fate and common oppression and in

---

1 Remarks at the Black Life Matters conference in Tucson, Arizona, on January 15, 2015. They were originally published in the Feminist Wire at: http://thefeministwire.com/2015/01/global-blackness/

many cases because the manifestations of global anti-Black violence are so similar.

In South Africa, for example, a booming prison industrial complex and accompanying State and non-State so-called 'security' apparatus is being established to protect capital from economically oppressed Black people rather than protecting the masses of Black people from the violence of capitalism. In the U.S., a Black person is killed every 28 hours, and in Brazil, approximately 118 Black people are murdered every day in what Afro-Brazilians are calling a silent genocide. One hundred and eighteen Black people are murdered every day!

The outpouring has highlighted not only the linked fate between the Black but also the asymmetry of how far the cries of indignation of les damnés carry. The cries of Ferguson echoes and have been heard across the globe. Yet, wherever one is, they must listen hard to hear the resistance in Burkina Faso, in Guinea, in Colombia, in Sudan, in the DRC. To remix CLR James, the only place where Black people do not revolt is in the pages of the capitalist media. Just as anti-Black oppression is global and takes many forms that are embedded in systems of white supremacists, hetero-patriarchy, ableist enablers and capitalism, resistance by Black people is also global. Thus, it is an all-Black and pro-Black responsibility to see, and listen to each other's cries, be inspired by one another and live in solidarity with one another.

In Colombia, Black women have been in permanent assembly in the offices of the Ministry of Interior of Giralda since November 27, 2014 as part of their fight to protect their lands and territories from mining, to end the war on their bodies and to resist displacement. In Madagascar, peasants and farmers resisted massive land grabs, their uprisings leading to an overturn of government. However, their gains are being reversed in the name of liberal democracy. More broadly, the fight against land grab in Africa is a fight for Black life and survival, for self-determined development and is a global fight for the future that all Black and their supporters need to be paying attention to.

With the collaboration of African governments and elites, about 20 million hectares of farmland has been grabbed since 2008, using the all too familiar justification that the land is unoccupied or unused. The land claims of pastoralists, women, peasants and small-scale farmers are marginalized from formal land rights processes and access to law and institutions by the colonial framework of land ownership that favours markets and businesses. Land use for non-commercial, including medicinal, spiritual or grazing (for pasture) activities, is ignored to make way for large-scale, high-yield 'production.' Biodiversity is being patented, flora and fauna commodified, and water grabbed – this is no longer the prediction of great writers like Octavia Butler but a terrifying reality.

Significant public relations efforts by, amongst others, Bill Gates in partnership with Monsanto, to persuade governments and farmers that GMOs offer the solution to food insecurity are obscuring the market-dependency that this and mono-cropping would create for already market-marginalized small-scale farmers on the continent. The sustainable future that global capitalism is envisioning and aggressively creating is one in which technology beats nature to maintain the luxury of a few. Black lives and lands remain commodities and disposables. Despite the threat, communities across Africa have been resisting land grab, and women have been organising beyond borders to claim 'we are the solution' to sustainable food production.

Globally, women and folks often described as queer, are resisting and building alternatives at the intersections of patriarchy and capitalism. In the U.S., it has been disheartening to see the erasure of Black cis and trans women's lives even within the Black Lives Matter movement. Where was the mass mobilization when Tanisha Anderson was murdered by the police? Where was the mass mobilization when Deshawnda Bradley was killed? Where is the movement for the sixty-four thousand Black women that are missing in the U.S.?

On the continent of Africa, there is the attempt to disappear Black women and queer lives and life from the very narrative of African identity. Armed with imported religious fundamentalisms, the promise of capitalist prosperity and the necessity for diversion and division, an alliance has formed to enshrine patriarchy, heteropatriarchy and transphobia into the fabric of Africa. It is important not to fall into the trap of asserting that oppression and oppressive practices are a manifestation of African culture or tradition. As Amilcar Cabral emphasised, culture is dynamic and perpetually being made. Culture can be used as a tool for liberation or for the purposes of domination: the choice sits with everyone. Patriarchy dominates the practices around but it should be rejected as a part of the African culture. It is vital to choose the traditions of freedom, respect, love and self-determination that are just as much embedded in the history and practices of the people of Africa.

Women and Queer Africans are choosing and creating an Africa outside of the bounds of patriarchy – from mobilising in Soweto for Pride – through hundreds of people taking to the streets of Nairobi in miniskirts when a woman was stripped naked for being indecently dressed – to demanding an end to violence against sex workers under the banner of Black Lives Matter. Black people came out globally to 'Bring Back our Girls' after about three hundred children were abducted from school in Chibok, Nigeria in April 2014. The response of the Chibok community and the Nigerian women's movement sounded the alarm and spurred global solidarity from Philadelphia to London, Cairo to Dakar and Johannesburg. But eight months later, the girls are still missing and many more Black lives have since been lost to the proxy battlegrounds of a global war that has been raging in a barrage of silence. When the demand rang out to 'Bring Back our Girls', the outcome was more U.S. troops with 'boots on the ground' in Africa.

Militarized responses from the U.S. are not new, but the humanitarian justification for U.S. military infiltration into Africa is none the less duplicitous, be it in the response to 'Bring Back our Girls' or to the Ebola epidemic that has taken nearly eight thousand lives in Guinea, Sierra Leone and Liberia. Ebola became an epidemic in Guinea, Sierra Leone and Liberia and not in Spain, the United States or the UK, where there were also cases, because of systemic and entrenched impoverishment and inequalities. In other words, the differential effects of Ebola are directly related to capitalist systems of exploitation. And it is capitalist interests that have maintained the attention of pharmaceutical corporations backed by the U.S. military in the Ebola crisis, not human solidarity. Because Black lives matter, the Black must build 'ways of being' that disrupt imperialism, patriarchy, militarism – disrupt the entire system and sustain Black life.

Despite the unprecedented Black presence in the U.S administration, the murder, mass incarceration and impoverishment of Black people continues. Similarly, for the last five years, African states have had African administrations that do not serve the interests of African peoples. When there is no justice, there is 'just us'. In this moment when the attention of so many is on the Black liberation movement in the U.S., there is significant pollical mileage in claiming ally-ship with the movement – the woodworks will be full. But genuine solidarity requires 'fighting on different terrains toward the same objectives', co-conspiracy rather than empty declarations of ally-ship. Co-conspiracy will require long-term commitment, introspection and practice. It might start with a hashtag or wearing a t-shirt, it certainly cannot end there. The consternation amongst sections of the Black community in the U.S., has been witnessed around the organising tactics and methods of the mobilizations for Black life and lives.

During the uprisings in Tunisia, a communist comrade recounted that every evening he wrote an analysis of what was happening and how it was happening. Every morning he tore up his analysis. In only a few hours, what he understood felt no longer applicable, relevant or even enough to understand what was happening. The people were creating revolution. Not from a text book, the red book or any other book, but from their own experience and knowledge. Learning in a con was the order of the day and a 'leaderful' not leaderless, movement was being created in the image of the aspirations of the people involved. It was definitely not a perfect uprising, there have been significant losses over the last four years but revolution is a process and without a doubt the uprisings changed Tunisia, Africa and the rest of the world in significant ways.

The uprisings in the U.S. feel similar in that they are grounded on years of organising and part of a transformative process, they are 'leaderful' not leaderless and they have swept the old guard to the side to make room for the articulation of the peoples' aspirations. In Tunisia, the call was for 'bread and dignity,' in the U.S. it is for Black lives. Both have clear affirmations and both affirmations challenge the economic, social and political global order in their demand. The systems of oppression that are challenged locally are global and there exists, a global Black village. Black people have a duty not only to indict the system or shut it down, but to build new ways of being, doing and sustaining. The Black must become, in the words of Assata, weapons of mass construction. Indeed, there is nothing to lose but the chains.

Alfred Moten makes an important distinction here on Black lives and Black life:

> We need to understand what the state is defending itself from and I think that in this respect, the particular instances of Michael Brown's murder and Eric Garner's murder are worth paying some attention to. Because what the drone, Darren Wilson, shot into that day was insurgent Black life walking down the street. I don't think he meant to violate the individual personhood of Michael Brown. He was... mobile Black sociality walking down the street in a way that he (Darren Wilson) understood implicitly constituted a threat to the order he represents and that he is sworn to protect. Eric Garner on an everyday basis initiated a new alternative kind of market place, another mode of social life. That's what they killed, ok? So, when we say that Black lives matter, I think what we do sometimes is obscure the fact that it's in fact Black life that matters. That insurgent Black social lives constitute a profound threat to the already existing order of things.

The movement is a Black Life matter.

WHITE SAVIORISM, VICTIMIZATION AND VIOLENCE

Firoze Manji

On October 31 2014, Blaise Campaoré, the despotic ruler of Burkina Faso, was overthrown by mass uprisings almost exactly 27 years after he had seized power through the assassination, on October 15, 1987, of Thomas Sankara – popularly referred to as the "Che Guevara of Africa". Burkina Faso provides an excellent case study for understanding the conditions under which the white saviour industry thrives or dies. The République de Haute-Volta (Upper Volta), as the country was formerly known, was once part of the French Union but obtained independence from France in 1960.

This tiny impoverished country was grossly underdeveloped, with an illiteracy rate of 90%, the world's highest infant mortality rate (280 deaths for every 1,000 births), inadequate basic social services, having one doctor per 50,000 people, an average yearly income of $150 per person, and unable to feed its population. Highly indebted, its people had been rendered into the perfect image that nourishes the white saviour complex, as Walter Rodney described, "A black child with a transparent rib-case, huge head, bloated stomach, protruding eyes and twigs as arms and legs was the favourite poster of the large British charitable operation known as Oxfam." Following a series of coups and counter-coups that eventually led Thomas Sankara and his comrades to power in 1983, an extraordinary revolution was launched in the country.

In the space of just four years, the country became self-sufficient in food, its infant mortality rate halved, school attendance doubled, 10 million trees were planted to halt desertification, and wheat production was doubled. Land and mineral resources were nationalized, railways and infrastructure constructed, and 2.5 million children immunized against meningitis, yellow fever and measles. Nearly 350 medical dispensaries and schools were constructed across the country by communities. Female genital mutilation (FGM), forced marriages and polygamy were outlawed, and women were actively involved in decision making at all levels. In order to achieve this, Sankara did not ask for aid – on the contrary, he shunned aid.

Moreover, he argued that the debt owed by the country was odious, therefore, should not be paid. Cotton production, therefore, was not directed to export but was used to support a thriving Burkinabé textile industry. The country was marked in particular by the almost complete absence of foreign aid agencies and their local counterparts, the development NGOs. Sankara's assassination at the hands of Blaise Campaoré, supported and celebrated by France and the rest of the imperial world, was to bring about a reversal of all the gains of that short period. Under Campaoré, the country quickly returned to the conditions of the former République de Haute-Volta. Cotton was once again grown for export comprising 30% of its GDP of $1500, making it one of the lowest in the world.

Today, Burkina Faso is classified as one of the highly indebted poor countries (HIPC), with more than 80% of its population living on less than $2 a day, and nearly 50% on less than $1 a day. Infant mortality rates have been increasing. Literacy levels have fallen back to around 12%, with less than 10% of primary school pupils reaching secondary school.

In contrast to the programme of 'land to the peasant' initiated under Sankara, Campaoré's policies were more like land to the parliamentarians and the president's family! Corruption is deep, with millions allegedly being syphoned off from aid and from handouts from mining companies. A large part of the economy is in fact funded by international aid. Privatization of water and other utilities has been the order of the day. A number of transnational mining corporations have been allowed to excavate gold and other minerals, with almost no benefit to the population at large. And the regime was not averse to using violence and assassinations to deal with its opponents. These were the conditions needed for the flowering of agents of the white saviour industry.

In contrast to Sankara's time, Campaoré's rule was characterized by the growth in the involvement of the transnational development NGOs and an exponential growth in the number of their local Burkinabé counterparts. Oxfam Québec's involvement in Burkina Faso, for example, escalated after Campaoré took power in 1987. The number of Burkinabé NGOs are thought to be in the hundreds, each depending on foreign aid, each ready to present Africans as victims in need of rescue, not least from themselves, as the basis for getting grants. They flourished under a regime that had retrenched from its responsibilities for providing social services, and which has systematically dispossessed its people by privatizing the commons. The regime actively encouraged this growth of NGOs supported by international aid as the basis for absolving itself of any responsibility for improving the lives of the majority.

For saviours to exist, there must be those in need of 'saving'. Put another way, saviours require victims. Victimization – that is, the process of making other human victims – is necessarily a fundamental requirement for there to be a saviour complex. And by definition, white savior complex is premised on the victimization of the African, the black body. Thus, it has become conventional in the West to describe Africans only in terms of what they are not. They are considered chaotic not ordered, traditional not modern, tribal not democratic, corrupt not honest, underdeveloped not developed, irrational not rational and lacking in all of those things the West presumes itself to be.

White Westerners are still today represented as the bearers of 'civilization', the brokers and arbiters of development, while black, post-colonial 'others' are still seen as uncivilised and unenlightened, destined to be development's exclusive objects. But to fulfill this image of Africa requires the complicity of the African state and African NGOs, each to carry out its own form of violence. First, as the case of Burkina Faso illustrates, it requires the violence associated with destroying the emergence of self-worth, self-determination and dignity that was the achievement of the short-lived revolution led by Sankara. That violence is also necessary if the new rulers are to use the state as a source of private accumulation by dispossession for the benefit of a few.

The local NGOs, whose survival is dependent of receiving handouts from the white saviour industry, are complicit in nurturing the image of the subservient, incapable, primitive African – the victim that needs saving. The complicity of African NGOs, and indeed of African leaders, in perpetuating a form of self-hate of the African identity, a modern manifestation of Fanon's Black Skins, White Masks, is a painful and too often unacknowledged form of violence. Saviours cannot thrive where a people retake control of their destinies, assert their dignity and humanity, create the structures for self-determination, organise to produce and make collective decisions, take pride in their own cultures, and seek neither aid, grants nor charity.

Indeed, the very name of the country, Burkina Faso, "the land of upright people", that Sankara introduced in 1984, is anathema to the white saviour industry. What Burkina Faso experienced over a period of nearly thirty years has all the hallmarks of the set of neoliberal economic policies imposed with varying degrees of violence across the continent. The result of these policies has been not only global economic and financial crises, but also crises of credibility of today's rulers, as demonstrated in the rise of a profound discontent amongst the people.

That Camporé was deposed through mass mobilization against his attempt to prolong his rule (and that of his family) should not have come as a surprise. The set of conditions that has so enraged the Burkinabé are similar to those that led to the mass mobilizations and removal of Ben Ali in Tunisia and Hosni Mubarak in Egypt. These are only the first of many uprisings to come in Africa. And in none of the uprisings to date, and I would venture, in none of those that are to come, will we witness banners proclaiming 'we want more aid' nor 'we want to be rescued by white saviours'.

What these uprisings, whether in Africa or beyond, require is neither rescue nor aid – they require solidarity. Speaking to popular movements recently, Pope Francis described the act of solidarity thus:

> It is to confront the destructive effects of the empire of money: forced displacements, painful emigrations, the traffic of persons, drugs, war, violence and all those realities that many of you suffer and that we are all called to transform. Solidarity, understood in its deepest sense, is a way of making history, and this is what the Popular Movements do.

And in that, everyone everywhere can participate.

WHY LAW CAN SAVE US

Femke Wijdekop

Which of you has ever seen a TED Talk that changed the course of your life? It happened to me. It was New Year's Day, 2013 and outside, it was 6 degrees. Grey clouds were blocking out the weak winter sun, rain dribbled down on my windows and when I looked outside, the street was deserted. I had some free time between my late breakfast and a visiting friend and decided to watch Polly Higgin's TED Talk on Ecocide. That, had been on my 'to do' list for some time. When I finished watching that talk, 18 minutes later, something had fundamentally changed inside of me. All of a sudden, I understood why I had become a lawyer, why I had left the world of law in my mid-twenties out of discontent, and most importantly, why it was now time for me to return to it. Two and a half years later, I am standing here, on the red dot of TEDx Haarlem, giving a talk on this year's topic of Enlightenment.

The Enlightenment

The Enlightenment was a crucial period in the development of the rule of law. It brought the separation of state powers and the fundamental rights and freedoms of man. Central to the Enlightenment was the ideal of liberation – the liberation of man from repressive traditions and religions, and from power abuse by all-mighty kings. The idea of individual autonomy took root and thanks to fundamental rights and freedoms – like the freedom of speech, the freedom of religion and the freedom of property – individuals were now free to think, act and believe as they chose as long as they did not violate other people's rights to do the same. The Enlightenment also further developed the philosophy of materialism, which says that physical matter is the only reality and that everything, including thoughts and feelings can be explained in terms of physical phenomena. Thanks to new scientific discoveries and technological innovations, people could now measure, understand and ultimately control these physical phenomena. By using reason and applying scientific methods, people could finally dominate nature (or so we thought!) and organise nature in neatly divided categories; another characteristic of the Enlightenment mindset was thinking in terms of separation.

The Enlightenment separated facts from values, reason from faith, and humans from nature. Nature lost its sacred dimension and became an "object" that we could control and exploit. The invention of the steam engine played a big part in this. It freed humans from the forces of nature and boosted the enormous projects of industrialisation and colonialism. Thanks to coals and the steam engine, ships could cross the world seas, independent of the direction and strength of the wind. Merchants and colonists now controlled their access to foreign lands and the raw materials they contained. The idea took root that not only foreign peoples, but nature itself could be conquered. Legislative assemblies passed laws that enabled economic expansion and chartered companies to 'go and conquer the earth'. Eighteenth century clergyman and philosopher, William Derham summarized the spirit of his time when he said: "We can ransack the whole globe, penetrate in to the bowels of the earth, descend to the boom of the deep, travel to the farthest regions of this world, to acquire wealth."

Extractive Mindset Enslaves the Earth

In the 20th and 21st centuries, the destructive effects of this 'extractive mindset' in combination with increasingly powerful technology became clear. Natural disasters caused by human-influenced climate change, and massive damage of ecosystems (Ecocides) through overfishing in the North Sea, the massive deforestation of the Amazon and the Fukushima nuclear disaster, are the talk of the day. The world has come face to face with the effects of an economic system that makes profit out of exploiting the Earth.

Over the last 50 years, environmental legislation has been on the rise. But Environmental law has not been able to stop the destructive effects of the exploitation by extractive industries. In the current legal system, nature is seen as property and the starting point is that not all of life is protected. Environmental law protects nature in a fragmented way, and environmental issues are treated as planning issues, ignoring the complex issues that arise when ecosystems are interfered with in an inter connected world.

Environmental law has failed to address the real flaw in the system, which is that the Earth is seen as a lifeless object instead of the living, super complex organism that it really is. While the Enlightenment liberated man, it contributed to the development of an extractive mindset that has come to enslave the Earth. Law has enabled this development and this lack of consciousness so greatly disillusioned me in my mid-twenties that I decided to leave the world of law behind. But seeing that TED talk on New

Year's Day 2013 opened my eyes. I realized that more and more lawyers are now waking up to the fact that enslaving the Earth endangers man's own hard-won fundamental rights and freedoms.

Without a clean and safe living environment, it is really challenging to enjoy the right to health, employment, freedom of expression and religion. A healthy and safe Earth is an absolute 'must' if man desires to flourish politically and economically. There are no human rights on a dead planet.

The Climate Case against the Dutch State

The realization of the absoluteness of a healthy and safe Earth lies at the basis of Urgenda's Climate Case against the Dutch State, which was presented on 14 April 2013. I joined the case as a co-plaintiff, together with almost 900 other Dutch citizens. It was a unique case in the Netherlands and in the world. According to Roger Cox, Urgenda's lawyer, the Dutch State falls short of its duty of care by not taking adequate steps to reduce CO_2 emissions fast enough to prevent catastrophic climate change in the future. The plaintiffs asserted the right to a clean and healthy environment on behalf of themselves and future generations and demanded that the State gets serious about its climate obligations. This is a powerful example of how the present generation can act as 'stewards' for future citizens, giving a voice to unborn generations who are voiceless but who will be greatly affected by the climate decisions the governments take today.

Earth Law

Other lawyers take it one step further. They leave the focus on humans behind and adopt an ecocentric point of view. Ecocentric means that they recognize that the natural world has intrinsic value regardless of its usefulness for humans, and should be treated with respect. These ecocentric or Earth lawyers advocate a shift in the way law treats the Earth. Instead of seeing the Earth as a lifeless object, as a property under law, they want to change the status of the Earth to one of possessing rights and dignity.

In this new way of seeing the world, humans do not own the Earth, but act as its caretaker. Human laws should harmonise with the laws of nature and citizens can even enforce nature's rights in court. It is this vision that so greatly excited me that I decided to immerse myself in the world of Earth La w. It made total sense to me on a gut level and I loved the intellectual challenge of building a bridge between Earth Law and the system we are in right now. Because, how do we anchor these wonderful ideas in our current reality? That is the big question. I started to do research, interview Earth

Lawyers, publish about these new developments, and joined national and international campaigns. And quicker than I could have fathomed two and half years ago, these 'heroes' became my colleagues and I was interviewed myself and invited as a speaker. I realized my break from the world of law had served to prepare me to come back to it, because now I could use my work experiences in communication, community and event organising that I gained in these years to spread the message of Earth Law. I also found like-minded people here in the Netherlands with whom we have established a documentary platform called Facing Crossroads to inject these ideas into the public debate.

Ecocide

The idea central to the work of Facing Crossroads and the topic of the TED Talk that sparked the change in my life, is the work of Scottish barrister Polly Higgins. Since 2010 she has been on a global mission to make Ecocide – massive damage and destruction of ecosystems – the 5th Crime against Peace (next to genocide, crimes of aggression, crimes against humanity and war crimes) under the Rome Statute which is the founding treaty of the International Criminal Court. The term Ecocide was invented in 1970 by American biologist Arthur Glaston. In the 1950s, Glaston worked in a laboratory where he helped prepare a chemical component, the notorious defoliant, 'Agent Orange' which was used in the Vietnam War. When Glaston saw how Agent Orange was put to use in Vietnam – destroying vegetation on a massive scale and poisoning human health – he was appalled. He turned into an anti-war activist over-night and was the first to call the massive damage and destruction of ecosystems "Ecocide."

Ecocide was put on the international agenda in the 1970s and 1980s, and was part of the draft Rome Statute in the early 1990s. However, the draft provision to make Ecocide a crime was withdrawn from the final treaty text. Today, Higgins is travelling the world to gather governments and civil societies' support for including Ecocide as the missing 5th Crime against Peace very soon. This mission could truly change the course of history, because making Ecocide a crime would change the rules of the game as to how business is done. No longer would it be legal for corporations to make profit out of destroying the Earth. It would be a great catalyst for the transition to a green economy.

Wild Law

South African Cormac Cullinan is another leader in the Earth Law movement who I interviewed. Cullinan, a white South African, became an anti-apartheid activist as a law student, fighting for social justice and racial equality. When apartheid ended, he worked as a lawyer and drafter of environmental legislation and was confronted with the flaws of a legal system that treats the natural world as property. He realized that after apartheid, the enslavement of the natural world is the new frontier. Cormac wrote a book called Wild Law in which he explored the possibility of a radically different legal system.

Wild Laws are human laws that balance the rights and responsibilities of humans against the rights of plants, animals, rivers and ecosystems. It starts with the idea that all of life is protected and creates a frame work or 'constitution' for an ecologically thriving world. This may sound very utopian, but in only a couple of years Wild Law principles found their way into the Ecuadorian constitution, which now states in its Chapter 7 that Nature or Pachamama has the right to exist, persist, maintain and regenerate its vital cycles. Bolivia now protects the rights of Mother Earth in its national legislation. Over 100 communities across the United States have included nature's rights in their ordinances.

In 2010, a Belize court ruled that a reef is not property but a living being, and cannot be sacrificed for commercial interests. In Europe, Switzerland recognises the dignity of all beings in its constitution. Spain recognises the rights of Apes. And European citizens, led by British lawyer Mumta Ito, are preparing the European Citizens Initiative to give Rights to Nature.

Environmental Defenders

Earth Law is correcting a system which has placed the costs of pollution on the natural world, thereby contaminating the soils, seas and air of the one and only planet Earth. It has done so to such a degree, that man's survival may be at stake. And for many people around the world, this is already the case. Small scale farmers, fishers and hunters, and especially indigenous peoples, are confronted with the destruction of forests, pollution of rivers and by the grabbing of their farmlands because big corporations want to take the natural resources – the coal, oil, wood – to make profit.

Many farmers and tribe leaders stand up against this destruction, on behalf of their communities, future generations and the Earth herself which is sacred to most indigenous peoples. They all are Environmental

Defenders and the tragedy is that being an Environmental Defender is an extremely dangerous form of speaking out. In the last four years, on an average, two Environmental Defenders were killed every week according to reports from Global Witness. Indra Pelani, a 22-year-old farmer from Indonesia, was killed for defending the rights of farmers against the corporate takeover of their lands.

Thanks to NGOs, the works of Environmental Defenders like Indra Pelani are now monitored internationally and being in 'the public eye', can make a huge difference for their personal safety. The Grrrowd Initiative even created a crowdfunding platform to garner support for these brave Environmental Defenders by helping to finance the costs of their David vs. Goliath-like bales.

Using Our Rights and Freedom to Defend the Earth

What Environmental Defenders and Earth Lawyers are doing is, using their fundamental rights and freedoms – the freedom of speech, the right to demonstrate, the right to form associations to protect nature – to help restore the health of the Earth. They realise that people can only be free on an Earth that is clean, healthy and safe. The sharp distinction between man and nature – an inheritance of the age of Enlightenment – is dropped and the truth that man is always connected to nature, and is part of nature becomes a guiding creed. In this Enlightenment 2.0, people's individual freedom and autonomy is not defined in isolation, but experienced in the context of a flourishing Earth community.

I have found my purpose in using my own freedom of speech and legal education to express my love for the Earth and for those who defend her. I took the inspiration I got from that TED Talk and with it, literally changed the course of my life. I discovered that when an idea calls to you so strongly, it is probably because you are meant to become one of its spokespersons. For me, this journey has been one of daring to take my space and speak up for something I believe in. And whenever I start to think it is all too much of an uphill bale, I remind myself of these words by Denis Levertov which always gives me great hope:

"But we have only begun to love the earth. We have only begun to imagine the fullness of life. How could we tire of hope? So much is in bud."

You too can speak up for the health of our Mother Earth, by signing petitions to end Ecocide at www.eradicangecocide.com, by supporting Environmental Defenders on Grrrowd.org and by becoming an Environmental Defender in your own sphere of influence.

BLASTING THE ROCK,
BLOWING AWAY OUR FUTURE

Godspower Martins

Urban-Rural Environmental Defenders (U-RED) is a non-governmental environmental advocacy organisation determined to contribute towards the preservation of the environment by resisting and discouraging all forms of unwholesome practices in the environment to uphold environmental justice and sustainability. The organisation is deeply disturbed by the alarming rate of indiscriminate blasting of rocks in host communities in Abuja. There have been endless complaints from indigenous host communities on the deadly effects of the blasts on their lives and environment. The hill and rocks in communities are supposed to be a blessing in many ways especially to the communities; they are part of a people's heritage. This seems not to be the case as hills and rocks are being blast and extracted in communities amidst their marginalization and exploitation. Apart from tampering with the aesthetic appeal of hills and rocks, there are many concerns agitating the mind as regards the careless blasting of the rocks.

Were environmental and social impact assessments carried out before these quarries are sited? Are the communities part of the EIA/ESIA processes? If no, how did the companies concerned get to the communities? Did the companies obtain the prior informed consent of the communities before blasting the rocks? How long will this environmental ill and injustice continue? Is government aware of this socio-environmental harm going on in these communities? If yes, what effort is being made to arrest the menace? When this hazardous blasting of the rocks and unhealthy quarrying stop, who restores and caters to the impacted environment, craters, security pits, cracks, compacted soil and the abandoned machineries?

With the above questions begging for answers and the affected communities along Airport Road, Abuja, calling for attention to their plight, U-RED went into action. The organisation initiated extensive environmental monitoring and investigations into the activities of quarry operators who recklessly blast rocks in the communities. Shocking revelations were made in terms of the deadly effects of rock blasting, the neglect of the communities, the slavery and dehumanising way the indigenous workers are treated at the quarries, to mention but a few. Based on the discoveries made, U-RED organised a dialogue/sensitization programme tagged "Blasting the rocks, blowing away our future." The aim of the programme was to explain the adverse effects of the extractive activities and share possible civil/legal templates on how to tackle the issues of unsafe approach to mining, economic exploitation, ecological abuse and injustice that threaten the existence of the community and the environment.

The dialogue was held in a cluster of communities: Toge (host), Baruwa and Dayinsa. Government agencies that participated included the Federal Ministry of Environment, National Environmental Standards Regulation and Enforcement Agency (NESREA), and Abuja Environmental Protection Board (AEPB). Through the dialogue, U-RED amplified the voice of the community regarding the deadly effects of the quarrying and blasting of rocks. There were discussions on the adverse health effects on the community members arising from the vibrations, dust, flying-rocks and poisonous metals all emanating from the activities. Other deadly effects discussed included: higher exposure to natural disaster such as windstorms as the communities are stripped of the cover provided by the hills and rocks which serve as wind breakers; distortion and destruction of natural aesthetic value of the hills and rocks; loss of community economic potentials and wealth that could have been created from eco-tourism and; increased poverty and environmental problems for the communities.

Other effects discussed included: life expectancy reduction, destruction of cultural heritage, possible landslide that can wipe out the entire community and beyond, displacement of fauna, loss of arable lands for agriculture to quarry sites, and compacted soil. Pollution (noise, air, water), abandoned wastes, deforestation, abandoned deadly craters and security pits, cracks and building collapse through vibrations, general inconveniences, and miscellaneous losses were amongst the matters tabled. During the meeting the local people repeatedly lamented their plight. It was clear that the people were in a terrible environmental crisis. The people recounted, with sorrow, pain and frustrations, their recent agony which led many residents to flee Toge community after a blast that shook the community to its foundation.

There were indications that the quarrying activities began without prior consent from the community members. According to a community youth:

We suddenly saw them (that is, the quarrying company) in our land. We were not part of the process that brought them into the community. We, including the chief of Toge, were threatened and chased away when we went for inquiry.

Unattended invitations were sent to CNC Quarry Nig. Ltd., a Chinese company, blasting the rocks in Toge community. The invitation was for both parties to meet, discuss and reach an understanding on how to best mitigate the deadly effects of the blast on the community and environment as stipulated in Nigerian law on quarrying and blasting operations of 2013. Speaking about the dangers of the presence of the destructive forces in their communities, a community person said "our hearts break daily with shocks from sudden blasts, our children get confused in the class while learning as the school is just few meters away from the site" – a situation they said can be verified from school teachers.

According to them, the trauma of community members can only be better imagined than experienced. Animals are no more in the communities because of the blasts and vibrations. There have been loss of trees and plants of economic and herbal values to quarry sites and roads that lead to quarries. Arable lands for farming, the people's main source of livelihood and income, have been destroyed. The people are surrounded with mining craters and over five meters deep so-called security pits dug round some quarry sites. Domestic animals and community members, especially during the raining season, have fallen into and lost their lives in such pits. The company blasts the rocks unannounced. Flying rocks, general inconveniences and miscellaneous losses threaten the land.

According to the people, their memorial graveyard (cemetery) has been lost though this time to a developer. They told a touching story of how recently, a bulldozer opening the road to the developer's site exhumed the bodies of their dead. The remains of a prominent member of the community who died 35 years ago was excavated recently. And they said strange things have been happening in Toge community after the reburial. The host communities expressed their worry and anger at the reckless impunity of quarry operators whose offensive activities threaten their existence and general survival in their ancestral land.

The people also regretted that "no government officials visited the community to check the effects of the exploiters' harmful activities, and the magnitude of their suffering". They complained of lacking the relevant skills and resources to prosecute the companies whose destructive actions are forcing them out of their ecological inheritance hence, deeply appreciated U-RED's intervention. The communities requested for U-RED and government to join and stand in solidarity with them to fight the injustice threatening their existence. They also pleaded with the media houses present for space for advocacy to publish the wickedness, abuse and threat to their existence for the entire world to see and join them to stop the forces of destruction. Government officials present in the programme from Federal Ministry of Environment, Abuja Environmental Protection Board (AEPB), and National Environmental Standards Regulation and Enforcement Agency (NESREA) seized the opportunity to reiterate government's stand against harmful mining, citing several legislations on quarrying and blasting operations, compliance monitoring and enforcement.

The government officials also acknowledged receiving numerous public complaints about quarry companies operating without due regards to the environment, health and economy of the communities. The officials said, government does not encourage destructive development hence it has worked hard to monitor, enforce environmental laws and, prosecute and punishe offenders to ensure safe environment for all. However, the officials said government cannot do the job alone. They stated that communities are government's extended-hand hence, advised them to work closely with the government to monitor and report any ongoing mining activities, especially quarries that are less than three kilometres to the community. Community members were urged to be bold, to confront exploiters and ask questions on what they are doing in their communities.

The chief of Toge community, HRH Auta Gbatsubwa on behalf of the other communities, said the meeting created a unique platform for the communities to interact and learn from each other's experiences. He commented that the programme came at the right time to douse the tension in the communities.

U-RED organised the programme on the premise that local communities and individuals have the right to a clean and healthy environment, to livelihood, to life, right of nature, right to participate in decision making on all matters that affect the community and environment especially on developments that may adversely affect the community and environment as stipulated in the LFN on quarry and blasting operations of 2013. The outcome of the programme was the immediate decision to set up Community Ecological Defence Action Committee (CEDAC) as recommended by U-RED for environmental monitoring, dialogue, justice and dignity employing every legal means available.

U-RED uses this forum to offer sincere thanks to the Almighty God; Global Green Grants Fund (GGF); Nnimmo Bassey, MFR (Executive Director, HOMEF); and to many who provided resources, guidance, and perspective for the programme. The community chiefs are also highly appreciated.

SYSTEM CHANGE WILL NOT BE NEGOTIATED

Nnimmo Bassey

We frequently hear calls for system change, at public mobilisations, in conference halls and even in negotiation halls. The calls come as slogans, they come in anger and they come as a strong rebuke to the systemic scaffold on which our pains, our exploitation and the denial of our voices and rights are hung. The necessity of system change is inescapable. The present system is dependent on the extreme exploitation and enslavement of nature and labour, built around an inherently unjust core. We are in the dying days of a civilisation driven by fossil fuels. This end is not coming merely because of the recorded and predicted severe species extinction, or by peak oil. It is, rather, being heralded by a looming climate catastrophe and by the reawakening of social forces realising that slavery persists as long as the enslaved is unaware of his state.

As Oilwatch International highlights, there are:

> similarities in the current pattern of resource exploitation in countries of the Global South, and in affected peoples in the rest of the world, which reflects historical legacy of disempowerment of peoples, plunder of natural resources and destruction of environment, and [Oilwatch] considers the recognition of the right of peoples to self-determination and cultural integrity as primary in the resolution of environmental problems.

Our urgent task is to reclaim the future, and this will not be attainable if the current system persists.

Green Capitalism

Green was once a colour. In today's system, it has turned into a silencing code that lulls us into accepting that Nature cannot be protected unless financial value is placed on her. The Rio + 20 summit served as a platform for the elevation of the concept of Green Economy as a major plank for global environmental governance, especially with regard to climate change. Green Economy permits the financialization of everything, through a plethora of instruments such as those intended to reduce emissions from deforestation and forest degradation (REDD, REDD plus), emissions trading schemes (ETS), clean development mechanisms (CDM) and the like.

Green economy is a neo-liberal idea that hoists the financialization of Nature and carbon offsetting as ideal tools for nature protection. It has been cooked up to entrench current capitalist production modes and power relations where might is right. Poor, vulnerable and cash-strapped nations that contribute little or nothing to global warming see the trickles that drop into their empty bowls from market mechanisms, while their citizens are displaced from their territories, forced to bear a disproportionate burden of real climate actions. With climate change neatly 'boxed' as a matter of means of handling carbon emissions, the world conveniently ignores the root cause of the crises – the origins of those emissions. This entrenched situation is neo-colonial and imperialist. It upturns every notion of justice, including the common but differentiated responsibilities anchor of pre-2011 climate negotiations.

A just climate regime ought not to scratch for funds to tackle the emergencies already throwing up climate refugees. A clear solution for climate finance can be found in the Peoples Agreement. The Agreement demands that countries cut their emissions by at least 50% at source between 2013and 2017, without recourse to offsets and other carbon trading schemes. It also demands that developed countries commit 6% of their GDP to finance adaptation and mitigation needs. The payment of climate debt is not seen as a mere demand for reparations, but as a means of decolonising the atmospheric space and redistributing what meagre space or carbon budget is left. It is a means towards obligating humans to take actions to restore disrupted natural cycles of Nature. Climate change negotiations offer us a clear lens to see that market environmentalism approaches are merely means of escape from responsibility and measureable action. A look at the Paris Agreement reached at COP21 reveals that the major cause of global warming – fossil fuels utilisation in production and transportation – is not recognised in the process of tackling global warming.

The notion that carbon emitted anywhere can be offset by carbon absorbed anywhere else has given rise to the concept of net emissions. This is offering polluting nations the ultimate escape hatch through which to retain their levels of pollution and consumption, while grabbing lands, forests and waters elsewhere to compensate. It is now well known that at least 80%of currently known fossil fuels reserves must be left untapped and unburned to keep temperature increases to below 2°C. What's troubling is that not only is this not being discussed at climate negotiations, but that new reserves are being sought, and extraction methods are being intensified. A clear throwback to fiddling while the city burns.

The fact that fossil fuels are not renewable does not deter the fossil addicts. In order to remove the cloud of dust (and doubt) over fossil fixations, the industry came up with the term clean coal, and the notions that carbon pollution can be tackled through carbon capture and storage or sequestration, or through geo-engineering. These unproven technologies are all ways of resisting the need for change and ensuring business as usual. The best possible outcome would be to postpone the evil day and build an uncertain future for the coming generation. Unfortunately, that day cannot be postponed much longer.

Centrality of Nature

The call for system change is a call to a common-sense path that would secure the survival of the human race. It is also a call for humans to recognise themselves as just one of the species on planet earth. Studies and observations have shown that species stand better chances of survival when they cooperate, live and work in solidarity rather than in competition; when they build bridges and not walls – give up some space and allow others to breathe. The Earth speaks. The sky speaks. The trees speak. All of Nature speaks. Communication is a vital tool for survival. Take for example the umbrella thorn acacias, a tree in the African savannah, which communicate via their thorns in order to avoid having their leaves being eaten up by the savanna animals. Researchers found that when giraffes start to eat the leaves of umbrella thorn acacias, the trees release some toxic substances (water soluble, carbon based compounds known as 'tannins') that offend the taste buds of the giraffes. This is a direct defence line to even the giraffes that appear immune to the 'devil thorns'.

The researchers noticed that the giraffes would then skip the next umbrella thorn acacia trees, and move by about 100 metres before resuming their dinner elsewhere. Why did they move over such a distance before resuming their feast? This is the explanation according to Wohlleben (2016):

> The acacia trees that were being eaten gave off warning gas (specifically, ethylene) that signalled to neighbouring trees of the same species that a crisis was at hand. Right away, all the forewarned trees also pumped toxins into their leaves to prepare themselves. The giraffes were wise to this game, therefore, moved farther away to a part of the savannah where they could find trees that were oblivious to what was going on.

Trees communicate by a variety of other ways, including through their root systems, affirming metaphorically that indeed, it takes roots to weather the storm.

Re-Source Democracy

We speak of the gifts of Nature as re-sources. Yes, re-sources, intentionally hyphenated because we are speaking not of commodities, but of the vital need for humans to return to the source, to reconnect to Nature and, to think of the source before lifting the chisel, hammer, shovel, drill or rig. Re-source democracy is a call for the recognition of the rights of Nature, including her right to regenerate and maintain her cycles. It is built on a clear understanding of the uses and intrinsic values of the gifts of Nature. Re-source democracy demands the interrogation of the meaning of progress and development, to help us draw the line between what we can accept or reject in our environment. Navdanya further gives clarity to this idea:

We need a new paradigm to respond to the fragmentation caused by various forms of fundamentalism. We need a new movement, which allows us to move from the dominant and pervasive culture of violence, destruction and death to a culture of non-violence, creative peace and life ... the Earth democracy movement ... provides an alternative worldview in which humans are embedded in the Earth Family, ... connected to each other through love, compassion, not hatred and violence and (in which); ecological responsibility and economic justice replaces greed, consumerism and competition as objectives of human life.

Convergence of Movements

System change will be birthed by a convergence of movements. It will be a matter for all. We have to continually remind ourselves that our lives and realities are formed by a web of relationships, issues and realities; that we require diversity of approaches to effectively confront and overcome them – with diversity of movements coalescing around common organising principles. For example, in the case of ecological resurgence, movements can come together using the Precautionary Principle as a pivot. Another basic impulse will be the recognition of the leadership of communities of peoples, especially indigenous women, on the frontlines of ecological defense and system change struggles.

System Change Will Not Be Negotiated

The present fossil-based civilization is running out of gas and its terminal point is imminent – whether planned or not. Our task is to hasten the demise of this destructive system, in which unjust relations are seen as opportunities for amassing profit. This is the time for drastic actions to bring about ecological health for all our communities and relatives on planet Earth. It is time to change the narrative that we can measure well-being by aggregating gross domestic product. The struggles of First Nation brothers and sisters in North America, the Ogoni in Nigeria's Niger Delta, the Yasunidos of Ecuador and many others show that the battle can be tough and abrasive. But we have no options.

Industrial growth societies have been built on the platforms of gross injustice. And those who benefit from the unjust, disruptive and unsustainable system – the handful of men that have more financial means than billions of men and women – will not listen to logical needs for system change. They have heard it over and over again. It is a system where the poor, no matter how wise, cannot sit at the official negotiation tables. It is a system that believes that, with the right financial means, one can make a dash for safety to another planet if apocalypse happens. History will judge the present generation very harshly if a transition is not made to a Life-Sustaining Society – a society in which humans and the environment are linked, not ranked. This society will come about only if we stand together with Earth Protectors and denounce the criminalisation of dissent and the constriction of democratic space that is fast becoming the norm. It is time to speak up and let a thousand solutions bloom. It is no time to be silent.[1]

System change will come about when the power of We the People becomes a rallying call and a pivot of action. We the People can redefine energy and own our clean, localised, energy generation and production systems. We the People can reclaim our streams, creeks and rivers and deny industry their privatisation and use as sewers. As the saying goes: freedom is not something that is given, it is taken. System change will not be negotiated. Change will come as fists burst through the cracks in the pavements just like saplings spring from hardened soils.

---

1 See more at http://www.homef.org/publication/re-source-democracy5Earth Democracy http://www. navdanya.org/earth-democracy

RESOURCE CONTROL, GENDER AND PEACE IN THE NIGER DELTA REGION

Nkoyo Esko Toyo

I have had to wrestle with a number of themes to arrive at the title of this presentation and hopefully will try, in a simplistic way, to weave different thoughts into a narrative that captures not only the essence of today and its pursuit of peace but the activist perspective of the organisations involved in this endeavour. Importantly, I will also examine the significance of HOMEF's descriptive engagement with Re-Source Democracy. In fact, I argue that Re-Source Democracy provides a basis to interrogate the place of gender relations in the resource appropriation debate and its differential implications for women and men. Overall, a resources lens underpins the entire argument, bringing into focus the crisis and conflicts around fossil fuel, the state of the Niger Delta region and its embattled but delicate ecosystem. Looking at the entire gamut of issues, at the core of the problem is the absence of peace and development in the Niger Delta. Why is the region readily identified and associated with crisis rather than peace? This has produced widespread frustration as citizens of the region cry for change.

The people cry for peace engendered by equitable development for men and women and, where the politics of the time allows the central administration, rule of law and accountable mechanisms to find a working balance. The root of the region's frustration is under-development despite huge resources and; a culture of endemic crisis eroding norms which should be at the root of peace and a sustainable culture of development. In making this presentation, one is reminded that the Niger Delta region, still faces unabated levels of violence, crime, militancy and destruction of human life and the environment. Given the levels of these challenges and the unacceptable damage caused by the exploitation of fossil fuel and its consequential impact on the environment, a new approach is needed. Even as we envisage change, there is the urgency to act on the exploitation of weak ecosystems, despoliation of ecology, disruptions of power relations between the so called "owners" of the resources and their exploiters. In fact, the very existence of the owner-exploiter relations has been defined and abused by the lack of respect for earth's endowments, privileges and rights. With these debasements of communities, there are accompanying unaddressed issues of gender, conflict and resource expropriation.

The dimensions of these issues vary depending on whether the argument is being made for resource control or the countervailing thoughts around Re-Source Democracy. A significant debate which seems unexplored yet holds sway in the region is around the question: What is the dominant logic of resource control given its interaction with the principles of fiscal federalism and the restructuring of the Nigerian state as envisaged by the 2014 National Conference? So, I interrogate the region's fixation with resource control and the issues it has spawned inside and outside the region. I accept as true that this is critical juncture for the region as the options available to her are narrowing. There is, hence, need to re-engage with the debate in ways that usher in new consciousness about existing or alternative facts. The debate needs to open other pathways towards prosperity, peace and the transformation on the Region.

Resource Control and/or Re-Source Democracy?

The opinions around resources and its ownership have been with us since the discovery of fossil fuels in the Niger Delta region. Much of the conflicts in the region are traceable to the exploitation of oil and how the Nigeria State has failed to address the needs of its citizens despite these resources. These failures and agitations have led to countless attempts, in the last two decades, to achieve meaningful constitutional reviews or reforms. In almost all instances, the efforts have been confronted by the singular question of how to manage and share the resources of the country in a more responsive manner. Nevertheless, not much has changed even though the region had some of the most strident advocates verbalizing its views at the 2005 and 2014 National Reform Conferences.

Rights activist Ms Annkio Briggs captures the mood of the region when she notes that:

> Despite our enormous resources in the Niger Delta, problems have remained unattended; the region is lacking access to basic necessities. That is why we must represent the aspiration of the people of Niger Delta making linkages between the advocacy of representatives and the people's reality.

Leader of Social Action Dr. Isaac Osuoka reviewed the history of the struggles in the region and noted that:

Some of the participants of today's conference, including some of our eminent leaders know that the idea of the Pan Niger Delta Conference dates back to the 1990s, especially during the late Abacha military junta. Following the genocide in Umuechem (Etche), Ogoniland and parts of Ijawland, organisations like the Chikoko Movement, Southern Minorities Movement (SMM), Movement for the Survival of Ogoni People (MOSOP), Rivers Coalition, Environmental Rights Action (ERA), and Ijaw Youth Council (IYC) started discussing the framework for a process of joint analysis and collaborative intervention in mobilising our peoples to promote the demands of self-determination within the Nigerian State, as guarantee for environmental and economic justice.

In summary, these advocates are challenged by a local logic which only partly addresses the larger issues of expropriation of resources. Where do they place the global imperatives such as those agreed upon at the Paris COP which promotes market environmentalist approaches that mask the responsibility for measurable action? Why will they continue to argue for resource control when in actual sense at least 80% of currently known fossil fuels reserves must be left untapped and unburned to keep temperature increases to below 2°C? What is even more troubling is that these issues are not conspicuously on the agenda of the region nor of the National Conferences that they attend. These dimensions have been dwarfed by the arguments for resource control, restructuring and fiscal federalism. Additionally, would it not be right to say that the region's call for resource control, is one for partial not full control? This is something to consider as even where the Niger Delta oversees its own resources, it may not amount to uncoupling the unsatisfactory relations with IOCs nor end the region's tendency to pursue non-strategic development.

The call in this paper to examine Re-source Democracy, is a call to revisit and broaden the argument for action not only against central governments but within the region, states, communities and, among groups of peoples, animals and all earth's publics, as a matter of rights. Celestine Akpobari, a participant during the Roundtable on the UNEP Report held in Port Harcourt, Nigeria, reminds us very vividly of this imperative when he spoke of the resource curse thus: "...to destroy a people, you destroy their environment."

Very often, the widely-canvassed notion of resource control, unlike Re-source democracy is not hinged on the recognition that what is known as 'resource' fundamentally belongs to nature. A nature-focused approach estimates the proper place of resource exploitation. It interprets resources through the prism of communities, species and peoples living in the region who have traditionally seen themselves as supervisors of what they own. Re-source Democracy is about stewardship and less about control or regulator rights. It recognises the stewardship towards the resource. It affirms the right of citizens to establish rules and act in line with traditional as well as best available knowledge – for safeguarding the soil, trees, crops, water and wildlife. Re-source Democracy allows those involved to enjoy nature's gifts as a necessary provision that supports their lives and livelihoods as well as the lives of future generations.

The Niger Delta Context and the Resource Question

In the Nigerian context, control is catechized based on the role of central governments as against their regional and local counterparts. Failure to interrogate the local context has often closed our eyes to how control is exercised and for who or what purpose. This presents another reason for seeking a shift from with the focus on resource control. In several communities in the region, the inequitable distribution of wealth has resulted in conflicts and growing incidences of militancy, cultism, crime, violence, hate and unhealthy rivalries. These objectionable outcomes make the point that the resource control model is not adequately advancing the development of the region nor giving appropriate value to its resources. The outcomes shows how multiple-layered the issues are. Another dimension to it all is the fact that women are often caught in the cross fire of resource conflicts, though they are not integral to the resource control agenda/ debate whether it be in its formulation, implementation, development of strategies, decisions and resolutions.

Women remain the closest to the impacted communities, and far from the direct benefits of resource control. Left as spectators within their communities and sometimes as victims, women are manipulated by local and global market forces that use their resources against their own good. Women, therefore, are bound to agonise and demand their participation in decisions that determine access to, and enjoyment of nature's gifts as well as in seeking ways to remove those obstacles erected by the politics of access and power. The resource politics must recognise women's participation in sharing the proceeds of resources. It must also attend to women's call for restraints to be put on extractive activities in fragile ecosystems or in locations of high cultural, religious or social significance in order to support the higher objective of clean and safe environments that support citizens' well-being.

Women, Gender and Re-Source Democracy

Going forward, we shall not return to the debate about women's expected roles as we do know that they have undergone extraordinary changes over the last four decades. In addition, there has been the phenomenal rise in women's education, employment, access to information and, gathering and mobilization through women-led movements and campaigns. Mobile phones and other new communication technologies have contributed greatly in providing information to women, giving them a basis to assess their actions and develop independence of thought. While there are actions to be taken by states to advance the rights and status of women, the norms that define the way women address their concerns must be worked out by women themselves through everyday actions led by ordinary people. Women must remember to build the control of resources around the centrality of safeguarding mother earth. This allows campaigners to go beyond the confines of existing publicly accepted norms to provide alternative practices which have the force of conviction to influence the way things are currently perceived and done. If we must get women into the role of influencing critical norms, they need to be a part of the debate and re-examine the fixation with resource control which has crystallised mindsets and emitted negative reactions.

Women must be conscious of the many ways they can communicate truth to power without inheriting the views which many associate with divisive politics. Such a shift in strategy and action must align with the ideology that resources, first and foremost, belong to mother earth – before region, states, community and families can lay claim. The challenge is to understand, domesticate and engage with Re-source Democracy in ways that uphold the values and norms of protection and preservation of the natural resources. It is time to develop, inculcate and incubate advocacies that promote harmony between different actors and nature's endowments. Taking a leap of faith in this direction will require extensive research into the politics of state and resources and, finding ways of delicately balancing state, law and accountabilities to nature and humanity.

A Paradigm Shift and the Charge

In her book 'How Change Happens', Duchan Green notes that the adoption and implementation of new human rights norms is conditioned by different nonlinear stages of change and norming. Engaging with Re-source Democracy requires that we adopt concepts that institute the co-existence of mother earth with its exploiters. Such an approach also needs to address the question and recognition of the rights of mother earth (a reproductive being) as a pre-condition to any exploratory rights. The repression of the rights of mother earth can be likened to the discrimination and marginalization that women suffer. These exclusions have engendered the debate that confronts those who refuse to acknowledge the pre-eminence of the female thus denying her qualities as crystallized by Mother Earth and her rights. There is work ahead – getting women who have been on the periphery of the resource debate to take action to: preserve, reject a culture of silence and confront actions that seek to de-legitimize both their voice and contributions and, particularly those that question their centrality. Like it was with Ken Saro-Wiwa, the process acknowledges that the new direction of the debate will be gradual and progress over time towards the institutionalization of Re-Source Democracy.

Such progression towards new values, open opportunities for women to participate and domesticate new standards which will subsequently be captured by enabling laws and institutions. As a matter of fact, many of the environmental regulatory bodies in Nigeria came on the heels of environmental rights campaign of the late 1990s. Researchers are important to this endeavour, in terms of creating understanding and instigating action on Re-Source Democracy; they bring clarity to who should be targeted and how strategies influence existing norms in the Niger Delta. The region must liberate itself from the skewed interpretation of 'control of resources' and open the conversation of resources to more democratic fundamentals.

Critical Juncture: Resource Dis-control as a Precursor to Inclusive Development

Acting and timing are crucial and the time to act is now. The current government has made efforts to address the rising tide of violent crimes in the Niger Delta. However, there have been discontent following the failure of institutions like the NDDC, Presidential Amnesty Programme, the Environmental Regulatory agencies and a host of other interventionist programmes including the UNEP programme for cleaning up Ogoni lands. This has brought significant pressure on the central government to respond to the issues presented by PANDEF when it met with President Buhari. In general, the current government seems to agree that 'business as usual' cannot continue. Hence, we need to change or perish. Those within the environmental and rights community see the danger ahead as the presence of fossil oil and the politics of its control will continue to cause untold crisis and support the festering of local and national disagreements. Consequently, there are serious reasons to seek an alternative agenda and act differently with an agenda that benefits all sides. This action includes seeking answers raised by the economic challenges currently facing the nation which is tied to the volatility of crude oil, the fall in the price of crude and the shift of buyers of our crude oil to shale oil. This means that sooner or later, fossil fuel development is bound to became outdated in the same way steam engines gave way to new technology and options.

Overall, the Niger Delta today is in a far weaker situation than it is ready to acknowledge. With the recession in the economy, the exit of many businesses from the region and deep concerns about the hostile business climate, things are no longer at ease. On the part of states, rather than struggle for excess crude funds and Paris club refunds, they must note that the time to run a profligate system is over. It is time to get hapless citizens who are victims of the distorted control of resources to live within a sustainable reality. These facts present an urgent call for diversification of the economy and awareness that the resource control arguments barely make the case for an inclusive approach to development. With high profile reviews of the economy by the FG, the urgent need to transit to a post-petroleum economy is evident. A Re-source democracy approach will be beneficial if it is allowed to guide planning to address issues such as inclusive development, environmental restoration, equitable use of resources and the post-petroleum Nigeria. The Re-source Democracy template affords the region the opportunity to say that a renewed Niger Delta is possible.

A REVIEW OF *GROSS DOMESTIC PROBLEM* BY LORENZO FIORAMONTI

Ukpono Bassey

The book *Gross Domestic Problem* by Lorenzo Fioramonti aims at revealing the politics behind Gross Domestic Product (GDP) and the urgency for the world to come up with better and sustainable measures of economic growth and development. The idea for the book came when Lorenzo was invited by the Italian National Institute of Statistics (ISTAT) to participate in a meeting on alternative measures to the gross domestic product.

The book focused on the history of GDP at the beginning and pointed out that the first attempt at measuring national income dates back to the seventeenth century (1600s). This happened when a physician with the British army, William Petty, was asked to conduct a systematic survey of the country's wealth in order to aid in the redistribution of land among the English military and political leader's (Oliver Cromwell) troops. As made clear in the book, it was noticed that Petty tried to place market value on both land and labour, in order to subject them to taxation. It was also noticed later on, that the survey helped Petty to increase his financial assets significantly. He acquired land in lieu of salary and thanks to the cheap purchase of land (that was declared 'unprofitable') from soldiers, the worth of his total assets increased significantly between 1652 and 1685.

During the great depression that happened between 1929 and 1941, the government who decided not to intervene at first, due to the believe that the market forces will work and gradually make the economy stable again, had to find ways of improving the economy as things were not getting any better. Simon Kuznets (a Russian-American economist) started to work on the conceptualization and measurement of national income in 1932. He was given the opportunity to put his theories to the test. Kuznets's idea was to condense all economic production by individuals, companies and the government into a single number. This method developed by Kuznets finally came together during the Second World War (1939-1945), GNP was then used as the main scorecard for the design and implementation of national economic policy. The GNP accounts turned to be a powerful instrument used to estimate militarization costs and to calculate the speed at which the economy needed to grow in order to 'pay for war'. The aim was to increase consumption within the country in order to be able to pay for the ammunitions used in war.

This same method which was used to help the country in the time of war remained and is still being used till this present time. This figure has been manipulated by political authorities overtime. In page 65 of the book, there is a graph that shows differences between the official GDP and the corrected GDP. The official GDP of course was noticed to be higher than the corrected GDP, which casts doubts on the creditability of the official GDP. The book makes it obvious that GDP figure is manipulated from time to time by political authorities in order to suit their political interests.

The book also focuses on the fact that GDP, though accepted and worshiped by many, is not as beautiful and majestic as it seems and is indeed a problem for all. It has caused people to engage in activities that put the environment in jeopardy (an example is the exploration and extraction of fossil fuels). It has also caused the neglect of the well-being of individuals and things that make living worthwhile. Lorenzo Fioramonti likens it to the book 'Frankenstein' written by Mary Shelley. He calls it the Frankenstein syndrome.

The book also talked about emerging forces coming up to dethrone GDP. The book identified the fact that progressive economists, intellectuals, think tanks, NGOs, foundations, governmental agencies and various types of civil society groups are trying to come up with better numbers and means of measuring economic growth and development. This can be noticed with the emergence of other indexes such as Measure of economic Welfare (MEW), Total Income System of Accounts (TISA), Index of Sustainable Economic Welfare, Physical quality of Life Index (PQLI), Human Suffering Index (HSI), Ecological Footprint, Gross National Happiness (GNH), and Human Development Index (HDI). GNH for example, is practiced in the Kingdom of Bhutan and when formulated, was based on four pillars namely: good governance, sustainable socio-economic development, cultural preservation and environmental conservation. This country, although regarded as poor (based on GDP), happens to be inhabited by one of the most satisfied people in the world, as they rank number eight in this respect.

The use of a 'dashboard' as a metaphor to represent a system where most of these indicators are used to determine the health of an economy and also serve as a guide for setting policies, is probably one of the most appealing approaches for getting a better barometer of economic growth and development. The better approaches like GNH takes an indicator such as GDP as a single dial that could represent 'how fast you are going' in a car setting, and points out that any reasonable driver (policymaker or political authority) would also want to know how much fuel is left, distance covered and any other vital information. In a nutshell, the better approaches suggest that other important indicators (such as people's lives, well-being, education and environment) should also be noticed and taken into serious consideration.

The book made it known that the change would have to start from below. It would have to start from society, communities, villages, etc. Different models are being introduced such as; the sandwich model, degrowth society, transition initiatives and others. The latter (transition initiative) aims at drastically reducing human dependence on fossil fuels in an effort to reduce environmental degradation and curb climate change. It points out that GDP development model is humanly and ecologically not sustainable. The transition initiative is also experimenting new forms of democracy and promotes self-governance as well.

Lorenzo Fioramonti ended by saying:

> GDP was designed as a war device. That war did not end in 1945, but has continued ever since. It turned into an endless war against social equilibria, natural environments and non-renewable resources, in which consumers become the new foot soldiers; ultimately, a war against our own future on this planet.

He also said in his book that "By reasserting the creativity of life over the fallacy of growth, we fight for the survival of humankind".

THE CENTRALITY OF CULTURE
IN THE STRUGGLE FOR A NEW WORLD:
AMILCAR CABRAL AND KEN SARO-WIWA

Firoze Manji[1]

There are two events in my life that have had a profound effect on my thinking and my politics. One was the assassination of Amilcar Cabral on January 20, 1973. The other was the assassination of Ken Saro-Wiwa on November 10, 1995. When Cabral was assassinated, I was at university in England and active in the solidarity movement in support of the liberation movements in the Portuguese colonies. His writings were, subsequently, to transform my thinking about the nature of colonialism and what it means to struggle for liberation, emancipation and freedom. And I was to discover later that he was, in fact, gunned down by his own comrades.

And when the Abacha regime killed Saro-Wiwa and his comrades. I was the Africa Director for Amnesty International at their headquarters in London. I remember how completely helpless and outraged I felt – here I was at the head of the Africa Programme of the world's largest human rights organisation yet, we had failed to prevent this crime. We had appealed to Western and African governments to intervene forcefully to obtain the release of Ken, but had been met with responses such as 'quiet diplomacy, not overt criticism or sanctions' would succeed, a response even made by the then recently newly elected South African government (the ANC's head office was at the time, after all, located in Shell House in Johannesburg). That experience was to transform my thinking about the meaning of neocolonialism, the complicity of transnational corporations and the degree to which our governments have become increasingly beholden to the corporations.

The two events helped me to understand the continuities between colonialism and neocolonialism, the first a product of liberalism, the second of neoliberalism. You can imagine, then, how delighted I was to be approached by colleagues at Maynooth University to help publish

1 A keynote address presented by Firoze Manji at the Annual Ken Saro-Wiwa Seminar held at Maynooth University Library, Maynooth University on 15 November 2018

Silence Would Be Treason: The Last Writings of Ken Saro-Wiwa exactly at the time that I was editing and about to publish the anthology *Claim No Easy Victories: The Legacy of Amilcar Cabral.* Before continuing, I would like to acknowledge here the efforts of Sister Majella and the solidarity movements in Ireland who during Saro-Wiwa's lifetime and imprisonment provided him with much needed sustenance, and since his assassination have, together with Maynooth University Library, helped keep him alive.

I want to share some thoughts about the commonalities between Amilcar Cabral and Ken Saro-Wiwa, especially in relation to culture and the centrality of culture in the struggle for freedom. Amilcar Cabral was the founder and leader of the Guinea-Bissau and Cabo Verde liberation movement, Partido Africano da Independência da Guinée Cabo Verde (PAIGC). He was a revolutionary, humanist, agronomist, poet, military strategist, and prolific writer on revolutionary theory, culture and liberation.

The struggles he led against Portuguese colonialism contributed to the collapse not only of Portugal's African empire, but also to the Portuguese revolution of 1974/5 and the downfall of the fascist dictatorship in Portugal, events that he was not to witness as he was assassinated in 1973. Cabral and Saro-Wiwa were separated by two eras, the one involving the struggle for independence in Africa, the other dealing with the consequences of the failures of independence and the rise of neoliberalism. There were continuities between the two eras. "Cabral and Saro-Wiwa sit together in this transformative and unfinished space," wrote Helen Fallon, "asking questions that remain important in Ireland as in Africa." Despite this separation, they had much in common. Both sought self-determination for their people. Both were clear that self-determination, not secession, was what they were fighting for. Self-determination and secession are often confused and considered synonymous.

Self-determination is about the struggle for justice, dignity and an attempt to establish an inclusive Universalist humanity, whereas secession is by definition an act of exclusion, defining the self through the exclusion of the other. The tragedy for Saro-Wiwa was that the struggle for self-determination for the Ogoni came in the wake of the Biafran war of secession, the leadership of which Saro-Wiwa was highly critical. The struggle of the Ogoni people for self-determination could easily come to be seen as a continuation of that secessionist movement, despite Saro-Wiwa's insistence against secession (although he was sometimes ambiguous about the distinction).

While Cabral and Saro-Wiwa were clearly exceptional individuals, it was the movements in which they were involved, and which they helped to create, that the credit must go to for organising and endeavouring to give birth to a new world. We often characterise such movements as being expressions of resistance. But I think they are more than that. Let me draw on Michelle Alexander's recent article in the New York Times, We are not the resistance. These movements were not the resistance. On the contrary, they sought to establish and give birth to a new world, just as the anti-fracking and environmental movements in Ireland, and the campaigns for "free, safe, legal" abortion following the pro-choice vote in the referendum in May. These are all movements seeking to give birth to a new world. We need to insist that it is the state and the corporations that are the resistance, not those seeking to give birth to a new world. It was the Portuguese colonial regime and the Abacha neocolonial regime in collaboration with Shell that were the resistance to the efforts of the movements that PAIGC and MOSSOP sought to birth.

Giving birth is always an act involving the struggle to overcome the violence of resistance. This is as true of a seedling emerging from the ground as it is for the child being born. Genuine movements for freedom never chose the path of violence, but they almost always face the violence of those that resist the birth of the world they are seeking to deliver. But in some cases, there is no choice but to use military means to defend the gains they have made. The struggle to give birth to Ireland was met with fierce, violent and terrorist resistance by the British state. There was no choice but to endeavour to defend it. But more importantly, it is community organising, that is the basis of defence. They may have to use arms as one of their tools, but without the organising, arms are worth nothing. So, let us agree: The state and corporations, not us, are the resistance. In Guinea Bissau, PAIGC had created liberated zones that, at the time of Cabral's assassination, covered some two-thirds of the country. There, completely new structures of popular democracy were established in which peasants were the decision makers.

The Portuguese currency was banned, and a system of barter exchange was established in its stead. Women played leading roles in political decision making. And the rekindling of culture and pride in their own histories, languages, stories and music flourished. New health, education and other services were established. They were creating a new world. But they had no choice than to ensure the movement had the means to defend the new society that had been built. PAIGC politics was not about promoting violence, but of defending the birth of a new society from the genocidal violence of Portuguese imperialism. Both Cabral (at the hands of his own comrades, those who were to become the neo-colonial rulers of the future) and Saro-Wiwa (at the hands of the neocolonial Abacha regime) paid the ultimate sacrifice for their audacity to both think and create in their time a new world. This is what distinguishes them from so many others: it was not only having a dream that another world was possible, but also having the courage to create that world in the present. It was that which presented such a threat to those who resist new births. I make this point because it is in the crucible of the struggle that real culture evolves as a weapon of liberation, a point that, as I will discuss, both Cabral and Saro-Wiwa make.

To be able to subject millions of humans to the barbarism of enslavement, slavery and colonial domination required defining them as non-humans or less than humans, and to do so required their dehumanisation. That process required a systematic and institutionalised attempt at the destruction of existing cultures, languages, histories; capacities to produce, organise, tell stories, invent, love, make music, sing songs, make poetry, produce art, philosophise, and to formulate in their minds that which they imagine before giving it concrete form and; all things that make a people human. This attempt to destroy the culture of Africans, as Cabral points out, turned out to be a signal failure.

Colonialism destroyed the institutions on the African continent. But the memories of their culture, institutions, art forms, music and all that which is associated with being human remained both on the continent and in the diaspora where the enslaved Africans found themselves. The enslavers, the slave owners, and all those who profited from these horrors, including the emerging capitalist classes of Europe, engaged in a systematic re-casting of human beings as non-humans or lesser beings – a process in which the Christian church and the European intelligentsia were deeply involved. Whatever the material aspects of domination, "it can be maintained only by the permanent and organised repression of the cultural life of the people concerned", wrote Cabral. The use of violence to dominate a people is "above all, to take up arms to destroy, or at least neutralize and to paralyze their cultural life. For as long as part of that people have a cultural life, foreign domination cannot be assured of its perpetuation." Such experiences must surely ring bells for people of Ireland whose own experiences of seeking freedom had so much in common with those of Africans. Famine, dispossession, displacement, attempts to silence song and language, enslavement and exile from their lands, all those things must surely resonate with you.

For Saro-Wiwa:

> The advent of British colonialism was to shatter Ogoni society and inflict on us a backwardness from which we are still struggling to escape. It was British colonialism which forced alien administrative structures on us and herded us into the domestic colonialism of Nigeria....As a result of domestic colonialism, the Ogoni people have virtually lost pride in themselves and their ability, have voted for the multiplicity of parties in elections, have regarded themselves as perpetual clients of other ethnic groups and have come to think that there is nowhere else to go but down... Yes, we merely exist; barely exist.

Culture, wrote Cabral, is

> the product of ... history just as a flower is the product of a plant. Like history, or because it is history, culture has as its material base the level of the productive forces and the mode of production. Culture plunges its roots into the physical reality of the environmental humus in which it develops, and reflects the organic nature of the society

You'd never guess he was an agronomist, would you? Culture, Cabral insists, is intimately linked to the struggle for freedom. While culture comprises many aspects, it "... grows deeper through the people's struggle, and not through songs, poems or folklore. ... One cannot expect African culture to advance unless one contributes realistically to the creation of the conditions necessary for this culture, i.e. the liberation of the continent." In other words, culture is not static and unchangeable, and it advances only through engagement in the struggle for freedom.

In this, Cabral echoes Frantz Fanon: "To fight for national culture, first of all, means fighting for the liberation of the nation, the tangible matrix from which culture can grow. One cannot divorce the combat for culture from the people's struggle for liberation." Furthermore:

> ... national culture takes form and shape during the fight, in prison, facing the guillotine and in the capture and destruction of the French military positions. ... National culture is no folklore ... [it] is the collective thought process of a people to describe, justify, and extol the actions whereby they have joined forces and remain strong.

Ken Saro-Wiwa's identity as a member of the Ogoni people, along with his political activism is inseparable from the content of his novels, for example *Sozaboy*. Saro-Wiwa is clear about the political role of his work:

As a result of this belief, *Sozaboy* possesses a sense of urgency and reflects from the perspective and language of the dispossessed, the conditions and dilemmas faced by the Ogoni (or the Dukana). "He becomes a 'martyr' who transcribes the struggles of the Ogoni people in the creation of the fictional Dukana people."

The television series *Basi and Company*, for example, targeted not just corrupt individuals but rather Nigeria's quote culture of cheating as a whole. Humorous and entertaining, the series was a political commentary. "The writer cannot be a mere storyteller," writes Saro-Wiwa. "He cannot merely x-ray societies' weaknesses, its ills, its perils. He or she must be actively involved in shaping its present and its future," he stated. "The most important thing for me is that I've used my talents as a writer to enable the Ogoni people to confront their tormentors. I was not able to do it as a politician or a businessman. My writing did it. And it sure makes me feel good! I'm mentally prepared for the worst, but hopeful for the best. I think I have the moral victory." Saro-Wiwa believed that "literature, in a critical situation such as Nigeria's, cannot be divorced from politics. Indeed, literature must serve society by steeping itself in politics, by intervention, and writers must not write merely to amuse... They must play an interventionist role."

For members of the community that produced billions of dollars of oil wealth but who, themselves, lack electricity and clean drinking water, however, "you must go into activism because if you're not into activism, then you are irresponsible" – Silence would, indeed, be treason! Saro Wiwa, like Cabral before him, believed that the writer "must take part in mass organisations" and "establish direct contact with the people". "What they (the authorities) cannot stand is that a writer should additionally give voice to the voiceless and organise them for action. In short, they do not want literature on the streets! And that is where, in Africa, it must be." As to language, Saro-Wiwa commented:

> Furthermore, I have examined myself very closely to see how writing or reading in English has colonised my mind. I am, I find, as Ogoni as ever. I am enmeshed in Ogoni culture. I devour Ogoni food. I sing Ogoni songs. I dance to Ogoni music. I'm anxious to see the Ogoni establish themselves in Nigeria and make their contribution to world civilisation. I, myself, am contributing to Ogoni life as fully, and possibly even more effectively than those of Ogoni who do not speak and write English. The fact that I appreciate Shakespeare, Dickens, Chaucer, Hemingway, et al.; the fact that I know something of European civilisation, its history and philosophy; the fact that I enjoy Mozart and Beethoven – is this a colonisation of

my mind? I cannot exactly complain about it. Historically, the Ogoni people have always been fierce and independent. They have been known to display an exceptional achievement in their original, abstract masks. As storytellers and in other forms of art, the Ogoni are gifted and hold their own easily. The Ogoni have made contributions of the first order to modern African literature in English.

The implicit appeal to a universalist and inclusive humanity is clear in these statements. Cabral had no hesitation in writing for a wider public in Portuguese, but he was insistent that in order to learn from the peasantry, we must have the ability to converse in their languages. "We must put the interests of our people higher," wrote Cabral, "in the context of the interests of mankind in general, and then we can put them in the context of the interests of Africa in general." :We must have the courage to state this clearly", he said, "No one should think that the culture of Africa – what is really African and so must be preserved for all time, for us to be Africans – is our weakness in the face of nature." "Indeed," says Saro-Wiwa, "literature must serve society by steeping itself in politics, by intervention; writers must not merely write to amuse or to take a bemused, critical look at society. They must play an interventionist role." He narrates: "My experience has been that African governments can ignore writers, taking comfort in the fact that only few can read and write, and that those who read, find little time for the luxury of literary consumption beyond the need to pass examinations based on set texts." Therefore, the writer must be l'homme engagé: The intellectual man of action. "He must take part in mass organisations. He must establish direct contact with the people and resort to the strength of African literature – oratory in the tongue." "...A writer who takes part in mass organisations will deliver his message more effectively than one who writes waiting for time to work its literary wonders."

"A reconversion of minds – of mental set – is, thus, indispensable to the true integration of people into the liberation movement," wrote Cabral. "Such reconversion – re-Africanization, in our case – may take place before the struggle, but it is complete only during the course of the struggle, through daily contact with the popular masses in the communion of sacrifice required by the struggle." I have, myself, just returned from South Africa where I was a jurist on the Permanent People's Tribunal on the Transnational Corporations in Southern Africa. We received moving testimony from DRC, Madagascar, South Africa, Malawi, Zambia, Zimbabwe, Mozambique, etc. The stories we heard recounted, over and over again, the culture of impunity, the destructive extraction of natural resources, the collusion of governments in the reaping of super profits and theft by transnational corporations, and the systematic attempts to destroy culture through land grabbing, dispossession and displacement. Knowledge of and connection with the land is at the heart of a people's history and culture. What took place with Shell and the Ogoni is not unique to Nigeria. It is being repeated across the continent even today.

As the writings of both Cabral and Saro-Wiwa show, culture is not a mere artefact or expression of aesthetics, custom or tradition. It is a means by which people assert their opposition to domination, a means to proclaim and invent their humanity, a means to assert agency and the capacity to make history. In a word, culture is one of the fundamental tools of the struggle for emancipation. The efforts of Sister Majella and the Maynooth University Library to bring these writings together and make them available to the world is an inspiring cultural act. It is an act with which Daraja Press is honoured to be associated.

WHAT ARE SYSTEMIC ALTERNATIVES?

Pablo Solon

The premise of systemic alternatives is that the environmental, economic, social, geopolitical, institutional and civilizational crises are part of a whole, interrelated and feed into one another. Therefore, it is impossible to resolve one of these crises without addressing the others as a whole. One-dimensional strategies are incapable of solving systemic crises and, on the contrary, can aggravate them. Systemic crises are caused by a set of factors like capitalism, xenophobia, racism, patriarchy, extractivism, anthropocentrism, plutocracy, productivism and colonialism. A systemic alternative seeks to confront and overcome the structural causes of the systemic crises. Systemic alternatives do not follow stages. They do not suggest that capitalism must first be overcome in order to confront patriarchy or anthropocentrism. Systemic alternatives affirm that capitalism, patriarchy, anthropocentrism and the other factors mentioned above are interdependent and are mutually reinforcing.

An alternative may be to begin to deal with one or some of these factors. But it'd still boil down to a systemic dynamic which is necessary to advance to challenge the other factors that are part of the underlying causes of the systemic crises. Generally, the alternatives arise from rejection such as STOP fossil fuels, END femicides, NO to authoritarianism, etc. From rejection, we start to build alternatives in order to give a positive answer. The proposal of renewable energies against fossil fuels is an alternative. Peace in opposition to war is an alternative. Agro-ecology against toxic agriculture is an alternative. These positive proposals are alternatives but not necessarily systemic alternatives. When can we say they are systemic alternatives? When those alternatives become multidimensional and start to challenge capitalism, productivism, extractivism, patriarchy, anthropocentrism, plutocracy, xenophobia, colonialism and other structural factors of the systemic crises.

The most important thing to define a systemic alternative is where it is going. If it remains in the one-dimensional framework, for example to propose only renewable energies, it is an alternative in relation to fossil fuels; but it is not yet a systemic alternative. The moment in which this proposal begins to state that the problem is not only the source of energy but also who controls it and how it is produced, distributed and consumed, it begins to have a broader and systemic dynamic that starts to question capitalism, productivism and extractivism. However, the process of building a systemic alternative has to go even further. If we see, for example, the issue of water, the recognition and application of the human right to water is an alternative, but it is not enough. To be a systemic alternative, it must question the privatization and commodification of water as well. The global water crisis cannot be addressed without overcoming extractivism, productivism and consumerism. Mining uses huge amounts of water and leaves rivers and ecosystems polluted. The large agro-industry is the sector with the highest water consumption. A kilo of meat requires 15,000 liters of water.

Without sustainable agroecology and changes in consumption patterns, it is impossible to face the water problem. The manufacturing of a car uses 148,000 liters of water. Productivism, whether under a capitalist or socialist logic, is a serious factor that must be confronted in order to face the world water crisis. Water can't be managed only under statist logic with a top-down approach. Different human groups of the countryside and the city must be involved in water management, promoting the practice of the commons. The issue of water and basic sanitation expresses, in a very visible way, the patriarchal system. On the planet, hundreds of millions of women walk more than an hour to collect water daily. The lack of basic sanitation is one of the factors that aggravates sexual aggressions and rapes against women.

According to the World Health Organisation, in the world, there are 2.1 billion people who do not have access to safe drinking water in their homes, and 4.5 billion people lack safe basic sanitation. This extremely critical situation is getting worse with climate change. Women spend more time than men in tasks related to water in agriculture, cooking, cleaning and family health. However, in general, women are subordinated in water management structures at different levels. The construction of systemic alternatives requires the feminization of water management in all instances. Water management must be comprehensive and encompass not only the human dimension but also the preservation of the vital cycle of water. To guarantee the human right to water, it is necessary to recognize and secure the rights of water. It is fundamental not to consider water as a simple resource, as an object, but to recognize that water is a subject that in its different forms of river, snow or ocean has the rights to flow, not to be contaminated, to live and give life. If rivers are subject to rights, then this must be reflected in the exercise of democracy in our municipalities, provinces, states and international integration spaces. A real democracy must include representation mechanisms for water. An anthropocentric democracy can't solve the systemic crisis of water.

The continuation of capitalism, globalization, anthropocentrism, patriarchy, extractivism, xenophobia and productivism is a source of increasing conflicts and wars over water. Water will be one of the most determining factors in geopolitical disputes between countries, regions, social sectors, ethnic and religious groups. Water does not recognize borders and its existence raises the need to rethink the boundaries of nations to move towards a shared management of watersheds. The global water crisis requires a new kind of international integration that is not dominated by capital and the geopolitical ambitions of the elites of nation states. An alternative can be multidimensional and yet not be anti-systemic. The capitalist, patriarchal and neocolonial systems also develop multidimensional proposals to adjust to the new realities in order to preserve their existence. There are alternatives that are born with an anti-systemic dynamic but are captured by the system. This is the case, for example, of the green economy that in its origins promoted a different relationship with nature but now has become a new way to commodify nature through initiatives such as REDD+ and payment for environmental services.

In other words, a systemic alternative doesn't have guarantees of an anti-systemic character for life. Everything depends on its dynamics, the process it follows, its implementation, how it evolves by adopting new perspectives and deepening of its own proposals to really address the different factors of the systemic crises. That is why systemic alternatives can't be reduced to a list of good practices. All good practices must deepen and transform themselves to become systemic alternatives. Without this evolution, which is not exempt from crises, contradictions and conflicts, a good practice may end up being captured by the system which once aspired to change. Systemic alternatives are in first place processes rather than given facts. That is why they can't be replicated and multiplied indiscriminately. There are no generic and universal systemic alternatives. Everything has a context, a history, a future and actors that can't be repeated mechanically in any situation.

The construction of systemic alternatives always has to start from the knowledge of the concrete realities and their dynamics. To build systemic alternatives, it is fundamental to start from the changing reality and from the theoretical postulates and practical experiences of different visions and approaches such as the commons, degrowth, Vivir Bien, ecosocialism, the rights of Mother Earth, ecofeminism, food sovereignty, just transition, deglobalization and many others. All these proposals are very valuable, but none of them can answer all the complexities of systemic crises. All of these approaches need to engage in processes of complementarity to forge systemic alternatives. Complementarity means to complement one another to form a whole that responds to the complexity of the problems we are facing. A process of complementarity requires to learn from the other vision, to see through the postulates of the other proposal, to discover the strengths of others, to explore your own weaknesses and the gaps that all visions share, and above all, to think in terms of the totality of the whole.

THE SLOTH AND THE BONFIRE

Pablo Solon[1]

In all the ways to die, the most painful is by fire. Feeling your skin char, the flames invading even your bone marrow – screaming until your voice melts – you plead for cardiac arrest. In the times of the inquisition, witches and heretics were burned at the stake. Today, human bonfires are prohibited. Since World War II and the Nazi Holocaust, the cremation of the living is considered a crime against humanity. No government would consider promoting policies of human incinerations, yet torching other living beings is on the rise in various countries on Earth. Supporting itself on a branch with its three claws, a sloth smiles, without sensing what is coming. It just finished eating a few leaves and it readies itself for its never-ending nap to aid digestion. Sloths are the slowest mammals on Earth. Their lives of repose have allowed them to survive for 64 million years, much longer than humans and other more agile animals. The fire remains unseen but travels at the speed of the wind. The sloth sleeps.

"The fire was an accident," exclaimed the politicians. In 2019, how can there be a fire that razes 957,000 hectares (3,700 square miles)? This is sixty times the area of Bolivia's capital of La Paz. It is almost the entirety of the Isiboro Sécure National Park and Indigenous Territory (TIPNIS). A fire of these dimensions is not the product of one or one hundred accidents; it is the product of thousands of fires all started in recent days. Every year, there is chaqueo (slashing-and-burning) but this time it has been multiplied a thousand-fold by the government's call to expand the agricultural frontier. Ethanol and biodiesel require hundreds of thousands of hectares for inputs like sugar cane and soy. To this, add meat exports to China which require millions of hectares of pasture for cattle.

There are also the political land grants and illegal settlements in forest areas. What is happening is no accident. Five years ago, the Vice President, Alvaro Garcia Linera, challenged Bolivian agro-industrialists to expand the agricultural frontier by one million hectares (3,860 square miles, or two-

1 Translation from Spanish by Tom Kruse. Culled from: https://www.paginasiete.bo/rascacielos /2019/8/25/ el-perezoso-la-hoguera-228197.html Originally published in Spanish on 25 August 2019 in Rascacielo (Skyscraper), the Sunday magazine of Pagina Siete.

thirds of Connecticut) per year. That target figure has been reached, but with lands devastated by fire, not productive agricultural lands.

The fire approaches. First a spark, then another. Ash falls on the fur that camouflages the sloth. It wakes, confused, without understanding what is happening. It feels burning pinpricks and lets out a painful moan as it slowly moves in search of refuge. This is Bolivia. The country where Mother Earth has rights – where there is a law that says forests, rivers and sloths have the right to life and to "maintain the integrity of the life systems and natural processes which sustain them" – country where schizophrenia is in power – where the President gives speeches at international meetings in defense of Pachamama, the Mother Earth revered by the indigenous people of the Andes, while in Bolivia the rights of Mother Earth are violated – a country where in just 24 hours the parliament unanimously approves a law for the massive expansion of biofuel production.

Not a single parliamentarian speaks for the forests that, even then was crackling at more than 300 degrees centigrade. The legislators all celebrated Bolivia's entry into the era of biofuels. The same happened with the export of meat to China. None demanded prior environmental impact studies. The fires this year (2019), are the product of a re-election strategy for national elections to be held in October. From a prior position of opposition to biofuels, the government flipped 180 degrees – without even blushing – to promoting ethanol and biodiesel as "green energy" sources.

The idea is to grow the agribusiness of Bolivia's eastern lowlands to win their support in the elections. It is the same with the cattle producers, and large refrigerated shipping companies. Following the example of Paraguay which devastated their forests to feed cattle, the Bolivian government cleared agribusiness as a pathway to export meat to China.

The dry leaves start to catch fire. The sloth hangs, climbing in slow motion until it reaches another tree. Anguish is reflected in its face. Smoke filling its lungs, it breathes with difficulty. Without hurrying or pausing it continues its climb. Occasionally wavering, it is sustained by claws and survival instinct. The candidates, who have said little or nothing about deforestation, biofuels and meat exports, run to the disaster areas for photo opportunities. Among themselves, they look for who to blame, but no one wants to point to the development model of agribusiness in the eastern lowland capital of Santa Cruz, which is responsible for most of Bolivia's deforestation.

In 2015, of the 240,000 hectares deforested in Bolivia, 204,000 hectares were in Santa Cruz. In 2012, when deforestation in Santa Cruz stood at 100,000 hectares, 91% was illegal. By 2017, with a stroke of the pen, the government had declared legal one-third of that deforestation. Nature should not be burned at the stake, legally or illegally. Setting fire to a forest or other living beings, human or not, is a crime that degrades the human condition. The sloth reaches the top of the highest tree, an imposing mapajo (ceiba pentandra) 70 meters tall. The horizon is in flames. It is said that the sloth lives slowly to not die fast. Now all depends on the fortitude of a 300-year-old tree.

Hopefully the winds will help. No chance of rain. In the distance the President's helicopter flies over the inferno. He talks of evacuating people without uttering a word about the sloth or the other beings of Mother Earth. In a few days, the candidates will return to campaigning, some to challenge totalitarianism and others to camouflage it, but none to denounce the anthropocentric totalitarianism we carry inside.

POLITICS OF TURBULENT WATERS

Nnimmo Bassey

The fact that Africa can be completely circumnavigated has advantages and disadvantages. One of the advantages is that the continent can be accessed by sea from any direction. This means that the seas can be a ready tool for wrapping up the continent and promoting regional integration and cooperation. We would be stating the obvious when we say that this spatial disposition has also made the continent prone to exploitation and assault. This position made it easy for Africans to be uprooted and relocated through slavery and this central location of the continent equally made it open to adventurers and colonizers. It is also noteworthy that key terrestrial infrastructure on the continent either begin or end at the shorelines. The sea means a lot to Africa and her littoral states. Africa's mineral resources and aquatic diversity have attracted entities with interest in legal activities and others with illegal intentions. The world is literally scrapping the bottom of the natural resource pot as scramble for the sea exacerbates. The scramble is propelled by the idea of limitless resources and opportunities of the sea which is marketed through the blue economy concept.

In the publication, Blue Economy Blues, HOMEF stated: To understand the blue economy, one needs to look at the concept that inspired its creation. That concept is that of the green economy. The green economy is another top-down concept that jars with the organic relationship between humans and their physical environment. It essentially deconstructs that relationship and builds upon a philosophy that distances humans and other species from the environment. The green economy concept presents the environment as a thing to be manipulated, transformed, and exploited in a way that delivers gains along subsisting unequal power alignments. African political leaders, including those at the African Union, are enamoured of the blue economy concept. This is particularly evident during deliberations concerning what can be done in the areas of fisheries, aquaculture, tourism, transport, shipbuilding, energy, bioprospecting, underwater mining, and related activities. The ocean and lakes simply appear to be spatially limitless and endowed with limitless resources. The truth is that these notions are not true.

Africa's waters are among some of the most overfished waters, and this is often not for consumption in the continent. Africa's fisheries provide nutrition to about 200 million Africans and employment for over 35 million coastal fishers. Nevertheless, about 25 percent of fish catch on Africa's waters are by non-African countries, according to an FAO report. The waters in West Africa that have been among the most fecund have seen shrunken fish populations due to overfishing, illegal fishing, and climate change. These illegal fishing activities are often carried out by large foreign industrial trawlers that travel over long distances with the help of harmful subsidies. It is said that about 65 percent of all known illegal, unregulated and unreported fishing takes place in the waters of the Gulf of Guinea.

The rush to exploit Africa's ocean has manifested in criminal activities including sea piracy, waste dumping (oil spills) and fish stealing. Shockingly, 95 percent of all kidnappings at sea is said to happen in the Gulf of Guinea. It is crucial to note that fish catch made by the industrial trawlers are said to end up being used to feed livestock in Europe and the USA. According to reports, these trawlers come from China, Russia, and countries in the European Union. They catch more fish in one day than what an artisanal fisher would catch in a year. These unregulated and illegal activities largely go unreported.

IPCC – Oceans Warming Faster than Expected

While the challenge of large foreign industrial trawlers persist, warming oceans continue to reduce fish populations and catch as fishes migrate to cooler waters and away from equatorial latitudes. Ocean warming has been fingered as triggering more violent cyclones such as cyclone Idai, Kenneth and Loise on the southeastern seaboard of Africa. The warming has also led to the destruction of coral reefs off the coast of East Africa. This clearly has impact on fish stocks.

The sixth assessment report of the Intergovernmental Panel on Climate Change (IPCC) affirmed that 1.5°C temperature rise above preindustrial levels may be reached by 2050 due to the continued dumping of greenhouse gases into the atmosphere. If drastic emissions cuts are not embarked on, the world is on track to overshoot the Paris Agreement targets thereby literally frying Africa and cooking its ocean. This will make nonsense of any notion of the blue economy, except that the ocean could become arenas for geoengineering experimentations aimed at sucking carbon out of the atmosphere or for some form of solar radiation management by pumping sea water into the clouds.

With temperatures rising and polar icecaps melting, the IPCC report assures that sea level rise will increase. As the floods come, submergence of coastal communities and cities will go from being a threat to becoming stark reality. We are already seeing deadly floods on virtually every continent. With sea level rise, comes loss of coastal land and infrastructure, as well as loss of freshwater systems through salinization.

For a continent that often suffers water stress and has the spectre of water conflicts hanging like the sword of Damocles, real action must be taken to counter climate change. One key action that must be taken is the outlawing of new oil or gas fields in Africa's ocean and other aquatic ecosystems. The oil rigs and FSPOs (Floating Productions Storage & Offloading) cut off fishing grounds and engender human rights abuses by security forces. They expose fishers to extreme danger just to maintain an expansive off-limits cordon ostensibly setup to protect oil company installations.

It is equally a time to halt the building of petrochemical refineries and other polluting industries (such as the one at Lekki Free Zone at Lagos) on seashores as they are sure to pollute the waters, poison biodiversity and negatively impact the food chain. A phosphate factory at Kpeme in Togo, for example, pumps its wastes into the Atlantic Ocean, literally fertilizing the continental shelf to death. Nutrient pollution can have devastating impacts on public health, aquatic ecosystems and the overall economy. Blue economy sails on the highway of pervasive market fundamentalism that seeks to shrink public involvement in productive endeavours and yield the space for the private enterprises. Market fundamentalism blinds policy makers to the fact that the so-called efficient and profitable private sectors depend on subsidies and securities provided by the public sector. One only needs to think of the bailouts of financial institutions during economic meltdowns, and the elimination of risks by pharmaceutical companies in the race for COVID-19 vaccines. These are, of course, justified by overriding public interests.

The drive to support industries such as those producing plastics, and the love for disposable products, permit highly polluting materials such as plastics to be unleashed into our environment – thereby, causing great harm to the ocean and aquatic creatures. It has been said that there would be more plastics than fish (by weight) in the ocean by 2050.

Reports indicate that the production of plastics increased twentyfold since 1964 and reached 311 million tonnes in 2014. This quantity is expected to double again over the next 20 years and almost quadruple by 2050. It should be noted that the volume of petroleum resources needed to make plastics has been increasing steadily. Despite the highly visible pollution impacts, the demand keep rising with only about 5 percent of plastics being effectively recycled and 40 percent ending up in landfill. About 30 percent of the plastics end up in sensitive ecosystems such as the world's ocean.

Already there is a plastic flotilla or a Great Plastic Patch in the Pacific Ocean that is euphemistically called the 8th continent. The patch is "three times the size of France and is the world's biggest ocean waste repository, with 1.8 billion pieces of floating plastic which kill thousands of marine animals each year." Sadly, those plastics will require hundreds of years to degrade if left floating out there. The politics of economic development and market fundamentalism, allow what would ordinarily be unthinkable to happen. Think, for example, on the fact that a drop of crude oil contaminates 25 litres of water making it unsuitable for drinking. Imagine how much water was polluted by Shell's 40,000 barrels Bonga Oil spill of December 2011 or Exxon's Idoho platform spill of similar volume in 1998. Then imagine the bane of the market fundamentalism.

Shell's Forcados terminal spill of 1979 dumped 570,000 barrels of crude oil into the estuary and creeks, while Chevron (then known as Texaco) released 400,000 barrels of crude oil in the Funiwa incident of 1980. Add to these, the Ororo-1 oil well blowout off the coast of Ondo State in April 2020 that has remained a crime scene more than a year after.

A Little Help from Nature

Once upon a time, our turbulent seas were embraced by verdant mangroves on our coastlines. Today, the mangrove forests have been deforested for energy or to make way for infrastructure or urbanisation. These forests are key components of a viable Gulf of Guinea. Without them, the region has no answer to rampaging waves and sea level rise. The spawning ground for fish species and nurseries for the juveniles gets eroded and lost as mangroves get depleted. Oil pollution turns the mangrove forests into dead zones.

The deforestation of the mangroves opens up space for invasive nipa palms introduced to the Niger Delta in 1906 by a horticultural adventurer. The call for restoration of mangrove forests must be supported and acted upon. This can be done in cooperation with community groups that are raising nurseries and demonstrating their efficacy through pilot efforts. Support by government can bring these efforts to scale and have greater impact. Alternative energy sources also need to be provided for communities that depend on mangroves for fuelwood. Protecting selected freshwater and marine ecosystems could be a way of securing thriving biodiversity in our oceans, seas, lakes and rivers. However, such areas must be delineated with close attention to indigenous knowledge and the cultural protection norms of communities that depend on them for their livelihoods.

Top-down approaches to establishing protected areas end up dislocating communities, harming their economies, and eroding their cultures, spirituality and dignity. Some of such areas are simply demarcated for officially sanctioned land and sea grabbing. They can, and have been used as tools of oppression and exploitation. In an article titled Protected areas must promote and respect rights of small-scale fishers, not dispossess them, Sibongiseni Gwebani stated, "The concept of protecting an identified fishing area, designating marine spatial territory and linking this to specific regulations has a long history in South Africa. These have been influenced by the apartheid spatial planning legislation introduced in the 1960s. Large proportions of coastal land were forcibly cleared for either forestry or marine conservation by using racial segregation laws. The histories of all of the major marine protected areas in South Africa are shaped by racially based removals through land and seascape during the 1970s and 1980s."

No Politics with our Seas

The statistics rolled out during Health of Mother Earth Foundation's (HOMEF) School of Ecology on the Politics of the Sea, show a very disturbing situation in the Gulf of Guinea. The gulf has become one of the most dangerous maritime areas in the world. The presenter informed that 90 percent of sea based environmental pollution footprint in the Gulf of Guinea takes place in Nigeria's waters. The region is very lankily policed and is a zone of plunder with hundreds of thousands of stolen crude oil moving unhindered. While gazing at the ocean, creek or river, it is vital to think about life below the surface, not as an SDG goal, but as creatures that have rights to live and thrive as children of Mother Earth. The water bodies must be seen as arenas of life. Humans must be reminded that they are just a tiny fraction of the biomass of living beings on earth. The seas offer a canvass for learning positive politics of life rather than scrambling to grab and trash whatever hands can be laid on.

RESTORATIVE JUSTICE:
A SUITABLE RESPONSE TO
ENVIRONMENTAL CRIME?

Femke Wijdekop

What if the wall of a dam containing highly toxic mining waste collapses, polluting the surrounding waterways and drinking water, decimating fish stocks and devastating the social and economic lives of the villagers dependent on these waterways? Even if the State upholds environmental law and charges the mining company with environmental offences, how will the imposition of a fine – the usual sanction for environmental offences -assist the individuals and communities whose lives have been shattered by the criminal negligence of the company? And while some victims, such as the fisherman whose livelihood is destroyed, may be readily identifiable, what about the polluted river or the landscape whose vegetation has been polluted by the toxic waste?[1]

The above extract demonstrates how the traditional way of addressing environmental violations can be inadequate for satisfying the victims' need for justice and restoration. This article will explore the concern of whether a restorative justice approach to environmental crime could lead to more satisfying results.

Restorative justice is a fast-growing social movement and set of practices that aim to redirect society's retributive (punishment-oriented) response to crime. Restorative justice views crime as a wrong against other members of the community not as a depersonalized breaking of the law. It attends to the broken relationships between three players: the offender, the victim, and the community. This means that restorative justice holds offenders directly accountable to the people they have harmed and that it restores, to the extent possible, the emotional and material losses of victims by providing a range of opportunities for dialogue, negotiation and problem solving.[2]

---

1 Justice Nicola Pain, Justice Rachel Pepper, Millicent McCreath, and John Zorzetto. (2016). Restorative justice for environmental crime: an antipodean experience. International Union for Conservation of Nature Academy of Environmental Law Colloquium 2016, Oslo Norway 22 June 2016, p. 1
2 https://charterforcompassion.org/restorative-justice/restorative-justice-some-facts-and-history

Moreover, it views criminal acts more comprehensively than the traditional judicial system does. This is because it recognizes how offenders harm victims, communities, and even themselves by their actions. It looks at the needs and obligations that result from those harms. Restorative justice uses inclusive, collaborative processes in which those with a stake in the situation (victims, offenders, community members; representatives of the criminal justice system), come together to collectively resolve how to deal with the aftermath of the offence and its implications for the future. Next to the goal of repairing the harm done, restorative justice has an aspiration for the future: to prevent recidivism by confronting the offender with their victim – instigating repentance and behavioural change.

Restorative justice processes have the following general objectives:

- to give victims a voice, encourage them to express their needs, enable and assist them participate in the resolution process;

- to repair relationships damaged by crime, in part, by arriving at a consensus on how best to respond to it;

- to renounce criminal behaviour as unacceptable and to reaffirm community values;

- to reduce recidivism by encouraging change in individual offenders and facilitating their integration into the community and;

- to identify factors that lead to crime and inform authorities responsible for crime reduction strategies about these factors.[3]

There are four main types of restorative processes[4]:

1. Victim-offender conferencing: a process which provides victims of crime the opportunity to meet the offender in a safe and structured setting, with the goal of holding the offender directly accountable for their behaviour while providing assistance and compensation to the victim.

2. Community and family group conferencing: a meeting between victims, offenders and their respective families and communities, led by a trained facilitator, in which the affected parties discuss how they have been harmed by the offence and how the offender might best repair the harm.

---

3 Hon. Justice Brian J. Preston. (2011). The use of restorative justice for environmental crime, *Criminal Law Journal*, 2011, 35(3):136-153

4 https://papers.ssrn.com/sol3/papers.cfm?abstract_id=1831822

3. Sentencing circles: a community-directed process, conducted in partnership with the criminal justice system, to develop consensus on an appropriate sentencing plan that addresses the concerns of all interested parties. These circles, which are sometimes called peace making circles, use traditional (indigenous) circle ritual and structures.

4. Community reparative boards, an alternative to the criminal justice system.

Restorative processes can be applied solely or alongside retributive sanctions (fines/imprisonment), as part of a convicts 'rehabilitation process, if the prosecution or judge so decides. Roots Restorative justice is a young field that emerged in North America during the 1970s when alternative approaches to the criminal justice system, such as alternative dispute resolution, were becoming a trend. It emerged alongside the victims' rights movement, which advocated greater involvement of crime victims in the criminal justice process, as well as for the use of restitution as compensation for losses.

A 1974 case in Kitchener, Ontario, Canada, is considered the beginning point of today's restorative justice movement. This "Kitchener experiment" required two teenagers to meet with and pay restitution to every one of the twenty-two people whose property they had vandalized.[5]

The Mennonite Church played a crucial role in rolling out these first Victim-Offender Reconciliation processes in Canada and the USA. At the same time, many of the values, principles and practices of restorative justice reflect those of indigenous cultures such as the Maori in New-Zealand and the First Nations People of Canada and the USA. In these indigenous cultures, community-members led by an elder, collectively participate in finding a solution for conflict. Until the Middle Ages, such participatory forms of conflict resolution were also used in Europe. But they were lost when the government took over the role of conflict-solver in the late Middle Ages[6], leaving little room for the victim (or the affected community) to play a part in conflict resolution.

Restorative justice has seen worldwide growth since the 1990s. Most academic studies suggest it makes offenders less likely to reoffend. A 2007 study also found out that it had the highest rate of victim satisfaction and offender accountability than any method of justice.[7] It is applied

5 https://charterforcompassion.org/restorative-justice/restorative-justice-some-facts-and-history
6 H. Zehr, *Changing Lenses. A New Focus for Crime and Justice*, Scottdale: Herald Press 2005, pp. 108-110.
7 https://en.wikipedia.org/wiki/Restorative_justice

to individual criminal cases and to system-wide offences, of which the South African Truth and Reconciliation Commission is the most famous example. In New Zealand and the Australian states of New South Wales and Victoria, restorative justice is applied to environmental crimes. This will be discussed in the next paragraph.

Application to environmental crime

Restorative justice can be applied to environmental crimes and the defendants' commitment to make amends can involve restoration of the natural environment. Environmental crime can result in the following:

1. Violations of the human right to health, to clean air, water, land, and quality life.

2. Violations of the right to property and amenity

3. Violation of natural and cultural heritage. In these cases, often aboriginal or indigenous people are the victim. An example is the Australian case Garrett vs. Williams[8], which concerned the destruction of Aboriginal artefacts during construction and exploration activities undertaken by a mining company. As part of the settlement of the case, a restorative justice conference was facilitated by the prosecutor and funded by the defendant. The Aboriginal people nominated a representative of the relevant local Aboriginal Land Council to represent them in the process. The Court appointed an independent facilitator who conducted interviews with representatives of the Broken Hill Local Aboriginal Land Council, archaeologists, representatives of mining company Pinnacle Hills and representatives of the prosecutor in preparation for the conference.

The conference itself provided the opportunity for the chairperson of the Broken Hill Aboriginal Land Council and the defendant to meet, and for the defendant to apologise for the harm caused. The parties produced a document outlining the agreement that was reached at the conference, which included financial contributions to be made to the victims, future training and employment opportunities for the local community, and a guarantee that the traditional owners would be involved in any salvage operations of Aboriginal artefacts. These results of the restorative justice intervention were taken into account by the judge in the sentencing process, but the restorative justice intervention

---

8 Garrett vs. Williams (2007) 151 LGERA 92; [2007] NSWLEC 96.

did not substitute the court sentence for the offences committed by the defendant.

4. Violation of the commons held in trust by the government.[9]

5. Violation of the rights of the environment itself with the environment as a victim. Increasingly, the rights of the natural world are recognised in court decisions and legislation.[10] In restorative justice conferences, trees and rivers can be represented by surrogate victims. This happened in the Waikato vs. Huntly case[11]. In this case, sediment laden stormwater was illegally discharged from the offender's quarry affecting the quality of the New Zealand Waikato River. The river was represented at the restorative justice conference by the chairperson of the Waikato River Enhancement Society. The conference outcome included payment of costs of the facilitator and a donation to the Lower Waikato River Enhancement Society instead of a fine.

6. Violation of the rights of future generations, who can be represented 'by proxy' in restorative processes, for example, by NGOs who protect the interest of future generations in their statutes.[12]

There are several possible restorative outcomes in the case of environmental crimes: apologies; restoration of environmental harm and prevention of future harm; compensatory restoration of environments elsewhere if the affected environment cannot be restored to its former condition and; payment of compensation to the victims and community service work. Measures addressing future behaviour, such as an environmental audit of the activities of the offending company, or environmental training and education of the company's employees, are also possible outcomes.[13]

Restorative Justice has been an important element in New Zealand sentencing since 2002. According to a 2012 report of the Ministry for Environment, between 1 July 2001 and 30 September 2012, a restorative justice process was used in 33 prosecutions under the Resource Management Act in New Zealand.[14] In Australia, the New South Wales

---

9 https://law.stanford.edu/2017/07/05/atmospheric-trust-litigation-paving-the-way-for-a-fossil-fuel-free-world/
10 http://www.harmonywithnatureun.org/
11 In Waikato Regional Council vs. Huntly Quarries Ltd and Ian Harrold Wedding, Auckland District Court (McElrea DCJ), 30 July 2003 and 28 October 2003.
12 See Minors Oposa vs. Secretary of the Department of Environment and Natural Resources 33 ILM173 (1994) at 185
13 https://papers.ssrn.com/sol3/papers.cfm?abstract_id=1831822
14 Justice Nicola Pain, Justice Rachel Pepper, Millicent McCreath, John Zorzetto, Restorative Justice for environmental crime: an antipodean experience, International Union for Conservation of Nature Academy of Environmental Law Colloquium 2016 Oslo Norway 22 June 2016, p. 15

Land and Environment Court also uses restorative processes in addressing environmental offences. The Australian Victorian Environmental Protection Agency uses restorative justice conferences in communities afflicted with environmental damage.

Finally, in the context of transitional justice, environmental restoration and conservation activities after (civil) war can help processes of reconciliation and peace making. Such processes took place in Mozambique in 1994, Afghanistan in 2003 and Nepal in 2006. Currently, the Colombian government wants former FARC-members to assist with the environmental restoration of landscapes that suffered from the Colombian civil war.

Letting the Offender and Systematic Injustices off the Hook?

Restorative justice has eye for the victim's emotional and material needs in the wake of crime. But does it let offenders off the hook by allowing them to take part in processes of reconciliation and rehabilitation? This is a reasonable question to ask. What is important to realize is that restorative justice does not necessarily replace retributive responses to crime. It is a tool which can be applied alongside traditional responses, such as fines and imprisonment. In that case, a positive outcome of a restorative justice process can make the judge decide to reduce the punishment.

Also, restorative justice is only applied when both victim and offender are willing to participate. It requires that the offender takes responsibility for committing the offense. Confronting the victims and committing to time consuming projects, such as re-planting trees, doing community work or attending environmental training, may be more of a deterrent for the offender than a non-restorative sentence such as a fine. Paying a fine may hurt financially, but it probably does not impact the offender on an emotional level, or challenge his/her assumptions about right and wrong behaviour. Meeting the victims and the community face-to-face and learning about the harm caused by the offence is more likely to leave a lasting effect on the offender[15]. Of course, this presumes that the offender has a conscience and is not partaking in restorative justice processes purely for selfish and tactical reasons ('faking' remorse in order to get a lower sentence). Discernment will be important when selecting cases and offenders that are suitable for a restorative justice intervention.

15 Justice Nicola Pain, Justice Rachel Pepper, Millicent McCreath, John Zorzetto, Restorative Justice for environmental crime: an antipodean experience, International Union for Conservation of Nature Academy of Environmental Law Colloquium 2016 Oslo Norway 22 June 2016, p. 17

Another possible point of criticism is that restorative justice legitimises existing economic and power relations by working towards reconciliation between victims and offenders. Is not a more assertive and confrontational approach, such as the recently launched climate case against Shell,[16] more appropriate to challenge the systemic way in which environmental pollution is allowed – and even rewarded – by our economic system? This is a valid point. But restorative justice can be part of an approach that is oriented to system-change, such as the campaign to make Ecocide a crime against peace. Polly Higgins proposes to add restorative justice processes to the sanction arsenal of a judge who decides in Ecocide-cases.[17] She proposes to offer it as an alternative sentencing option when there is victim and offender consent, and when the offender – probably a company, bank or state official – accepts responsibility for restoring territories adversely impacted by ecocide.

Another angle is that restorative justice actually empowers change from the bottom up, because it is a way for communities to develop social capital, social networks and civic interconnectedness. Participation in restorative process offers citizens the chance to mobilize their community to challenge systemic socio-economic injustice. It can encourage citizens to challenge norms and stimulate political debate. It also gives space for rights-of-nature approaches to what constitutes an environmental violation and who can be a victim of such a violation. As happened in the Waikato vs. Huntly case described above, nature itself can be represented in restorative justice conferences as a victim in its own right. The outcome of such conferences can include the obligation to restore the environment that has been harmed. The fact that restorative justice uses indigenous processes, such as peace-making circles, can create a conducive environment for rights-of-nature approaches which lean towards indigenous worldviews, to gain strength.

Conclusion

Restorative justice holds promise as an alternative response to environmental crime. Studies show that offenders are less likely to reoffend, and that restorative justice produces a high rate of victim satisfaction and offender accountability. However, the question if restorative justice is a suitable response to environmental crime has to be answered on a case-by-case basis. There will be cases which will not qualify for a restorative approach,

16 https://en.milieudefensie.nl/climate-case-shell
17 https://www.theguardian.com/law/2012/jun/04/ecocide-earth-business-extract

for example, where the offender does not take responsibility for the offense, or when victims do not feel safe to take part in restorative processes because they fear the offender might retaliate behind the scenes if they raise their voices publicly. In such cases, the environmental offense is embedded in a broader culture of impunity and intimidation, or lack of rule of law. If the culture is more conducive to upholding environmental law and to restoration of broken relationships, restorative justice seems to have a lot to offer. If we consider the example used in the introduction – of the pollution caused by toxic mining waste – engaging in a restorative justice process can give a voice to those victims who are impacted by the crime of pollution but who would normally be excluded from its resolution.

Proxies can be appointed to represent the polluted river and land. A conference offers the opportunity for the offender to directly apologise to victims, to first-hand understand how the crime has affected the victims and harmed the social fabric of the community. It can diminish the chances of recidivism and educate the offender in the norms and values of environmental law. If anything, applying restorative justice to environmental disputes that have come to a standstill might proof to be worth the try. This is what a small group of Quakers is committed to do regarding the 1984 Bhopal disaster in which no justice has yet been achieved three decades after the disaster which killed ten thousands of people. The Quakers started a 'Restorative Action for Bhopal' and are currently trying to engage the offending company in a restorative process.[18] It will be interesting to keep an eye on this bold initiative to hold a multinational accountable for environmental and human rights violations in a restorative way.

---

18 https://www.prospectmagazine.co.uk/world/three-decades-after-the-bhopal-disaster-a-new-approach-offers-hope

OF EXTRACTIVISM AND DISCONTENTMENT

Stephen Oduware

Extractivism, they say, is the practice of extracting natural resources to trade in the world market. Globally, economies strive on competitive and senseless extraction of these resources irrespective of a growing discontentment from those negatively impacted. Market forces have been created around extractivism to support demand and supply. Economies have made it an index to watch out for in the measurement of growth or progress. For example, in 2018, the oil sector accounted for 90 percent of Nigeria's foreign exchange. In June 2019, the then Group Managing Director of Nigerian National Petroleum Corporation (NNPC), Mr Maikanti Baru, said NNPC would resume oil exploration in Chad Basin. He remarked: "We will go back there as soon as we receive security clearance. There seems to be some prospects there because Niger Republic drilled over 600 wells and now, they are producing while we [Nigeria] have only drilled 23 wells."

This is the kind of competition that allows collusion between multinationals and the government to exploit even the most fragile ecosystems. In 2017, President Donald Trump vowed to revive the coal industry despite the moratorium on coal leasing on federal lands placed by former President Barrack Obama's administration. Continuous exploitation of these resources has huge negative impacts on the environment, livelihoods and the wellbeing of peoples of the world. They are known to release greenhouse gases (which absorb infrared radiation, thereby trapping heat and causing warming in the atmosphere), radionuclides, heavy metals etc. to the atmosphere.

The extractive industry has become the economic mainstay of global governance, displacing indigenous people from their ancestral lands. Pollution and oppressions are also tied to the industry. In Africa, there have been various conflicts and wars all tied to the mindless exploitation of natural resources. In Nigeria, for instance, there has been face-offs between communities and oil giants in the past, leading to heavy militarization, oppression, repression and violation of the human rights of community people. The problem is far more than this! In the midst of the existential global climate chaos, pollution is going on unabated in the Niger Delta, and it seems that the more the pollution in the region, the greater the quest to explore new fields.

Part of the problems encountered with regards to resource extractions, lies with the World Bank; they encourage and promote these extractive industries, providing them with loans and funds. They encourage the migration of these industries to the less developed countries. Nnimmo Bassey, in his book *To Cook a Continent* analyzed three reasons behind the World Bank's involvement in promoting the extractive industries. The first is that the measurement of the cost of health-impairing pollution depends on the foregone earnings from increased morbidity and mortality. That is to say, health-impairing pollution should be done in a country with the lowest cost so that more profits can be made from the peoples' suffering. He added that the cost of pollution is impeccable, and the developing nations of the world should face up to that as well as get discontented with such ideologies. Second, the costs of pollution are likely to be non-linear as the initial increments of pollution probably have very low cost in the developing regions of the world.

Third, the demands for a clean environment for aesthetic and health reasons are likely to have a very high income–elasticity. With these reasons, one can see clearly that pollution in developing countries does not happen by chance. Poverty and ill-health are apparently engineered through ideological mindsets that will only secure the wealth of the mighty even if it kills or diminishes the capacity of the weak to survive. Extractivism can be likened to an act of robbing Peter to pay Paul, impoverishing the grassroots communities while enriching a few people. Africa today is seen as the extractive base of nations from the Global North, milking the continent dry of its natural resources while leaving the people stranded and dependent on aids from them.

The hunger to probe more for resources to extract is on an exponential increase and the competition to be within the purview of power and dominance is rife among countries. The negative effects of extrativism are global, but countries in the Global South feel the greatest impacts. There is, therefore, a need to pursue development that is in sync with nature. A new world is possible –let us demand a shift from a polluting age to an age of renewable energy, shared prosperity and Ubuntu!

Positive Green Criminology: Becoming Ecologically Awake System Changers

Femke Wijdekop

It is heartening and inspiring to see the legal innovations that lawyers have come up with in response to biodiversity and climate crises. Particularly of interest is their use of the legal notion of duty of care. Lawyers use this notion to force governments into climate action such as in the Dutch Urgenda climate case. The notion is also used to advocate the criminalization of massive environmental destruction, for example, Stop Ecocide movement or to establish a governing body to safeguard the rights of future generations such as the Future Generations Commissioner for Wales. These developments indicate a movement away from the 'right to exploit natural resources and pollute' towards a 'duty of care' for the environment. A legal duty of care to avoid causing harm to others through climate change or environmental destruction is externally imposed by the justice system. In a recent publication in the Conscious Lawyer, criminologist Anneke van Hoek and myself explore whether environmentally caring behaviour can also be stimulated in ways that speak to our intrinsic motivation.

In the words of the Synod of Bishops for the Amazon that convened in October 2019, caring for our common home requires deep ecological conversion. Positive Green Criminology is concerned with intrinsically motivated care for nature. It is a term that Anneke and I coined for criminological research into the prevention and remediation of environmental harm, and it is related to the fields of positive psychology and positive criminology. Positive psychology studies how people can flourish and live their best lives. Positive Criminology was coined by the Dutch criminologist Marc Schuilenburg. It researches how we can create safety by strengthening positive feelings such as connection and security, care and belonging.

Positive Green Criminology is informed by insights from ecopsychology, restorative justice, research into eudemonic values, affective commoning and stimulating care through storytelling. Each of these elements are explained in the following paragraphs

1. **Ecopsychology**: This term was coined in 1992 by Theodore Roszak in his book 'The Voice of the Earth'. It studies the relationship between human beings and the natural world through ecological and psychological principles. It seeks to develop and understand ways of expanding the emotional connection between individuals and the natural world, thereby, assisting individuals with developing sustainable lifestyles and remedying alienation from nature. A central premise of ecopsychology is that human beings have an innate instinct to care about and connect emotionally with nature. Evidence suggests that many environmentally damaging behaviours are addictive at some level, and more effectively addressed through positive emotional fulfilment rather than by inflicting shame.

Ecopsychology has developed various methods of positive motivation for adopting sustainable practices in its applied practice called Ecotherapy. These methods include psychotherapy, forest bathing, garden therapy, wilderness therapy, green mindfulness and involvement in outdoor conservation activities. Such interventions from ecotherapy can assist in developing an intrinsic attitude of care towards the environment.

2. **Restorative justice**: Restorative justice is a process whereby all the parties with a stake in a particular offence voluntarily come together to collectively resolve how to deal with the aftermath of the offence and its implications for the future. Restorative justice emphasizes the healing of damaged relationships. It searches for the roots of harmful behaviour. Its community and forward-looking orientation makes it well-positioned to address environmental harms. In countries such as New Zealand, Australia, Canada and Brazil, restorative justice has been successfully applied to environmental offences. Some beneficial outcomes of these cases include apologies, restoration of environmental harm and prevention of future harm through environmental training and education of the offender; environmental audits of the activities of the offending company; compensatory restoration of environments elsewhere and community service work. In New Zealand and Canada, trees and rivers have been recognised as victims of environmental crime in their own right and have been represented by indigenous organisations in the restorative process. In Brazil, Dominic Barter's work with restorative circles in the aftermath of the Rio Doce ecocide has contributed to the awakening that the river Doce is an entity with its own rights which needs to be restored to health.

The confrontation with human and represented non-human victims during a restorative justice conference can educate the offenders about the harmful environmental effects of their behaviour and ideally contribute to their ecological awakening. Engaging in environmental restoration work following a conference can also foster in the offender, a sense of belonging and connectedness to the natural world, according to insights from ecopsychology.

3. **Research into eudemonic values:** Researchers of the EU-funded BIOMOT project recognised the importance of eudemonic values (expressing the meaningful life) as a motivating force for nature conservation. The researchers interviewed 105 committed actors for nature and found out that the key concept for understanding their committed action for nature is meaningfulness. People act for nature because nature is meaningful to them, connected to a life that makes sense and a difference in the world. All the committed actors in the study had intense encounters with nature in childhood. Such experiences during childhood seem to be essential for the development of a relationship with nature, and for inspiring action for nature later in life.

A way to connect to nature encounters in childhood is by writing down your green life story. Guided by questions, you return to early childhood experiences of connection and interaction with the Earth, but you also look at patterns of alienation that caused ecological woundedness and possible 'unfinished Earth business'. One of the recommendations of the BIOMOT researchers to policymakers is to ensure, through educational curricula and town planning, that children have access to nature. And would it not be interesting to ask people to write their green life story as part of an ecotherapeutic intervention or as part of ecoliteracy coaching?

4. **Affective Commoning:** Associate Professor and Geographer Neera Singh (University of Toronto) in her research found that through community-based conservation, villagers in Odisha, India, developed "affective ties with the growing plants, trees, birds and animals." And in so doing, "forests are transformed from nature out there and become a part of the self that is nurtured through care." She calls this 'affective commoning'. This entails that people who are engaged in the conservation of their natural environment, through the act of taking care of their environment, become "environmental subjects" who apply their subjective human talents, imagination and commitments and become stewards of elements of nature (rather than owners or users). For clarity, commoning is the practice of collaborating and sharing (outside of the State and

market) to meet everyday needs and achieve the well-being of individuals, communities and lived-in environments.

5. **Storytelling:** Finally, a study from the Yale Program on Climate Change Communication found out that sharing personal anecdotes about how the climate crisis is changing our lives for the worse, can invite people, including conservatives, to care for nature. In two experiments, people listened to a short radio clip from 2015 about Richard Mode, a 66-year-old North Carolinian who enjoys hunting and fishing. In heartfelt tones, Mode describes how he has seen the climate changing first-hand as ducks migrate later in the year and trout disappear from their old territories. After listening to the segment, the study participants – who identified as conservatives or moderates – reported greater concern about climate change and greater acceptance that climate change is happening and caused by humans. This study suggests that storytelling, rather than relying heavily on facts and evidence, can motivate people to care for the environment.

These five elements give clues about how to stimulate intrinsically motived care for nature. Through childhood nature-experiences, touching encounters in restorative justice settings, empathic listening to moving narratives, writing own green life stories, affective commoning and ecotherapy interventions, humans can nurture and enable feelings of belonging and connection to the natural world. This potentially giving us positive emotional fulfilment and a sense of meaningfulness. As Earthlings, we are wired for connection with each other and with the Earth. So, when we re-connect (overcome our alienation) to the Earth community, it feels emotionally fulfilling and profoundly meaningful.

Quantum Social Change

But how does such embodied care for nature on the level of the individual relate to the system change we so much need? Professor Karen O'Brien's (Oslo University – Dept. of Human Geography & Sociology) theory of Quantum Social Change comes to mind. According to O'Brien, history tells us that progressive social changes, such as the abolition of slavery, equal rights for women and marriage equality, have been the result of small groups of individuals who see their world in new ways and act from deeper and more inclusive values.

These groups, with an expanded sense of social consciousness, ascribed rights to previously excluded groups and worked for social and political change. Could this apply as well to groups with an expanded sense of ecological consciousness who ascribe rights to nature? O'Brien's theory of Quantum Social Change explains why their agency could generate such transformative change and, more importantly, how we might access this same quality of agency in response to the climate and biodiversity crises. According to O'Brien, Quantum social change means being self-aware and self-reflective about the beliefs we hold about the future. When we ground our speech and actions in universal values (such as Polly Higgins' credo 'first do no harm'), we generate quantum fractals that replicate these values across all levels and scales.

When we connect to others from a place of interconnectedness (also known as 'interbeing'), we transcend separation and are able to access our collective intelligence; our actions will be impactful beyond linear logic and help materialise new realities that reflect a culture of interbeing; and the potential for an equitable and thriving world exists in every moment, and we can realize this potential by consciously choosing to "be" the new paradigm. The more often people embody the fractal of interbeing, the sooner we will notice a transformative change in society.

This raises the question: When we connect to the Earth from an experience of interbeing, are we able to access the intelligence of the Earth herself? Polly Higgins and Cormac Cullinan the author of 'Wild Law' told me that they experienced this and that their innovative ideas on ecocide law and rights of nature came to them after spending time in nature. There are also lots of stories about meaningful 'coincidence' or synchronicity. A bigger intelligence – the Earth herself - seems to be at play and bring ecological change-makers together at the right time and place in order to help generate system (and quantum!) change.

Conclusion

Being ecologically 'awake' – aware of our interconnectedness with the natural world of which we are an inseparable part – means to be aware of our interbeing with the natural world. O'Brien's research seems promising! It indicates that ecologically awake people have powerful agency when they put their knowledge, expertise and heart-wisdom in the service of system change. So, how then could we, as ecologically sensitive citizens, be a part of the much-needed system change towards a flourishing, ecologically 'literate' civilization? What would assist us in harnessing this kind of agency with the potency to move mountains?

ABOUT THE CONTRIBUTORS

Ako Amadi is the director of Nigerian Conservation Foundation, and technical advisor/analyst with the Canadian International Development Agency, Abuja.

Babawale Obayanju is a climate justice campaigner with Environmental Rights Action (ERA)/Friends of the Earth Nigeria (FoEN), communicator with Friends of the Earth Africa, and content creator, storyteller and photographer at TellThatStory.

Benita Siloko is an environmentalist, an associate lecturer, a researcher and PhD candidate at the Centre for Global Development in Northumbria University Newcastle. She is associate member, Institute of Environmental Management and Assessment (AIEMA) United Kingdom, Nigerian Environmental Society (MNES) and Nigerian Institute of Management (NIM).

Cadmus Atake-Enade is a climate and environmental justice campaigner. He currently leads the Community and Culture Desk in Health of Mother Earth Foundation (HOMEF).

Femke Wijdekop is a legal counsel at Stop Ecocide Netherlands, a member of the Environmental Restorative Justice working group of the European Forum for Restorative Justice and an Earth-centered law expert at the UN Harmony with Nature initiative.

Fidelis Allen is professor of development studies in the University of Port Harcourt and a visiting fellow at Institute for Pan- African Thought and Conversations in University of Johannesburg, South Africa.

Firoze Manji is a Kenyan-born expert on international development, health, human rights and political organising. He is a member of the Daraja Press collective, founder and former editor-in-chief of the pan-African social justice platform, Pambazuka News and Pambazuka Press as well as the founder of the Fahamu Networks for Social Justice. He has authored and edited a wide range of books.

Gbadebo Rhodes-Vivour, popularly known as GRV, is an architect, politician, businessman, activist, MIT alumni and the 2023 Lagos State governorship candidate under the Labour Party (LP).

209

God'spower Martins is the executive director of Urban-Rural Environmental Defenders (U-RED).

Hakima Abbas is a policy analyst, trainer, strategist and researcher. She is the co-founder and co-executive director of Black Feminist Fund.

Hamza Hamouchene is an Algerian researcher-activist, commentator and a founding member of Algeria Solidarity Campaign (ASC) and Environmental Justice North Africa (EJNA). He is the author of "The Struggle for Energy Democracy in the Maghreb" (2017) and "The Coming Revolution to North Africa: The Struggle for Climate Justice" (2015).

Hannibal Rhoades is a contributing writer at Intercontinental Cry Magazine, a citizen journalist, indigenous and environmental rights advocate, and Yes to Life, No to Mining regional coordinator for Northern Europe.

Hans R. Herren is a researcher and an expert on biological pest control and sustainable agriculture. He is the president and CEO of the Millennium Institute, founder and president of the Biovision Foundation. He is a recipient of the 1995 World Food Prize and the 2013 Alternative Nobel Prize laureate.

Hocine Malti is an oil engineer who participated in the creation of Sonatrach, where he was vice-president from 1972 to 1975. He was advisor to the Secretary General of OPAEP (Kuwait) from 1975 to 1977, and director general of the Arab Petroleum Services Company (Tripoli) until 1982.

Jibrin Ibrahim is a professor of political science with Institute of Political Studies at the University of Bordeaux in France, a development consultant/ expert, director of Centre for Democracy & Development and chair of the Editorial Board of Premium Times.

Joyce Ebebeinwe is a food sovereignty and public health activist. She is the director of programmes and leads the Hunger Politics Desk in Health of Mother Earth Foundation (HOMEF). She is board member, Alliance for Food Sovereignty in Africa (AFSA) and coordinates AFSA's youth forum as well as the Alliance for Action on Pesticides in Nigeria.

Lidy Nacpil is the co-founder of the Fight Inequality Alliance, an activist, coordinator of the Asian Peoples' Movement on Debt and Development, co-coordinator of the Global Campaign to Demand Climate Justice, member of the global Coordinating Committee of the Global Alliance on

Tax Justice, and convener of the Philippine Movement for Climate Justice as well as vice president of the Freedom from Debt Coalition.

Magdalene Ime Idiang is a feminist, an environmental justice campaigner and project officer with Health of Mother Earth Foundation where she is in charge of the Gender, Monitoring and Evaluation Desk.

Mariann Bassey Orovwuje is Food Sovereignty campaigner for Friends of the Earth Africa and deputy executive director, Environmental Rights Action/Friends of the Earth, Nigeria (FoEN). She is listed among the 2023 "Nigeria Women Annual 100 Leading Women".

Mary Lou Malig is a researcher, policy analyst, and campaigner now currently based in Bolivia. She has written on the issues of trade particularly the World Trade Organization (WTO), EU- Mercosur, also, climate change, and agriculture. She is co-author of the book, "The Anti-Development State: The Political Economy of Permanent Crisis in the Philippines" and other more recent publications such as "Decoding the Digital Economy".

Mfoniso Antia is an environmental scientist, researcher and climate justice advocate. She works with Health of Mother Earth Foundation (HOMEF) as programmes manger and project lead overseeing HOMEF's learning spaces, Ikike. She is also the Anglophone coordinator of Africa Technology Assessment Platform (AfriTAP) and co-leads the Hands Off Mother Earth Africa Working Group on Geoengineering.

Nduka Otiono is a writer, Associate Professor and Graduate Programme Coordinator at the Institute of African Studies, Carleton University, Canada. He is an award-winning author and co-editor of eight books of creative writing and academic research. Formerly a journalist and General Secretary of the Association of Nigerian Authors, his professional honors include: Capital Educator's Award for Excellence in Teaching; Carleton University Faculty of Arts and Social Sciences Early Career Award for Research Excellence; Carnegie African Diaspora Fellowship, and 2018 Black History Ottawa Community Builder Award.

Nkoyo Esuko Toyo is a lawyer, development activist, and politician. She served as a member of the Nigerian House of Representatives, and as Ambassador to Ethiopia and Djibouti. She co-founded Gender and Development Action (GADA), an organisation improving access to economic and political opportunities for women in Nigeria.

Nnimmo Bassey is a Nigerian architect, environmental activist, author and poet. He has authored several books including *We Thought It Was*

*Oil, But it Was Blood, I will not Dance to Your Beat, To Cook a Continent –
Destructive Extraction and the Climate Crisis in Africa,* and *Oil Politics –
Echoes of Ecological Wars* and he is recipient of the 2010 Right Livelihood
Award (Alternative Nobel Prize) and 2012 Rafto Human Rights Award,
and the executive director of Health of Mother Earth Foundation.

Ogechi Okanya Cookey is an environmental and climate justice advocate,
a researcher, communication expert, editor, reviewer and an academic. She
is research and publications lead at Health of Mother Earth Foundation,
partner at Omega Resilience Awards and pioneer of GrassRoots Data Hub.

Oluwafunmilayo Oyatogun is an environmentalist and a travel business
executive. She studied Environmental Studies and Geography as an
undergraduate and enjoys working for sustainable development.

Pablo Solon, a Bolivian social and environmental activist, is the director
of Fundación Solón and former executive director of Focus on the Global
South. He is a researcher and policy analyst in the areas of water, climate,
the environment, trade, finance and systemic alternatives. He was the
Ambassador of Bolivia to the United Nations from 2009 to 2011.

Patti Lynn is the executive director of Corporate Accountability. She stays
inspired by working shoulder to shoulder with allies in Lagos, Nigeria and
across the Global South toward justice and a better world.

Richard Steiner is Professor Emeritus of Semitic Languages and
Literatures, an honorary member of the Academy of the Hebrew Language
and the Mekize Nirdamim Society, a former Starr Fellow (Harvard
University), and two-time fellow of the Institute for Advanced Studies
(Hebrew University).

Sonali Narang worked for 10 years as research scholar with the Center for
the Study of Geopolitics, Panjab University Chandigarh, India.

Stephen Oduware is an environmental/climate justice campaigner,
grassroots campaigner and a researcher. He is programme manager
and project lead for the fossil politics desk at Health of Mother Earth
Foundation (HOMEF). His work in HOMEF puts him at the forefront
of organising meetings with fossil-impacted communities (in Nigeria and
other African countries).

Timothy A. Wise is a researcher, and a senior advisor at the Institute for
Agriculture and Trade Policy (IATP) and at the Small Planet Institute. He
was research fellow at Tufts University and is the author of *Eating Tomorrow:
Agribusiness, Family Farmers, and the Battle for the Future of Food.*

Tom Kruse is programme director for the Global Challenges portion of the Democratic Practice Program of the Rockefeller Brothers Fund. He served as an advisor to the Bolivian government on trade and investment policy, the continuation of trade preference programs, and debt relief.

Ukpono Bassey is a graphic designer, into 3d modelling and 3d animation voice overs. He works in the Youth Action unit of the Community and Culture Desk in Health of Mother Earth Foundation (HOMEF).

Vandana Shiva is an eco-activist, agro-ecologist, environmental thinker, feminist, philosopher of science, writer and science policy advocate. She is the founder of Navdanya Research Foundation for Science, Technology and Ecology (India) and president of Navdanya International. She is a recipient of many awards, including the Right Livelihood Award.

ABOUT HOMEF

Health of Mother Earth Foundation (HOMEF) is an ecological think tank advocating for socio-ecological justice and food sovereignty in Nigeria and Africa at large. HOMEF recognises that the global crises have systemic roots and the current paradigm of development and growth based on competition will lead to the critical destruction of biodiversity and continued destructive extraction of natural resources as well as dependency on risky technologies.

HOMEF works on Fossil Politics and Hunger Politics using cultural tools to build and share knowledge through her Ikike platforms.

Vision
An ecologically just world where all beings live in harmony with Mother Earth

Mission
To build ecological knowledge, propagate re-source democracy and support wholesome socio-ecologically cohesive communities where people live in solidarity and dignity.

Website **https://homef.org**
Email: **home@homef.org**
Head Office: #30, 19th Street, Ugbowo, Benin City 300212, Nigeria

www.ingramcontent.com/pod-product-compliance
Lightning Source LLC
Chambersburg PA
CBHW070247290326
41930CB00042B/2788